Film stars

Published in our
centenary year
∾ **2004** ∾
MANCHESTER
UNIVERSITY
PRESS

Inside Popular Film

General editors Mark Jancovich and Eric Schaefer

Inside Popular Film is a forum for writers who are working to develop new ways of analysing popular film. Each book offers a critical introduction to existing debates while also exploring new approaches. In general, the books give historically informed accounts of popular film, which present this area as altogether more complex than is commonly suggested by established film theories.

Developments over the past decade have led to a broader understanding of film, which moves beyond the traditional oppositions between high and low culture, popular and avant-garde. The analysis of film has also moved beyond a concentration on the textual forms of films, to include an analysis of both the social situations within which films are consumed by audiences, and the relationship between film and other popular forms. The series therefore addresses issues such as the complex intertextual systems that link film, literature, art and music, as well as the production and consumption of film through a variety of hybrid media, including video, cable and satellite.

The authors take interdisciplinary approaches, which bring together a variety of theoretical and critical debates that have developed in film, media and cultural studies. They neither embrace nor condemn popular film, but explore specific forms and genres within the contexts of their production and consumption.

Already published:

Film stars

Hollywood and beyond

Edited by
Andy Willis

Manchester University Press

Manchester and New York

distributed exclusively in the USA by Palgrave

Published by Manchester University Press
Oxford Road, Manchester M13 9NR, UK
and Room 400, 175 Fifth Avenue, New York, NY 10010, USA
www.manchesteruniversitypress.co.uk

Distributed exclusively in the USA by
Palgrave, 175 Fifth Avenue, New York,
NY 10010, USA

Distributed exclusively in Canada by
UBC Press, University of British Columbia, 2029 West Mall,
Vancouver, BC, Canada V6T 1Z2

British Library Cataloguing-in-Publication Data
A catalogue record for this book is available from the British Library

Library of Congress Cataloging-in-Publication Data applied for

ISBN 0 7190 5644 6 *hardback*
　　 0 7190 5645 4 *paperback*

First published 2004

13 12 11 10 09 08 07 06 05 04　　　　10 9 8 7 6 5 4 3 2 1

Typeset in Sabon with Frutiger
by Northern Phototypesetting Co. Ltd, Bolton

Printed in Great Britain
by Bell & Bain Ltd, Glasgow

Contents

Notes on contributors

Nick Cox is a lecturer in English at Leeds Metropolitan University. His publications and research interests have focused on early modern literature and culture, popular resistance, the body and Foucault.

Phillip Drake is a lecturer in Media and Cultural Studies at the University of Paisley, Scotland. He has contributed articles and chapters on post-classical comedians, comedy and music and memory to a number of recent collections. He is currently working on the political economy of stardom and on star performance.

Cynthia Felando is a lecturer in Film at the University of California at Santa Barbara.

Mark Gallagher is Visiting Assistant Professor of English and Film Studies at the University of Missouri-Columbia. He has taught film at the University of Oregon, Georgia State University and Oklahoma State University. His work has appeared in *Jump Cut*, *Velvet Light Trap*, the *Journal of Popular Film and Television*, the *Quarterly Review of Film and Video*, the *Journal of Film and Video* and other journals and anthologies. His work analyses configurations of masculinity, race and power in popular and independent cinema and television.

Jane Hendler is a freelance lecturer and the author of *Best-Sellers and Their Film Adaptations in Post-War America: From Here to Eternity, Sayonara, Giant, Auntie Mame, Peyton Place* (Peter Lang, 2001).

Mark Jancovich is Professor and Director of the Institute of Film Studies at the University of Nottingham. He has written and edited several books, including: *Approaches to Popular Film* (with Joanne Hollows) (Manchester University Press, 1995); *Rational Fears: American Horror in the 1950s* (Manchester University Press, 1996) *The Film Studies Reader* (with Joanne Hollows and Peter Hutchings) (Arnold, 2000); *Horror, The Film Reader*

(Routledge, 2002) *The Place of the Audience: Cultural Geographies of Film Consumption* (with Lucy Faire and Sarah Stubbings) (BFI, 2003). He is the editor (with Eric Schaefer) of the MUP series *Inside Popular Film*, and a founding editor of *Scope: An Online Journal of Film Studies*.

Peter Krämer teaches Film Studies at the University of East Anglia. He has published essays on American film and media history, and on the relationship between Hollywood and Europe, in *Screen*, *The Velvet Light Trap*, *Theatre History Studies*, *The Historical Journal of Film*, *Radio and Television*, *History Today*, *Film Studies*, and *Scope: An Online Journal of Film Studies*. He has edited and co-edited numerous collections including *Screen Acting* (Routledge, 1999) and *The Silent Cinema Reader* (Routledge, 2003). He is also the co-author of a children's book entitled *American Film: An A–Z Guide* (Franklin Watts, 2003).

Lisa Taylor is a Senior Lecturer in Media and Cultural Studies at the University of Wolverhampton. She is co-author of *Media Studies: Texts Institutions and Audiences* (Blackwell, 1999). Her current research and publications are concerned with the cultural space of gardens.

Andy Willis is a Senior Lecturer in Media and Performance at the University of Salford. He is the co-author (with Lisa Taylor) of *Media Studies: Texts, Institutions and Audiences* (Blackwell, 1999), co-editor (with Antonio Lázaro-Reboll) of *Spanish Popular Cinema* (Manchester University Press, 2004) and co-editor (with Mark Jancovich, Antonio Lázaro-Reboll and Julian Stringer) of *Defining Cult Movies: The Cultural Politics of Oppositional Taste* (Manchester University Press, 2003).

Acknowledgements

A book such as this is clearly the work of many people. As editor, I would like to take the opportunity to thank all the contributors for their patience throughout what has been a fairly long process from initial idea to publication. I am also grateful to Matthew Frost and Kate Fox at Manchester University Press for their continued help and assistance. The arguments in my own chapter were rehearsed in a very different form in my contribution to *Consuming for Pleasure: Selected Essays on Popular Fiction*, edited by Julia Hallam and Nickianne Moody (Liverpool John Moores University). In a similar fashion those contained in Mark Gallagher's chapter owe a debt to his 'Masculinity in Translation: Jackie Chan's Transcultural Star Text', *Velvet Light Trap* (Spring 1997), 39. Part of Chapter 2 on Rosalind Russell originally appeared as part of *Best-Sellers and their Film Adaptations in Postwar America* (Peter Lang, 2001). It is reprinted with permission. Finally, I would like to thank Mark Jancovich for his continued support and encouragement and without whom this volume would not exist.

Andy Willis

Introduction

Andy Willis

The idea of a star has become somewhat blurred after decades of use. Indeed, today everyone from a television soap actor to a member of the *Big Brother* household seems to be able to assume the mantle 'star'. As Christine Geraghty (2000) has pointed out, film stars no longer represent a standard notion of stardom as they once did. Rather, today they compete with a range of personalities from an ever-increasing array of media. Again as Geraghty notes, whereas in the 1940s magazines would carry pin-ups of just film stars, today they are as likely to feature celebrities from the worlds of television, pop music and, increasingly, sports such as football. This clearly indicates that the definition and meaning of stars and stardom may shift significantly across different historical moments and in different production contexts. This collection therefore reflects this notion, drawing upon studies of film stars from the 1920s up to the present day, and from various contexts within increasingly global film industries. The shifting nature of the term 'star' has encouraged each contributor to draw on a variety of different approaches to popular cinema, each showing that his or her approach may assist our understanding of the subjects, the film industry that produced them, and their moment of stardom. Indeed, at the core of this book is the assumption that stars are central to any understanding of the popular film text, the industries that produce and circulate such work and the audiences that pay money to see these actors on the screen.

A general assumption, therefore, is that stars are absolutely essential to mainstream film production, be that in Hollywood or the popular national cinemas across the globe. Page upon page in the popular press have been devoted to star biography and to gossip about their private lives. However, when one casts an eye across the literature of film studies, proportionately, there is not nearly enough work produced that addresses this area. The majority of the work that has been undertaken has focused exclusively on mainstream Hollywood performers, although there have been some notable exceptions – for example, Gandhy and Thomas (1991), Teo (1997), Vincendeau (2000), Mishra (2002). As its title suggests, this book is designed to contribute to the serious study of film stars drawn from both Hollywood and beyond. Indeed, it was a desire to explore the increasing variety of stars that initiated the book that follows.

Stars and the film industry

Without doubt, stars are a key element in the overall film package. The transference of 'image' from one context or one medium to another has increasingly become a weapon in the armoury of the film financiers. Music, television and even sports stars – perhaps most notably 'blaxploitation' figures O. J. Simpson and Jim Brown – have been used to try and ensure an audience for films. This has also extended to the transference of popular performers from a range of national cinemas to Hollywood. The drive to include a familiar element within a film package is due to the ease with which distributors feel they will then be able to promote it. Again, the way in which stars translate from different contexts informs a number of the chapters that follow.

Undoubtedly most filmgoers' choices about what to watch revolve around stars, their image and their reputation. In fact, today's cinema audiences, especially in the environment of the modern multiplex, increasingly decide what to consume based on choices dictated by their awareness of star personas and the vehicles they are associated with. It is therefore not surprising that recently star studies have moved towards an analysis of audiences and their inter-action and use of stars and their images. Indeed, the questions about how far stars are made by marketing departments and how far by fans remain important ones. Certainly, as Justin Wyatt argues in his book *High Concept* (1994), the popularity of a star-driven film is dependent upon the marketing connected with its process being effective. Within his version of 'high concept', Wyatt argues that stars need to appear in the right type of vehicle for their already existing image or persona. Logically, then, it is possible to argue that stars only ensure the success of a film when they appear in a work that complements the public's view of them. If they appear in something radically different their stardom may not be enough to ensure success. Stars therefore cannot be separated from the industrial contexts of their production and their films distribution and exhibition. This confirms that whilst many are given the label 'star', there are in fact very few stars whose mere presence will secure a big opening weekend for a film. The vehicle has to fit the audience's idea of the star, or be of sufficient interest as a 'left-field' experiment to intrigue them. Thus, when Eddie Murphy achieved wide popularity once again after his post-*Beverly Hills Cop* (1984) lean period, with remakes of *The Nutty Professor* (1996) and *Dr Dolittle* (1998), audiences would only accept him when in fat rubber suits or with talking animals. Attempts to re-present his comedy action persona, such as *Metro* (1997), were not box-office successes, thus indicating that a new audience now associated him with rather different types of films and only flocked to see him in vehicles that fitted this new idea of 'Eddie Murphy'.

The sudden decline of stars' box-office fortunes reveals that audience reactions to stars can therefore never simply be assumed by the film industry. The dip in popularity of recent stars, from Arnold Schwarzenegger to Adam Sandler, clearly reveals that however much one feels it is possible to predict audience responses they are always fluid. This factor has led some writers to choose to conduct studies that actually engage with audiences in order to understand the way they react to and use star images. One of the most notable of these audience-based studies was conducted by Jackie Stacey. Drawing on approaches associated with cultural studies, her *Star Gazing* (1994) analyses the ways in which British women in the 1940s reacted to film stars, revealing a variety of possible ways in which audiences take something from the performers who appear on the cinema screen and beyond. Stacey's work indicates how far the meaning of film stars is historically, culturally and socially specific. Her writings on the older star figures from the history of Hollywood offer ways of considering these performers that acknowledge that their meaning and our understanding of them may change over time as more information appears relating to their careers.

Within star studies there has been a primary focus on Hollywood performers. As Hollywood is the most influential industry within the global film economy, that is hardly surprising. However, this concentration has sometimes overshadowed the operation of stardom within other, particularly large markets, most notably East and South Asia. Indeed, it is possible to argue that at certain historical moments such as the late 1970s and 1980s *the* most globally watched film stars came from these markets – in no small part due to the large cinema attendances in these areas. In fact if these eastern stars were able to find a place in western markets their potential is clearly massive. Certainly, Jackie Chan, thanks to careful marketing, has become such a global phenomenon since the crossover of his Hong Kong produced *Rumble in the Bronx* (1996) into the US market and his appearance in the Hollywood produced hits *Rush Hour* (1998), *Shanghai Noon* (2000) and *Rush Hour 2* (2001).

Stardom has also played an important part in the popular cinemas of Europe. Again, when compared to the volume of work produced on Hollywood this been given little space within star studies. This is due in part to the fact that European cinema still suffers from an equation with art-house products. Popular actors from Spain, France and Italy, for example, have usually only received any real academic interest when they have crossed over into the more global sphere of Hollywood. Then, they are usually discussed in terms of representations of national stereotypes. For example, Antonio Banderas, it may be argued, fits the archetypal image of the Latin lover and therefore can be sold to US audiences in this shorthand manner. European performers have often therefore had their chances limited when they attempt to challenge these simplistic definitions.

Less familiar to western audiences is the Indian screen legend Amitabh Bachchan. A star of the popular Hindi cinema since the mid-1970s, Bachchan, due to the large number of cinemagoers in India and the distribution of his vehicles in markets as diverse as Africa and the former USSR, is perhaps the second most recognised star in the world behind Jackie Chan. The difference is that most of those who are instantly familiar with his image live outside the West. However, it is only relatively recently that studies of the Hong Kong and Indian popular cinemas have begun to appear within the mainstream of film studies. For example, groundbreaking star studies that focused on Indian popular cinema, such as that by Gandhy and Thomas (1991), have only recently been followed up in any substantial way. It might also be argued that this is because academic work produced in countries such as India has only recently gained any widespread readership in the West. That is not to say that no work has been undertaken regarding these performers. Recent studies of Hindi cinema have

considered Bachchan's centrality to the development of the popular
film industry in the 1970s and 1980s (Mishra, 2001).

Alongside this, important work is now appearing that focuses
on stars and stardom within particular national film industries in
Europe. For example, Bruce Babbington's *British Film Stars* (2001)
offers a range of studies of stars from different historical moments
within the British film industry. The need for such studies is put
forward by Ginette Vincendeau, who states that,

> Yes, in the sense that stars are crucial to the economy of French
> cinema: most mainstream films feature stars who in turn organize
> its narrative hierarchy and publicity . . . France has a star system by
> virtue of the number of major film stars in activity, the length of their
> filmographies and the discursive production that exists around them:
> press, radio and television coverage, award ceremonies (the Caesars)
> and festivals, especially Cannes. (2000: 1)

Such studies show that the study of film stars and the idea of
stardom still has a key place within film studies in the future. As star
studies collide with other areas of film studies such as institutional
and audience-based approaches it is likely to shift to a more central
position. All the chapters that make up this collection draw on
a variety of approaches in order to understand the multi-faceted
entities that are film stars.

The collection opens with a number of chapters that address stars
from Hollywood's past. Collectively they suggest ways in which
stars need to be considered in their production contexts, and how
particular career trajectories reveal much about the organisation of
the Hollywood film industry and its relationship with its audience.
Cynthia Felando offers a clear reading of 1920s star Clara Bow,
arguing that her persona must be linked with wider social movements, revealing a shifting position for women in American society.
By describing how Bow was the archetypal 'flapper', Felando goes
on to suggest that her star status offered a challenge to other more
passive representations of women. Rosalind Russell is the subject of
Jane Hendler's chapter. She argues that Russell may be read pro-
gressively because she assumes particular feminine roles, often challenging, like Bow, and certainly suggesting that femininity is a role
that can be assumed to deliver particular results. Hendler also
explores the association of Russell with the role of Auntie Mame, as
she appeared on Broadway in the same role, creating a 'fit' between

the star and role. Both Felando and Hendler move from a general discussion of their chosen star to a particular reading of their presence in a particular film. The final contribution analysing stars from Hollywood's past is Mark Jancovich's study of Charlton Heston. Here we are offered an analysis that links this star's career to the changing production trends in Hollywood from the 1950s to the present. Jancovich also uses Heston as a way of exploring his association with other forms of acting, such as the classical stage, and his use of such forms as a way of legitimising his position as an 'actor'.

Contemporary Hollywood offers another set of questions. In the next cluster of chapters, Philip Drake's study of comedy star Jim Carrey uses the performer as a starting point for an exploration of the charges that Hollywood is 'dumbing down'. His study reveals how criticisms of stars such as Carrey are used to, once again, legitimise certain tastes and value judgements. Peter Krämer's chapter on Sandra Bullock charts the rise, decline and slow re-establishment of her as a top box-office attraction. The industrial decisions made regarding the roles offered to her and those she has accepted have clearly had an impact on Bullock's position at the box office. However, as Krämer argues, they also reflect wider issues, and ask important questions about, female stars and starmaking in contemporary Hollywood. Mark Gallagher's chapter on Jackie Chan marks a shift in emphasis. Here he looks at how Chan's star persona has been adapted to fit into the confines of Hollywood. He goes on to suggest that Chan, in his difference to earlier muscle-bound action heroes, offers a new and interesting manifestation of the action star in the late 1990s and early twenty-first century. A key factor in Gallagher's study is, of course, an exploration of Chan's East Asian identity. Touching upon some of the areas that Jancovich explores, Nick Cox takes actor Kenneth Branagh as his focus. He utilises the work of Pierre Bourdieu to suggest ways in which Branagh has used his association with classical Shakespearean theatre as a way of elevating the perceived social status of his film work: Branagh seemingly wants to present a persona that draws on the cultural status of theatre to distinguish him from other 'popular' film performers.

The final two chapters in the collection analyse stars who exist, in different ways, on the margins of the film industry. Lisa Taylor considers music star Prince to examine the ways in which performers' star status often depends upon how close they remain to audiences' pre-existing ideas of them. Prince therefore was enormously successful in

Purple Rain, which saw him re-present his music persona on screen, but a massive flop when he strayed away from it in the self-directed *Under the Cherry Moon*. The final chapter in the collection looks at, perhaps, one of the most marginalised aspects of recent US cinema: martial arts films of the 1990s, and in particular actress and video star Cynthia Rothrock. I argue that Rothrock's status as a 'real' martial artist has led to particular representations that have ultimately meant she has remained in the ghetto of exploitation cinema.

References

Babbington, Bruce (2001) *British Film Stars*, Manchester: Manchester University Press.

Gandhy, Behroze and Rosie Thomas (1991) 'Three Indian Film Stars', in Christine Gledhill (ed.) *Stardom: Industry of Desire*, London: Routledge.

Geraghty, Christine (2000) 'Re-examining Stardom: Questions of Texts, Bodies and Performance', in Christine Gledhill and Linda Williams (eds) *Reinventing Film Studies*, London: Arnold.

Gledhill, Christine (ed.) (1991) *Stardom: Industry of Desire*, London: Routledge.

Mishra, Vijay (2002) *Bollywood Cinema: Temples of Desire*, London: Routledge.

Stacey, Jackie (1994) *Star Gazing: Hollywood Cinema and Female Spectatorship*, London: Routledge.

Teo, Stephen (1997) *Hong Kong Cinema: The Extra Dimensions*, London: British Film Institute.

Vincendeau, Ginette (2000) *Stars and Stardom in French Cinema*, London: Continuum.

Wyatt, Justin (1994) *High Concept: Movies and Marketing in Hollywood*, Austin: University of Texas Press.

1

Clara Bow is *It*

Cynthia Felando

> She was the girl of the year, the 'it' girl, the girl for whose services
> every studio was in violent competition. This girl was the real thing,
> someone to stir every pulse in the nation. (F. S. Fitzgerald in Reid,
> 1927: 104)

In 1926, a year before the comedy-romance *It* was released, *Photo-play* magazine asked a rather provocative rhetorical question: 'What is this quivering – pulsating – throbbing – beating – palpitating IT? Undeniably It is a product of this decade. Indeed, you might say It is a product of this hour. But what is It?' (Spensley, 1926: 30). As nearly everyone at the time knew, and as *Photoplay*'s question implied, the term 'It' was slang for 'sex appeal'. And soon it was synonymous with the movie star Clara Bow. When the film *It* was released in January 1927, it proved to be a popular phenomenon of extraordinary proportions and, since then, it has been fixed in popular memory as the quintessential 'Jazz Age' movie. It was both a smash hit and a distinctive example of the 'flapper movie', which foregrounded and helped to redefine feminine sexuality during the 1920s (see Stenn, 1988: 86–7). Moreover, *It* assured Clara Bow's status as the era's most popular icon of youthful sexuality and as an idol of her generation.

This chapter reads *It* against the context of Clara Bow's star persona and in relation to her performance as Betty Lou, the film's flapper heroine. A close analysis of her performance reveals that her dynamic physical movements and gestures had the following effects: they shaped the movie's rhythm; they complemented the narrative's emphasis on disturbing conservative feminine proprieties; and they undermined the narrative's conventional ending, which promises marriage for Bow's character. Such an analysis helps to provide a more nuanced understanding of the historical definitions of femininity and sexuality that predominated in the 1920s.

Clara Bow's spirited performance can be understood in relation to the emergent changes in femininity, as the newly mobile, modern young woman started to displace the nineteenth century's genteel feminine ideal, which required a quiet, serene demeanour. Indeed, as late as the 1890s, girls and young women were taught that it was vulgar to swing their arms as they walked (see Steele, 1985: 213; Schwartz, 1992: 107). Also, while the earlier period favoured the fuller contours of the mature woman, increasingly in the early twentieth century, and especially during the 1920s, a young, slender ideal predominated. The corresponding changes in women's fashion were profound: in the earlier period, women's clothing – including long skirts, long sleeves, petticoats and corsets – functioned to restrict movement and was meant to convey an 'inner spiritual beauty'; but by the 1920s, clothing was designed to accommodate the newly dynamic feminine style. Most importantly, as fashion historian Valerie Steele notes, women's clothing was designed to be 'seen at [its] best either in an instant of walking or dancing, conversing or gesturing, or posed as if pausing' (1985: 222). Further, women's arms and legs were exposed to an unprecedented degree, which helped to accentuate the mobility of the entire body, rather than just the movement of the garments. Designers in the 1920s, like the internationally renowned Lucien Lelong, characterised the fashionable silhouette as 'predominately kinetic'; that is, although dresses and skirts gave the appearance of being slim, pleats or gathers at the waist permitted the 'absolute freedom of movement which modern life requires' (Lelong, 1927: 21). Not surprisingly perhaps, the movies helped encourage the more dynamic feminine style. For example, as fashion historian Anne Hollander observes: 'It was naturally the movies that confirmed women's visual locomotion . . . [By the 1920s], feminine gesture and posture was freer and more expressive' (1975: 340–4). Further, the modesty and demure poses favoured in the earlier period were challenged by a more visible sexuality. Hollander puts it well: 'Women strove for the erotic appeal inherent in the racehorse and the sports car. . . . Immanent sexuality, best expressed in a condition of stasis, was no longer the foundation of feminine allure. The look of possible movement became a necessary element in fashion. . . . Women, once thought to glide, were seen to walk' (1975: 153).

Notably, in the 1920s, descriptions of modern femininity and modern youth were remarkably similar – both were spoken of as hyperkinetic. As the popular magazine *Century* remarked in 1921: 'It seems that the young people have taken the bit between their teeth and are running wild. They . . . show no disposition to impose a speed limit upon themselves . . . the pace only gets hotter' (quoted in Donovan, 1967: 192). The connections between youth and femininity during the early twentieth century can be understood in relation to the emergence of new ideals of morality for youth that supplanted an earlier ideal. In terms of young women specifically, in the nineteenth century they were expected to live with their parents until marriage and to be refined and sexually temperate in preparation for motherhood and other domestic duties (Deland, 1910: 296). This ideal was challenged by a 'new morality', whereby young women no longer were expected to sublimate their sexuality, but rather to find partners who offered passion and eroticism in marriage. Havelock Ellis, for example, advocated the pursuit of sexual pleasure rather than self-control and, for youth especially, he favoured a period of sexual experimentation in order to ensure the sexual compatibility of marital partners (see Dell, 1930; D'Emilio and Freedman, 1988). In commentary that increasingly defined contemporary youth in sexual and moral terms, they were dubbed 'flaming', 'wild' and 'jazz mad'. Of course, the quintessential icon of the dynamic and youthful femininity during the 1920s was the flapper, who sported a cynical attitude and a candid interest in sex. According to a self-proclaimed flapper, the type was 'shameless, selfish and honest, but at the same time she considers these three attributes virtues' (quoted in Mowry, 1963). Clara Bow, arguably the most important flapper movie star of the 1920s, not only embodied the changes in fashion, femininity, youth and morality, they were crucial elements of her appeal in the 1920s.

Inspired by an obsession with flappers in the popular press and literature, Hollywood produced a cycle of flapper movies, starting with *Flaming Youth* in 1923, and followed by equally provocatively titled movies such as *Love 'Em and Leave 'Em* (1926), *Our Dancing Daughters* (1928), and *The Wild Party* (1929). In the typical flapper movie, a naive young woman in the Big City enthusiastically indulges in the freedom and manners of 'flaming youth' by drinking, dancing, smoking, 'joyriding' and 'petting'. Then, on the brink of defilement and/or death, she is rescued by a formerly rejected suitor, whereupon she renounces her modern ways and the movie ends with the promise of a marriage that her Victorian grandparents would embrace. However, as the following discussion suggests, neither the movie *It* nor Clara Bow's performance was typical of the cycle.

Paramount produced the flapper movie *It* specifically as a vehicle for contract player Bow, whose star was then soaring in Hollywood. By the time she was cast in the film as Betty Lou, which would become her most famous role, Bow already was well known to moviegoers and her status as a popular movie flapper had been established. She had played flappers in several successful movies, including *Black Oxen* (1925), *The Plastic Age* (1925), *Dancing Mothers* (1926), and *Mantrap* (1926). In addition, the press had noted her popularity as a movie flapper. For example, in 1926 the fan magazine *Motion Picture Classic* declared that Bow was 'the spirit of youth. She is Young America rampant, the symbol of flapperdom' (Stenn, 1988: 48). And, at the end of 1926, *Weekly Variety* commented upon her accelerating popularity and accurately predicated that she would prove to be Paramount's most important female performer in 1927 (Ungar, 1926). Finally, in 1927, *Film Daily Yearbook* named Bow one of the twelve 'Best Players of 1926' as a result of her performances in *Dancing Mothers* and *Mantrap*. Interestingly, despite the fact that the film had been undertaken specifically to capitalise on Bow's popularity, much of the studio's huge publicity campaign for *It* promoted the myth that she had been cast because she perfectly represented the newly important quality, 'It'.[1] So, several months before the movie was released, the more specific answer to the burning question, 'What is "It"?' was well known: Clara Bow was 'It' – as the movie's poster graphically underscored.

Movie flappers provided especially enticing and influential models of the new femininity, in part because they expressed themselves through 'constant, vibrant movement' (Banner, 1983: 279). But it was movie flapper Clara Bow who best embodied the modern ideal. She was bouncy and full of pep – especially in *It*. Her Betty Lou is a strikingly active dynamo whose sexuality dominates the movie and is conveyed via her physical confidence, her agility, and her tactile ease with other characters, as well as by her facial expressions. Bow's performance persuasively communicates her character's modern youthfulness, while underscoring the radical discontinuity between the past and present – in terms of feminine ideals. At this point, it is useful to make a distinction between Bow and another important movie flapper, Colleen Moore. As a result of her appearance in the first flapper movie, the extraordinarily popular *Flaming Youth* from 1923, Moore was dubbed 'the original screen flapper' (Walker, 1967: 38); but, as she herself acknowledged, her flapper image was far more tame than Bow's. Although the flappers Moore played certainly were young and spirited, Bow's flapper image was more sexually charged. As Moore explained, 'Clara Bow was my chief rival, but we were quite different in our styles. . . . I would say that she was obviously very sexy in her approach and mine was not' (quoted in Drew, 1989: 172). Another observer similarly recalled the distinction between the two stars and cleverly noted Bow's combination of youthful naivety and modern femininity: 'Colleen Moore's Flapper, while she moved in the free and easy spirit of the Jazz Age, was about as sexy as a Shirley Temple doll. Clara Bow, on and off the screen, was somebody else. She smashed through any lingering conventions' (Rogers St John, 1978: 229).

Before turning to an examination of Bow's performance in *It*, a description of the film's plot is in order: Clara Bow plays lingerie clerk Betty Lou Spence, who sets her romantic sights on her boss, Cyrus Waltham, the recent inheritor of the 'World's Largest Department Store'. Upon seeing him for the first time, she exclaims, 'Sweet Santa Claus. Give me him!' But rather than wait for Christmas, Betty Lou pursues Cyrus with aggressive determination, first by wrangling a date to the Ritz with his best friend, where she manages a formal introduction, and then by suggesting a date with him to Coney Island, despite her knowledge that he is romantically involved with another woman. Soon, with little regard for his impending engagement to Adela Van Norman, a haughty young society woman, Cyrus becomes hopelessly charmed by Betty Lou. On their first date Betty Lou and Cyrus fall in love, but they soon break up when he believes a false rumour that she is a fallen woman with a fatherless baby – a story that Betty Lou herself has fabricated in order to protect her friend, the baby's real mother (who is unemployed and in ill health), from the nosy social workers who have threatened to seize the child 'for its own good'. Cyrus then makes an old-fashioned proposal – to keep Betty Lou as his well-appointed mistress, an offer she tearfully rejects. After his unseemly offer, and in protest, Betty Lou quits her job. Then, furious because 'he wouldn't even give me the benefit of the doubt', she plots her revenge against Cyrus, declaring: 'I'll make him propose to me – and when he does, I'll laugh in his face!' With the reluctant assistance of his best friend, Betty Lou crashes Cyrus's yachting party by masquerading as a society femme, 'Miss Van Cortlandt'. Soon Betty Lou has charmed Cyrus again, and when he learns the truth about Betty Lou's 'baby', he apologises and proposes marriage. But, according to her original plan, she scoffs at him. Eventually, however, she has tearful regrets and, after a near-catastrophe during the yachting party, the couple reconciles and the movie ends happily.

Certainly, Bow's performance in *It* derived much of its effect from the parallels between her sexy off-screen persona and her on-screen flapper characters. The interaction between Bow's star persona and her performance as the heroine of *It* can be read in relation to Richard Dyer's notion of the 'fit' between a star's image and the character he or she plays in a particular movie. Correspondingly, it is the 'misfit' between image and character that encourages alternative readings that can illuminate the ideological struggle within which a movie is situated. As Dyer further suggests, one can examine a performance for its explicit meanings, as well as to consider the possibility that stars may resist their narrative material, 'not only by what they inescapably signify (i.e., via miscasting), but also through performance' (1978: 97). Inasmuch as a movie star's image is constructed from both film appearances and publicity, the star brings an image as an 'already signifying complex of meaning and affect' (Dyer, 1978: 92) to his or her films, which can trouble narrative intentions – as demonstrated by Bow's performance as Betty Lou in *It*.

Throughout 1926, the year before *It*'s release, the popular press was filled with often apocryphal stories about Bow's many lovers and the problems she had keeping track of them as she fulfilled her duties as a busy actress. In particular, the fan press published several reports that Bow was engaged to be married, but they were inevitably followed by announcements that the engagements were cancelled or had proven to be false rumours. Arguably, both the publicity for the movie, and Bow's star image as a 'playgirl' (see Rogers St Johns 1978: 233) disturbed the narrative promise of marriage for *It*'s heroine, and, along with her 'flirtatious' performance as Betty Lou, made it possible to read the movie as a tacit endorsement of a new morality of eroticism for young women and as a rejection of the sexuality of the nineteenth century's virtues of 'piety, purity, submissiveness, and domesticity' (Welter, 1966). That is, the speed with which Bow moved, her repertoire of gestures, and the association of her persona, both by critics and fans, with her movie roles as sexually aware flappers were all important factors in her depiction of a distinctly modern, youthful femininity. As film scholar Gaylyn Studlar notes, the weakness in *It*'s attempt to contain Betty Lou's 'symbolic eroticism', is due in large part to Bow's 'overwhelming dynamic eroticism', which remains undeterred by narrative closure (Studlar, 1990: 20).

The terms popular critics used to describe Bow's performance in *It* were 'dynamic', 'flirtatious', 'vivacious', 'spontaneous' and 'spirited'. Critics generally agreed that Bow's 'spirited' performance was the movie's singular strength. As *Variety* (9 February 1927) concluded in its review of the film: 'you can't get away from this Bow girl. She . . . just runs away with the film'. *Motion Picture News* (18 February 1927) raved: 'That much-discussed and bandied word ['it'] certainly fits the star . . . [Bow] . . . is so dynamic, so sure of her stuff, so abundantly vital – that she makes the film entertaining in spite of itself.' As the use of terms such as 'flirtatious' suggests, critics tended to read her predilection for dynamic movement in sexual terms without regard to the movie's conventional romantic ending, thus supporting Dyer's argument that it is through movement that women on screen can escape the controlling patriarchal gaze or narrative that is typical of 'classical Hollywood' cinema, at least as explicated by Laura Mulvey (Dyer, 1978: 97).

Throughout *It*, Clara Bow exudes a jazzy physical exuberance. In the film's medium and long shots, her movements often evoke the seductive 'shimmying and shaking' associated with popular 1920s dances – as when she bounces and shifts from foot to foot while waiting to put on her dress for her date at the Ritz. Yet, at other times, her movements suggest a simpler youthful exuberance – when she runs rather than walks to cross a room, to board a yacht, or, in the best example, when she delightedly breaks into a full run to escape Waltham's Department Store at the end of her workday. Bow's stunningly vigorous performance style occasionally prompted observers to overstate her propensity for movement, as they declared that she was 'hyperkinetic', in 'perpetual motion' (Higashi, 1978: 105), or 'alarmingly active' (Kael, 1991: 170). Thus, Paramount executive Adolph Zukor asserted that Bow 'danced even when her feet were not moving. Some part of her was in motion in all her waking moments' (Zukor, 1953: 245).

Clara Bow's reputation as a uniquely energetic performer preceded her appearance in *It*. For example, a few months before the movie was released, the fan magazine *Photoplay* published a feature that described the favourite 'camera angles' of several popular actors and actresses, including other flapper stars such as Colleen Moore, Bebe Daniels and Joan Crawford. But it was only Bow whose alleged favourite was characterised as problematic. Despite the fact that the motion picture camera functions precisely to record movement, *Photoplay* implied that Bow's dynamic style was troublesome: 'Unfortunately [her favourite angle] is a tricky one and cannot be used too often . . . the three-quarter view of the face, caught as [she] looks over [her] shoulder', with a provocative and spontaneous 'catch-me-if-you-can glance' (*Photoplay*, November, 1926). Significantly, the movie poster for *It*, a serigraph not a photograph, portrays Bow in this very pose: against a large full moon, she looks seductively over her bare shoulder with up-cast eyes and slightly parted lips.

To illustrate Bow's performance style and some of the specific methods she used to render her character in *It*, I have selected three moments for close analysis. The first moment evokes classical film theorist Béla Balázs's conceptions of the 'silent soliloquy' – 'in which a face can speak with the subtlest shades of meaning without appearing unnatural and arousing the distaste of the spectators', as well as his related notion of the 'polyphonic play of features' – in which there is a quick succession of contradictory expressions on a film performer's face (Balázs, 1952: 162–5). Specifically, the scene early in the film that introduces Bow/Betty Lou includes a series of point-of-view and reaction shots when she sees Cyrus for the first time. In response to her co-worker's exclamation, 'Hot socks – the new boss!', Bow/Betty Lou is shown looking off camera while raptly gazing at Cyrus: she parts her lips slightly, widens her eyes, and leans forward as she looks very interested in, almost surprised by, the vision of him. Following a point-of-view shot, a medium-shot shows Bow/Betty Lou comfortably leaning on the lingerie display case, unaware of the co-workers gathering behind her; her lips are still parted and she is smiling as she continues to examine Cyrus – though not lustily. The next shot, the first real close-up in the segment, is the scene's most provocative: with her chin in her hand,

Bow/Betty Lou continues to gaze at Cyrus but her expression quickly changes as she narrows her eyes, purses her lips and says (silently), 'Oh yes!' with a slight shake of her head. The last expression in her 'silent soliloquy' is unmistakably sultry and passionate. But then, as we return to a longer shot, Bow/Betty Lou is again innocently smiling rather than looking as though she is thinking lusty thoughts. Interestingly, Bow was acutely aware of the importance of cultivating sympathy for her still unconventional flapper character, and she had planned the quick succession of facial expressions in order to have the widest appeal:

> that first expression was for the lovesick dames in the audience, and . . . the second expression, that passionate stuff, was for the boys and their papas, and that . . . third expression – well, . . . just about the time all the old women in the audience had become shocked and scandalized by the passionate part, they'd suddenly see that third expression, become absorbed in it, and change their minds about me having naughty ideas, and go home thinking how pure and innocent I was; and having got me mixed up personally with this character I'm playing, they'd come again when my next picture showed up. (quoted in Card, 1957: 188–9)

The second important performance moment is a private one. Again, Dyer's work is useful. He persuasively argues that, in Hollywood's rhetoric of character construction, it is often private moments that are the moments of truth: 'What they tell us about the character is privileged over what the character says (and even does) in public' (Dyer, 1978: 95). After their first date at Coney Island, Betty Lou and Cyrus return to her apartment building in his automobile, whereupon Cyrus tries to sneak a kiss and Bow/Betty Lou responds by chastising him both verbally and by slapping him ('So you're one of those minute men – the minute you know a girl you think you can kiss her!'). She then angrily gets out of the car and dashes into her apartment building where she stands momentarily, apparently cursing his audacity, whereupon she runs upstairs to her room to secretly watch him leave. First, she gazes at him from her window but when she turns away, Bow/Betty Lou conveys a far different set of emotions than anger as she lightly and sensuously strokes her lip with her fingertip and seems to dreamily recall Cyrus's kiss. She then quickly picks up the stuffed dog in her lap and playfully snuggles, hugs and spanks it; then, she turns the dog around and, in a gesture that fellow actress Louise Brooks singled out as 'completely original', she lifts its tail to peek at its 'private parts' (quoted in Paris, 1989: 27).

Conducted in private, Bow's series of gestures has unmistakable sexual implications that go beyond Betty Lou's deception as provided in the narrative. Certainly her performance in this scene adds a certain level of ambiguity that led to a number of unusual interpretations. For one conservative trade critic who read the scene without regard to Bow's private performance, the scene's resolution was morally unobjectionable: 'In one situation it is handled delicately' (*Harrison's Reports*, 12 February 1927). Also, when Betty Lou becomes 'angry' with Cyrus for kissing her, Bow briefly employs a different mode of acting from that used in the immediately preceding and subsequent sequences, so as to convey her fierce 'disgust' at his presumption. Specifically, she adopts a more exaggerated expression as she purses her lips, stiffens her body jerkily. The exaggerated style contrasts markedly with the easier, fluid, freely gesturing style that she uses, for example, just before Cyrus's kiss, as she laughs, happily sways her head, playfully pushes her stuffed dog into his chin, and casually rests her head upon the car seat as she looks lovingly at him. The more exaggerated moment can be read as a parody of the vehemently emotive facial expressions associated with the acting style that had predominated in an earlier period of cinema history, and, as a result, it complicates the narrative suggestion that Betty Lou really is disturbed by Cyrus's amorous advances.

Unlike more conventional flapper movie narratives, *It*'s final sequence depicts the strength of an independent modern woman who needs no man to rescue her, and the final performance moment to be examined occurs during this sequence. Interestingly, it recalls the ending of the original flapper movie, *Flaming Youth*, but with a remarkable difference. In *Flaming Youth*, the heroine is forced to jump overboard from a yacht in order to escape the advances of an anarchist Lothario, whereupon she is rescued by a sailor at the very moment the rich, worthy man she really loves happens to be passing on a nearby ship. But *It* ends quite differently: after Adela is accidentally tossed into the sea when Cyrus's yacht suddenly capsizes, Betty Lou deftly and without hesitation swims to the rescue of her flailing nemesis. After saving her, Betty Lou swims to safety – alone. Without being seen, she climbs onto the yacht's hoisted anchor, whereupon she attracts Cyrus's attention by dropping her shoe on his head and he joins her on the anchor for a happy reunion and a sexy, wet embrace, and their first shared kiss. In terms of her performance specifically, Bow appears more highly eroticised here than at any other time in the movie: precariously perched on the anchor, her wet, light-coloured dress clings seductively to her body and is hiked up to reveal her thighs, which are highlighted by her apparently half-hearted attempts to pull the dress down. As they start to embrace, the couple briefly pull apart, strategically revealing the yacht's name 'IT' between them, then, as they start to kiss, Bow/Betty Lou reaches to lightly touch Cyrus's cheek near his lips with her fingertips, and she completes the gesture with a compelling flourish that suggests a frankly knowing sexual desire. Specifically, starting at his cheek, she deftly sweeps her hands over the side and back of his head, using her fingers and the palm of her hand as the film fades to black on her continuing caress.

Critics and historians argued that *It*'s ending implied that Betty Lou would entirely sacrifice her identity for marriage, but the film's final scenes indicate that the formation of this couple is not so one-sided. Certainly, Betty Lou wins her rich prince, but there is nothing to suggest that she will become a docile or decorous princess. Arguably, *It* endorses the then-emergent morality of passion and eroticism for young women and rejects the morality of the nineteenth century's pious and pure 'womanly woman', whose primary responsibilities were to her family rather than to her own personal pleasures. Indeed, Cyrus's relationship with the wealthy Adela is depicted as devoid of the passion and spontaneity between compatible partners that was the crux of the new morality, while his relationship with Betty Lou promises considerably more excitement and mutual erotic pleasure. Although *It* upholds certain flapper movie conventions, including an ending that promises marriage, it is the heroine's sexuality that is foregrounded by Bow's enchanting, kinetically charged performance. If her impending marriage to Cyrus is a narrative attempt to recuperate Betty Lou's independence, Bow's performance resists the attempt because she communicates a more knowing sexuality than is suggested by the narrative alone or than was typical of other flapper movies.

Both *It*'s narrative and Bow's performance helped to reconfigure the conventions of the flapper movie and the Cinderella myth that informs it. Accordingly, instead of the narrative trajectory of the classical romance – boy meets girl, boy loses girl, and boy gets girl back – in the movie *It*, girl meets boy, boy loses girl, and girl 'hooks'

boy – on her own terms and without regard to genteel feminine proprieties. Although in the strictest sense Bow's character remains
'chaste', *It* antagonised the feminine sexual ideal of absolute purity
because its heroine has unabashed designs on the hero's body that
are emphasised by Bow's kinetically charged and sexually captivat-
ing performance of modern femininity. In addition, *It* articulates the
possibility of heterosexual female desire outside the realm of domesticity via the depiction of the new morality of passion and erotic rec-
iprocity between male and female 'partners'.

Variety applauded *It* as 'one of those pretty little Cinderella stories' (9 February 1927). Certainly, there are a number of references
to the Cinderella fairy tale – the pre-eminent girl's fantasy – woven
into *It*'s narrative, which function both to self-reflexively critique
the fairy tale and to trouble the romantic narrative of flapper movies
in general. For example, with shop girl Betty Lou as Cinderella,
Cyrus is the Prince whose kingdom is the 'world largest department
store', and the glass slipper into which the Prince fits Cinderella's
diminutive foot becomes the shoe that Betty Lou unceremoniously
drops on Cyrus's head as he searches frantically for her at the end
of the movie. One sequence in *It* offers an especially compelling
reworking of a crucial moment in the Cinderella story, and provides
a representative example of Bow's performance style. Like Cinderella, Betty Lou undertakes what fashion magazines nowadays call
a 'day-to-evening makeover'. The difference between the two is
significant: whereas the poor, passive Cinderella is magically transformed by her fairy godmother into a perfect, class-transcendent
princess, Betty Lou's makeover is achieved with the assistance of her
friend and solidly working-class roommate Molly. It becomes, at
least at this point in *It*'s narrative, more an attempt to be chic than
to masquerade as middle or upper class. The movie's most romantic
and magical sequence, it includes a sophisticated series of glamour
shots and dissolves that reveal Betty Lou's delighted preparations for
an evening at the Ritz with Cyrus's friend Monty. Notably, Betty
Lou's enjoyment has as much to do with the process of dressing up
with her friend as it does with the outcome of her makeover efforts.
That is, she confidently and playfully transforms her plain work
dress into a dramatic cocktail chemise by boldly snipping away
strategic areas, selecting loud accessories (a long net scarf and a
large, crushed bouquet of artificial flowers), and posing vamp-like
for Molly's amusement. Later, her trip through the elegant dining

room of the Ritz with its formally attired guests is self-assured, despite the obvious disdain of the restaurant captain and her date for her garish, working-class display, and – although Betty Lou is utterly enchanted by the Ritz's luxury, whose large dining room features chandeliers, lavish draperies, grand arches and columns –she refuses to alter her manners accordingly. For example, when the restaurant captain looks her over disapprovingly and then offers the couple a discreet corner table, she refuses ('When I'm with the goldfish I want to be in the swim!'); instead, with Monty in tow, she skips to a more centrally located one – which attracts the attention of several diners.

Betty Lou contrasts sharply with two other important female characters in *It* – specifically the sympathetic, working-class Molly and the wealthy, supercilious Adela. The contrasts are rendered not only in terms of physical appearance and behaviour, but also by means of performance style and transgressive narrative elements. Whereas other flapper movies typically posed oppositions between a moderately flaming, but still-virginal flapper heroine, and a more modern, mobile, urban, and sexually experienced young woman, Betty Lou is contrasted with her roommate Molly. She is a rather surprising 'fallen woman'; that is, although she is a single mother, and thereby has a compromised morality, Molly looks and acts more like an old-fashioned girl with her long, pinned-up hair, and her shy, fragile demeanour. In what can be read as a mocking allusion to contemporary theories about the widely deplored 'masculinisation' of modern young women, Betty Lou is both the provider and protector in her surrogate family, which consists of Molly and her baby.

Betty Lou is also vastly different from Cyrus's wealthy girlfriend, the 'proper', aloof, and statuesque Adela. The pointedly brief sequence that introduces Adela is intercut with the scene that depicts Betty Lou's makeover, as she is shown sitting at the vanity in her palatial bedroom preparing for her date with Cyrus while chatting with her well-dressed mother. Adela remains nearly motionless while her maid scurries about attending to her and the sequence ends as she slowly stands and lifts her arms for the maid to dress her. The juxtaposition of the two sequences reveals and emphasises the disparate class positions of Betty Lou and Adela. Interestingly, although Adela is close to Betty Lou's age and her appearance is more modern than Molly's, she nonetheless is depicted as more old-fashioned – she is never shown without her mother and she openly deplores what she calls Betty Lou's 'lack of reserve'. Even when

Adela is walking, her longer dresses obscure her movements. And, although her blond hair is bobbed, it appears to be marcelled and evokes an older hair fashion. In contrast, as Betty Lou, Bow's hair is fashionably shingled and tousled and looks younger, sexier, and more amenable to – or the result of – movement.

The phenomenal effect of Clara Bow and her performance in *It* was dramatic: after the film's release she gained an even larger following of young fans and she inspired scores of young women to imitate her 'It Girl' style. Accordingly, feminist historian Lois Banner was prompted to argue, Bow's movie flapper provided the most influential model of femininity for American women during the 1920s (1983: 279). Among the indicators of her influence are that sales of red henna hair colouring increased, as did requests for the 'Bow bob' in beauty salons throughout the United States. National retailers immediately capitalised on Bow's enormous appeal to young women by offering products endorsed by Bow. Even the 1927 Sears catalogue included a display advertisement for 'Clara Bow Hats'. Sears marketed the inexpensive hats 'Posed by the Famous Paramount Picture Star' specifically to 'young women and misses'.

Interestingly, when 1970s feminist film scholars took up the subject of 1920s movie heroines, they referred to *It* and to Clara Bow only briefly, despite the movie and its star's extraordinary popularity and cultural impact. Furthermore, typically plot-oriented, they tended to neglect Bow's performance. Sumiko Higashi, for example, argued that *It* provided a 'negative' model of femininity, because the heroine, a working-class 'sexual predator', schemes to achieve her ultimate goal – marriage to and economic dependence upon a rich man, rather than her own career and independence (1978: 105). Similarly, historian Molly Haskell suggested that the new morality promoted in flapper movies such as *It* was 'more rhetorical than real', since the heroines were only superficially uninhibited with regard to matters of sexuality (1987: 79). That is, movie flappers were characterised as flirtatious but chaste at heart. Even the 'It girl', Haskell said, 'was not as naughty as she seemed; instead she was a disturber of the peace redeemable by marriage' (1987: 45).

Yet given the popular commentary unleashed by *It*, most of which focused on Clara Bow, it is clear that her performance touched a rather sensitive socio-cultural nerve among critics and audiences. To conservative critics, her depiction of a spirited young woman enjoying the new morality posed a serious threat to already weak genteel feminine ideals, and to the social order in general. *A New Republic* writer, for example, complained obliquely about Bow's 'lack of charm' and her forthright sexuality onscreen; instead, he endorsed the 'childlike' sexuality portrayed by Douglas Fairbanks and Mary Pickford (Bishop, 1927: 338). On the other hand, a more liberal observer, the famous American juvenile court judge Benjamin Lindsey, offered awkward reassurances to *Photoplay* readers that although Clara Bow 'may be increasing the idea of flirting and easy infatuation . . . [I]f it is to bring the idea of Love and Sex from under cover . . . it is to prove an eventual advantage' (Biery, 1927: 29).

Additional evidence of Bow's significance as a model of femininity during the 1920s is provided by conservative, censorship-oriented critics who objected in particular to depictions of or allusions to sex and sexuality, and who characterised Bow as an especially appealing but dangerously immoral model for young women. For example, Marjorie Daw's *Motion Picture Reviews*, a trade journal for exhibitors that routinely printed warnings about films with potentially troubling themes and stories, alerted readers to the meanings that viewers might infer from Bow's performance in *It*: 'Miss Bow indicates that if a young girl wriggles, struts, simpers, fondles, ogles, and otherwise makes up to her employer, the girl . . . engages his affections as well, and ends by marrying him. Surely not a healthy point of view for the girl at the ribbon counter' (quoted in Short, 1928: 129). Apparently, as conservative critics feared, at least some young women considered Bow's performance quite persuasive. When the Payne Fund Studies released their findings from research conducted between 1929 and 1933, which ostensibly 'proved' the pernicious effects of movies on young people, one aspect of the research concerned the effects of movies that featured the themes of 'love and sex' on young women in particular. Specifically, when the researchers asked young women about the effects of movies on their behaviours and attitudes about love and sex, several acknowledged that they were especially drawn to *It* by Bow and they referred to her performance in particular. As one young woman confessed: 'Sometimes, when I feel sort of blue, and I go to see Clara Bow . . . I feel like flirting with everybody when I get out of the theater' (Blumer, 1933: 105). Another young woman remarked that without the enticing example Bow provided, 'where would we get the idea of being "hot"?' (Forman, 1933: 167). Such young women were hardly alone in their admiration of Bow. Shortly after *It* was released, no less an authority on the subject of youth than F. Scott Fitzgerald proclaimed that 'Clara Bow is the quintessence of what the term "flapper" signifies. . . . Pretty, impudent, superbly assured, as worldly wise, briefly clad and "hard-berled" as possible. There were hundreds of them – her prototypes. Now . . . there are thousands more – patterning themselves after her' (Reid, 1927: 104). Indeed, depending on where one stood, that was precisely the problem – and the promise – of Clara Bow.

Note

1   Information taken from the clipping file for *It* at the Margaret Herrick Library, Academy of Motion Picture Arts and Sciences, Los Angeles.

Bibliography

Balázs, Béla (1952) *Theory of Film (Character and Growth of a New Art)*, London: Dennis Dobson.

Banner, Lois W. (1983) *American Beauty*, New York: Alfred A. Knopf.

Biery, Ruth (1927) 'Judge Ben Lindsey Defends Flapper Movies', *Photoplay*, November, 32.

Bishop, John Peale (1927) 'Sex Appeal in the Movies', *The New Republic*, 16 November.

Blum, Stella (ed.) (1981) *Everyday Fashions of the Twenties as Pictured in Sears and other Catalogs*, New York: Dover.

Blumer, Herbert (1933) *Movies and Conduct*, New York: Macmillan.

Card, James (1957) 'Winners of the Second Festival of Film Artists', *Image*, 6(8), October: 188–9.

Deland, Margaret (1910) 'The Change in the Feminine Ideal', *Atlantic Monthly*, March 1910.

Dell, Floyd (1930) *Love in the Machine Age: A Psychological Study of the Transformation from Patriarchy*, New York: Farrar & Rinehart.

D'Emilio, John and Estelle B. Freedman (1988) *Intimate Matters: A History of Sexuality in America*, New York: Harper and Row.

Donovan, Frank R. (1967) *Wild Kids: How Youth has Shocked its Elders Then and Now*, Harrisburg: Stackpole Books.

Drew, William M. (1989) *Speaking of Silents: First Ladies of the Screen*, New York: The Vestal Press.

Dyer, Richard (1978) 'Resistance Through Charisma', in E. Ann Kaplan (ed.), *Women in Film Noir*, London: British Film Institute.

Forman, Henry James (1933) *Our Movie Made Children*, New York: Macmillan.

Haskell, Molly (1987) *From Reverence to Rape: The Treatment of Women in the Movies*, Chicago: The University of Chicago Press.

Higashi, Sumiko (1978) *Virgins, Vamps and Flappers: The American Silent Movie Heroine*, Quebec: Eden Press Women's Publications.

Hollander, Anne (1975) *Seeing Through Clothes*, New York: Viking.

Kael, Pauline (1991) *5001 Nights at the Movies*, New York: Henry Holt.

Lelong, Lucien (1927) 'Fashioned So Slenderly', *Delineator*, May.

Mowry, George W. (ed.) (1963) *The Twenties: Fords, Flappers & Fanatics*, New Jersey: Prentice Hall.

Paris, Barry (1989) *Louise Brooks*, New York: Alfred A. Knopf.

Reid, Margaret (1927) 'Has the Flapper Changed? F. Scott Fitzgerald Discusses the Cinema Descendants of the Type he has Made so Well Known', *Motion Picture Magazine*, July.

Rogers St Johns, Adela (1979) *Love, Laughter, Tears: My Hollywood Story*, New York: Doubleday.

Schwartz, Hillel (1992) 'Torque: The New Kinaesthetic of the Twentieth Century', in Jonathan Crary and Sanford Kwinter (eds) *Incorporations*, vol. 6, New York: Zone.

Short, William H. (1928) *A Generation of Motion Pictures: A Review of Social Values in Recreational Films*, New York: The National Committee for the Study of Social Values in Motion Pictures.

Spensley, Dorothy (1926) 'What is IT?', *Photoplay*, February.

Steele, Valerie (1985) *Fashion and Eroticism: Ideals of Feminine Beauty from the Victorian Era to the Jazz Age*, New York: Oxford University Press.

Stenn, David (1988) *Clara Bow: Runnin' Wild*, New York: Doubleday.

Studlar, Gaylyn (1990) 'The Perils of Pleasure? Fan Magazine Discourse as Women's Commodified Culture in the 1920s', *Wide Angle*, 13.

Ungar, Arthur (1926) 'Ranking of Stars, Featured Actors and Companies', *Weekly Variety*, 29 December.

Walker, Alexander (1967) *The Celluloid Sacrifice: Aspects of Sex in the Movies*, New York: Hawthorn.

Welter, Barbara (1966) 'The Cult of Womanhood', *American Quarterly*, 18, Summer.

Zukor, Adolph with Dale Kramer (1953) *The Public is Never Wrong*, New York: G. P. Putnam's.

2

Contesting the feminine mystique:
Rosalind Russell, *Auntie Mame*
and gender performativity

Jane Hendler

In a tribute following her death in November 1976, one writer eulo-
gised Rosalind Russell as 'too smart and sassy for her own good,
a women's libber far ahead of her time' (Sarris, 1976: 57). In a
similar vein, theatre critic Arthur Bell expanded on this assessment
of her star power: 'There was both strength and vulnerability, both
masculinity and femininity in almost every part Roz played. Unwittingly, she represented liberation: not only women's liberation, but,
in some strange, odd way, gay liberation, before there was such a
thing' (Bell, 1976: 119). Curiously, neither Russell's career nor this
mid-1970s perception of her as a star associated with gender mobility and feminism has drawn the full attention of film scholars, leaving open to question precisely how and to what extent her image
may have functioned historically as a 'progressive' figure in relation
to dominant gender ideologies.

Russell's acting career, spanning nearly four decades, began in
1934 at Metro-GoldwynMayer (MGM) when she was already in her
mid-twenties – considered an 'advanced' age for most aspiring starlets at that time. With her characteristic humour, Russell described
herself as a 'second echelon' actress whose function was to replace
top stars such as Myrna Loy in case they became 'difficult' (Russell
and Chase, 1977: 60). Russell admittedly did not cultivate the glamour queen image, nor did she present herself as soft or vulnerable.
While her characters were usually destined to fall in love, however,
they inevitably appeared to be the stronger ones in the relationship.
On screen, Russell seemed to be in charge, if only because she
appeared to be constantly animated and confident; she walked with
a purposeful stride, even at times a swagger. Off screen, she was
credited with the ability, in *Time*'s words, to be the 'master [sic] of

her own destiny' (*Time*, 1953: 40). She is perhaps best known for her sophisticated comedy and quick wit, although occasionally she took dramatic roles, most notably *Sister Kenny* (1946), a biography of an Australian nurse who crusaded for polio treatment, and *Mourning Becomes Electra* (1947), both films for which she received Academy Award nominations. After her smash success in *Auntie Mame* (1958), the high point in her career, Russell continued to act throughout the 1960s and early 1970s, her later films being a mixed bag of less critically successful comedies and dramas, such as *A Majority of One* (1961), *Gypsy* (1962), and *The Trouble With Angels* (1967).

In her early roles in Hollywood films Russell appeared as the perennial career woman. Perhaps, then, it comes as no surprise that she was remembered as a kind of liberatory figure. Pre-war filmgoers, in particular, would have been able to recall her numerous films of the 1930s and 1940s, such as *His Girl Friday* (1939), *Take a Letter, Darling* (1942), and *What a Woman!* (1943), in which she played an overly independent, brisk professional woman. This competent female was, of course, recuperated in the closing moments of the films, Russell herself being quick to note, in the *Minneapolis Tribune* (9 June 1957), that these pin-striped, wise-cracking towers of strength would melt into the arms of a 'big hunk like Fred Mac-Murray' in the last reel, leaving her leading men to say, 'You're not really hard at all'. Nonetheless, the image of the 'superwoman', to borrow Molly Haskell's term (1973: 214),[1] seems to have prevented the films' closures from fully affirming the heterosexual couple and traditional femininity. Indeed, Russell's portrayals of career women earned her an award from the National Federation of Business and Professional Women's Clubs in 1950, and the tag 'career girl' not only continued to define Russell in publicity articles well into that decade, but reappeared some twenty-five years later in several of her obituaries in the popular press.

While Russell may have acquired the image of perennial 'career girl', the ambitious, independent female, the 'hard' woman, as it were, had virtually disappeared as a positive onscreen image by the 1950s, and where this figure remained, she generally was construed as either dangerous or neurotic. As Peter Biskind reminds us, 'Career women [in 1950s films] ran the risk of being criminalized, neuroticized, failing, falling ill or under cars. Or, being just plain unhappy' (1983: 263).[2] Post-war Hollywood had taken a conservative turn in responding to the emerging national politics of the Cold War, which, in part, involved symbolically linking democracy and national self-image with orthodox representations of gender and a stable family life.[3] The film industry also echoed the national post-war resettlement effort to reinstate veterans in the workplace and as heads of the household, while enticing women from their factory jobs back into the home. This is not to say that all post-war films uncritically celebrated the traditional home and family life – recall, for example, Douglas Sirk's melodramas or teen pictures such as *Rebel Without a Cause* (1955) in which the family is disintegrating or embroiled in conflict – but they did suggest that exclusion from family and domesticity was the formula for greater social upheaval and that ambitious women were clearly a danger to society.

Recognising these changes in the film industry and finding her career stagnating after years of being typecast as a brittle career women in a number of films – including *She Wouldn't Say Yes* (1945), *Tell It To The Judge* (1949), and *A Woman of Distinction* (1950), where she played a psychiatrist, a judge and a college dean, respectively – Russell risked a plunge into obscurity by leaving Hollywood in 1950 to return to the stage. Russell admitted to being at a low point in her career; Hedda Hopper seemed to confirm Russell's own assessment by pronouncing her 'old hat' (Hopper, 1955: 1). She revived her flagging confidence with a starring role as an enchanting sorceress in the national touring company of *Bell, Book and Candle* (1950) and went on to receive unanimous critical acclaim in the commercially successful Broadway productions of *Wonderful Town* (1953) and *Auntie Mame* (1956). Following this success, Russell returned to Hollywood to co-star in *Picnic* (1956) and take the lead in *Auntie Mame* (1958), the apogee of her career and, by her own account, 'the biggest success [she'd] ever had' (Hyams, 1957: 22).

What is notable about Russell's career at this critical juncture is that she accomplished her greatest acting achievements and reached the peak of her success in her forties, a point at which many female actors find it more difficult to secure leading roles and sustain their box-office draw.[4] On leaving Hollywood after nearly twenty years, Russell, always shrewd about self-promotion, assured her fans that 'her career had only begun', implicitly affirming the value of women approaching middle-age (Graham, 1955: n.p.). She began to experiment with various dramatic and comedic roles throughout the

1950s, both in film and on stage, continuing to play, if not the swaggering career woman, the woman who did not quite fit with conventional patterns of femininity. Reflecting on why she was able to revive her career at this point, Russell stated: 'I call many of our "stars" two-year girls – they come and go. They're stacked, shall we say, but they fall as they grow older. The ones who stay on top in this business – I'm a 20–year girl myself – have the quality to go on against odds. The industry has changed' (Hopper: 1955: 1). Thus, in terms of how both Russell and the entertainment industry promoted and used her stardom in the 1950s, she remained positioned somewhere between the sexy, glamour queens of the day and the actresses who inevitably played character roles; yet she was considered a leading female star, a position she sustained after receiving critical notice in her breakthrough film, *The Women* (1939). As entertainment critic Joe Hyams said of her, 'Trying to pin Rosalind Russell on paper is like trying to catch a firefly with a thimble ... she won't be typed, catalogued or filed – and that's the secret of her success' (1957: 22).

My interest in Russell lies in this construction of her 1950s star image in relation to the orthodox representation of female gender identity in post-war American culture. This chapter will examine the particular associations that accrued around 'Rosalind Russell' in order to argue that her persona functioned as a register of the contradictions inherent in post-war America's dominant gender ideologies, and that she presented an alternative to the standardised view in the decade that gender was a natural, stable, binarised category. Because Russell's persona in the 1950s became inextricably entwined with her character Mame Dennis in *Auntie Mame*, I use this extremely popular film as an especially revealing example of how star and role became mutually reinforcing representations of nonconformity and unorthodox femininity. For fans and critics alike the 'truth' about this dynamic, irrepressible female figure became inseparable from the 'truth' about Rosalind Russell, a phenomenon that Richard Dyer calls 'audience-star identification', in this case, a 'perfect fit' (Dyer, 1979: 145). As one of several critics put it, 'As Auntie Mame, Roz plays herself' (*Minneapolis Tribune*, 9 June 1957). The following investigation of Russell's star text focuses on what she brought to Mame in terms of her former roles, extra-textual images, and her screen performances, all of which functioned to amplify the 'progressive' aspects of both Russell and Mame in terms of how they were gendered. The chapter concludes with a reading of Russell's performance in *Auntie Mame*. Drawing on Judith Butler's theory that gender is performative, I argue that Auntie Mame and Rosalind Russell troubled the prevailing notion in the 1950s of an essential femininity by foregrounding gender as masquerade and parody. Gender formation, according to Butler, involves 'a stylized repetition of acts', or the manipulation of signs through bodily gestures, acts and style, which produces the *effect* of gender and 'the illusion of an abiding gendered self' (Butler, 1990: 140). What postures as an identity originating as a natural consequence of anatomical sex is merely an effect of performance or masquerade, one regulated through the dominant discourses that rule cultural practices of male and female identities. Through ongoing performances or masquerades, which make gendered acts visible on screen, viewing audiences were able to see Russell and Auntie Mame playing up and playing on the theatricality of femininity. Moviegoers, therefore, may have gained a sense that women do not embody the 'natural', but, in fact, construct their gendered 'selves' through a series of corporeal effects, such as voice, gesture and bearing, and within particular cultural and historical contexts.

The orthodox construction of gender in post-war America, in which I contextualise Russell's image and her character Auntie Mame, was largely constituted by the discourses of Freudian psychoanalysis, which understood sex as both an innate biological drive 'expressed' in accordance with a fixed binary of 'male' and 'female' and a key determinant of personality. More simply, biological sex ('male', 'female') certified gender ('masculinity', 'femininity'). In this paradigm, biological females should naturally possess feminine qualities, such as receptivity, passivity and objectivity. These qualities were key components of what Betty Friedan described as the 'feminine mystique', the ideal of feminine fulfilment that had widespread cultural currency in post-war America and had accumulated 'scientific' backing from the psychomedical establishment. For women invested in this ideal, Friedan states, 'Their only dream was to be perfect wives and mothers; their highest ambition to have five children and a beautiful house, their only fight to get and keep their husbands. They had no thought for the unfeminine problems of the world outside the home; they wanted the men to make the major decisions' (Friedan, 1963: 18). Of course, the way in which post-war women understood their roles and lived their daily lives is more

complicated and contradictory than this representation of female
sex roles would allow. As historian Joanne Meyerowitz maintains,
there were multiple histories and multiple constructions of gender
in post-war America, along with subcultural challenges to the feminine ideal and a wide range of experiences that did not correspond
with Friedan's description of white, middle-class women's lives
(Meyerowitz, 1994: 1–13). However, because this stereotypical
image held such powerful sway in the entertainment media and the
popular press as an ideal to which women in general should aspire,
it serves here as an appropriate, if admittedly somewhat reductive,
construction of post-war femininity.

Because Russell's image in the 1950s existed within and between
post-war gender ideologies and thus contained, and at times recon-
ciled, various contradictions, her persona in some respects foregrounded the regulatory nature of post-war sex roles as evidenced
in her stage and film roles, her publicity statements, and her *Reader's
Digest* articles on dating and marriage. For example, as Dyer suggests is the case with many stars (1979: 49–50), she exemplified the
specialness and success of stardom, while at the same time presenting herself as an 'ordinary' gal and 'just a custard pie kid at heart'
(Thompson, 1952: n.p.). Her family, she joked, descended from
'horse thieves' and 'good Irish peasant stock' (Hyams, 1957: 22). Yet
Russell also was frequently cited as one of America's best dressed
women and, for a short time, even marketed her own clothing line,
featuring hats, sweaters and jewellery. Her association with consumption and providing wardrobe advice to middle-class women
prompted one Detroit journalist to complain that 'she has made a
living hell for John Q. Citizen who is married to the average house-
wife' and who cannot afford to keep his wife in style (Pooler, 1952:
7). Likewise, her business acumen proved that she was good at playing a man's game, while endorsing a competitive market economy
that inevitably marginalised and oppressed both men and women.

If indeed these aspects of the Russell image may have precluded
radical engagement with the prevailing gender and class ideologies,
at the same time, the image was constituted by elements that countered dominant constructions of femininity. Considering the parts
Russell played just prior to *Auntie Mame*, we would see very different 'Russells' as the practical sister, Ruth Sherwood, who has literary aspirations but trouble attracting men in *Wonderful Town*, or the
'old maid' school teacher Rosemary Sydney in the film *Picnic*, who

in a self-abasing moment begs her long-time suitor, Howard, to marry her. Rather than simply reinforcing the feminine mystique by suggesting that marriage is the only positive option for women, Rosemary's abasement foregrounds the subjugation of self that she must undergo in order to be married, as symbolised by her crawling on her knees along the front porch after Howard. While these two earlier roles were far removed from the wise, sophisticated Mame, who obviously enjoys her single life, they share in common Russell's propensity in the 1950s for playing female figures that did not quite fit in with the orthodox brand of femininity. Whether playing the unromantic Ruth, the bitter spinster Rosemary or the iconoclastic single aunt, Russell portrayed women who acted 'different', women who either 'failed' or refused to comply with the injunction that women were subservient to and existed as sexual objects for men. Considering these roles, we can see how Russell became associated with parodying or satirising the notion that women's happiness was contingent on their snagging a husband and subordinating their own ambitions to romance.

Russell's post-war star image was built up around her pre-war roles, as well, which served to reinforce her feminist image. Russell appeared in more than forty Hollywood films prior to *Auntie Mame*; thus filmgoers were no doubt inclined to formulate certain expectations about Auntie Mame prior to stepping foot in a theatre, priming them to see Mame as an empowered woman. By her own account, Russell told *Newsweek* readers in 1957 that she had played,

> about 23 [career girls] in a row . . . doctor, college dean, head of advertising agency, crack reporter – you name it and I've done it. It got so when I picked up a script I didn't read it, just asked: 'How many telephones on my beautiful blond desk this time – four or six.' Judging from that, I could start ordering my costumes. I'd need a couple of business suits – gray flannel, one blue, and maybe one black – for the first scenes when I was ordering big hulks like Fred MacMurray and Melvyn Douglas around. (Wenning, 1957: 68–9)

Although Auntie Mame is not a career woman *per se*, Russell made this connection explicit in her memoirs, *Life is a Banquet*, that 'even in all those career-women pictures I'd been Mame, so when I finally played her, it was nothing new to me, she was the same character, only a bit more exaggerated and with a little boy instead of a leading man for a foil' (1977: 200–1). Post-war filmgoers may well have remembered her roles in films such as *His Girl Friday*, in which she played the brassy and bold Hildy Johnson, a journalist who distinguishes herself in a male-dominated profession by her quick, witty rejoinders, her ambition and her competitive spirit. (Viewers also may have recalled that in the original stage version of *His Girl Friday*, Hildy's part was written for a male actor.) These resonances with her career woman persona may have fostered the impression that Russell was tailor-made for the buoyant, unflappable Mame Dennis.

In addition, publicity about the 'real' Rosalind Russell played up the similarities between Russell and the strong, dynamic female characters she played in the stage performances in *Wonderful Town* and *Auntie Mame*. Following her explosive success in *Wonderful Town* (a remake of the 1942 film *My Sister Eileen*, for which Russell received her first Oscar nomination), *Time* magazine featured her on its cover along with a substantial biographical sketch of her. The article credits her twenty-year success in film and stage to her 'bubbling confidence', 'boundless energy', and 'shrewd sense of what is best for Rosalind Russell'. It continues by saying, 'those who have known Ros longest and best say that her part in *Wonderful Town* is simply an enlargement of her own personality. She has always been forthright, both "musically and noisily inclined", and has operated under a full head of steam' (30 March 1953: 40). *Newsweek*'s 1957 review of Broadway's *Auntie Mame* made a similar comparison: 'the same sort of raffish spirit' that Russell attributed to her character Mame could also describe Russell herself (Wenning, 1957: 70). *Cosmopolitan* spoke of 'her phenomenal energy, a power source roughly comparable to a nuclear reactor' (Whitcomb, 1958: 19), and a theatre critic, making no distinction between actress and role, observed, 'we haven't been bothered much by hurricanes this year. They were afraid of the competition' (Kerr, 1956: n.p.). Such articles consistently glossed Auntie Mame through Rosalind Russell, the confident, take-charge, ebullient actress and shrewd businesswoman. Indeed, columnist Earl Wilson called Russell 'quite a business babe' (1956: n.p.), and she and husband Fred Brisson ran a successful production company, Independent Artists, which had grossed five million dollars on two movie ventures.

Furthermore, Russell's publicity repeatedly mentioned her confidence and her willingness to take risks and learn from her 'flops'. In one interview, she advised her female fans to emulate Auntie Mame and avoid becoming 'victims of convention': 'I think every woman could profit by acquiring some of Auntie Mame's attitude of not being too influenced by what people will think of any change she wants to make in herself' (Lane, 1958: 14).

Russell's refusal to conform fully to the culture's entrenched version of gender differences began, according to her press, as a young girl. *Time* told its reader that Russell had been a tomboy:

> Ros enlisted early in the war between the sexes. In proving herself the equal of the neighborhood boys, she broke her left leg jumping out of a hayloft, her left wrist falling off a wall, her left collarbone tripping over a curb, her left arm twice – once falling off a horse, the other time when she was pushed off a chair. At summer camp, she was forever winning the cup as the best all-around athlete. She always had the self-confidence necessary to bluff her way through tough situations. (*Time*, 1953: 40)

Time associates her inclination toward 'boyish' behaviour with her later roles, particularly Ruth in *Wonderful Town*. One of Russell's best-known songs from this play, 'One Hundred Easy Ways to Lose a Man', describes Ruth's inability to keep a man because she is too quick to upstage them: 'just throw your knowledge in his face,' she crows, 'he'll never try for second base'. Russell admits that this situation did not differ much from her own experiences as a young actress; in fact, she took credit for helping to write the lyrics, adding, 'the song is the story of my life' (*World Telegram and Sun*, 22 September 1959: n.p.). Wondering why men did not flock around her as they did other young women in Hollywood, she asked her roommate, actress Charlotte Winters, what she did wrong. Winters replied, 'Ros, you just *talk* too much'.

In a droll treatment of contemporary courtship rituals published in a 1953 issue of the *Reader's Digest*, Russell ostensibly offered helpful advice to single women, so that they might avoid her 'mistakes' of scaring off prospective suitors. However, her advice, in fact, satirised the traditional assumptions of male superiority and female passivity and dependency, which effectively made competent, intelligent women less attractive as romantic partners. With tongue in cheek, Russell poked fun at the masquerade of femininity that young women felt compelled to perform in order to 'get a man', confessing that she, too, had tried acting helpless around men by asking them to get 'poor little me a drink of water'. With her typical gibe, she then delivered the punchline: 'Sometimes I had to show them where the faucet was and get the glass' (Russell, 1953: 29). In the *World Telegram*, Russell joked about her 'blunder' of being too intelligent and independent, noting that she used to insist on going home by herself on dates: 'While plodding up a mountain he'd be taking home the dumb blonde who didn't even know where she lived. Those blondes still terrify me. While you're discussing Khrushchev, they're playing kneesies under the table'.

In a later edition of the *Reader's Digest*, Russell again offered advice, this time in a serious vein, to single men and women about marriage. Marry later rather than younger, she urged, in order to increase the likelihood of success and happiness in the partnership. Using her own prolonged 'bachelorhood' as a positive example ('I was 29 when I said "I do" – that's ten years later than most girls wed nowadays'), Russell urged young women to 'go out and get a job' as opposed to marrying in their teens or early twenties (Russell, 1958: 75). Although her counsel ultimately affirmed traditional thinking about sex roles, in that women's careers would better prepare them for their future roles as wives and managers of the household, her advice may have offered a different outlook for young women, leading them to life-long careers and the possibility of choice. Elsewhere, though, Russell eschewed the idea of fixed 'stages' of women's lives (first a career, then marriage and motherhood). When asked by columnist Sheilah Graham if she approved of dual-career marriages, Russell replied, 'That noise about husband and wife both having careers and it can't work out is crazy' (1958: n.p.).

Even in her first years in Hollywood, Russell made a conscious decision to go against the grain. She declined to present herself as excessively feminine and 'sexy' as did other aspiring starlets, and as a result caused problems for Universal with regard to casting her in suitable roles (she had her first screen tests at Universal, prior to her signing on with MGM). Russell was never considered a sex symbol or a glamour girl – the result of her own choice as much as Hollywood's casting decisions. Thus, in her earlier films, she was typically cast as the foil for leading actresses. In *Life is a Banquet*, Russell recalls:

> I was put into movies with Joan Crawford and Jean Harlow, and I was always taking their men away from them. Temporarily. It was ludicrous. There would be Jean, all alabaster skin and cleft chin, savory as a ripe peach, and I'd be saying disdainfully (and usually with an English accent) to Gable or to Bob Montgomery, 'How can you spend time with *her*? She's rahther [sic] vulgar, isn't she?' (Russell and Chase, 1977: 60)

Russell admits she did not work very hard at changing her 'girl who didn't get the man' status, and while this may have been unusual in an industry that equated success with romantic leading roles, she claims to have wanted to retain some balance between the demands of Hollywood and her private life. Russell also said she was 'sensible enough to know [she] wasn't a sex symbol and never could be', and she disclosed that love scenes were 'murder' since she was not very convincing lying on a couch (Russell and Chase, 1977: 67). She was at MGM for five years before anyone ever asked if she had had a make-up test. Furthermore, she rejected any opportunity, in her own words, to 'have my name changed or my teeth capped, or my hair-line redesigned'. Even after MGM boss Louis B. Mayer said to her, 'you're a wonderful girl, but you represent yourself as a cold New England woman', Russell remained unperturbed. 'If my style was off-putting, so much the better; it made my working life easier. Nobody chased me around a desk, I wasn't the type' (Russell and Chase, 1977: 64–5).

If not being the 'type' allowed Russell to disengage from some of the sexual politics within her profession, it also informed the way her screen image became gendered. Her performance in *The Women* – the film in which she first drew acclaim as a first-rate comedienne – illustrates this point. Russell literally stole the show, declared *Time*:

> Of the 135 actresses (including Joan Crawford, Norma Shearer and Paulette Goddard) in *The Women*, Rosalind Russell is the one usually best remembered by the millions who saw the picture. She became firmly established as the idol of a generation of less-than-beautiful movie-going girls who had to use smart clothes and bright chatter to lure men away from more luscious-looking females. (*Time*, 1953: 40)

If indeed Russell became an idol for less-than-beautiful girls, a kind of 'regular gal', she also illustrated that femininity was a fabrication of particular effects, in this case, clothes and bright chatter. This is interesting in light of Haskell's claim that Russell 'was not a favorite with men': 'Like Dietrich, the combination of comic intelligence (and she had the best timing in the business) and femininity was overwhelming. Men preferred . . . to believe that her femininity was either absent or fake' (Haskell, 1973: 133). Although Haskell does not elaborate on this latter point, I think that this is what makes Russell's brand of femininity so fascinating as well as subversive: if her 'femininity' were absent or fake, then this calls into question any notion of female sexual identity as essence. That is, femininity is *both* absent and fake: absent because it exists only through its discursive production, which must then be reproduced by individual female subjects through repetition, and fake because gender has no claim to ontological status.

When Russell nabbed the role of Auntie Mame, then, her star persona – constituted through her images of the young tomboy, the shrewd businesswoman, the inexhaustible dynamo, and the actress who played self-assured career women – undoubtedly contributed to the expectation and image of Mame as a 'progressive' figure. Likewise Auntie Mame's association with role-playing and masquerade, which by itself provides a reading of the performative nature of gender, reinforced Russell's own association with gender mobility and fabrication of femininity. Moreover, Auntie Mame's popularity and power most likely derived from filmgoers' identification with her loathing of conformity and her determination to shake up the status quo. Based on Patrick Dennis's 1955 bestseller, the film *Auntie Mame* consists of a series of raucous episodic adventures involving Mame Dennis, a wealthy high-spirited nonconformist, who becomes the guardian of her orphaned nephew, Patrick (Jan Handzlik). The narrative trajectory leads full circle, beginning with Mame's attempts to instil in her ten-year-old nephew her own liberal values. As a young adult, Patrick's (Roger Smith) short-lived engagement to a vacuous, self-absorbed debutante – 'an Aryan from Darien' – threatens to override Mame's influence. But the film's closure presents viewers with a more 'suitable' match for Patrick, the intelligent, vivacious Pegeen (Pippa Scott), and an opportunity for the eccentric Mame to whisk her new charge, Patrick and Pegeen's son, off to India to experience Eastern mysticism.

Auntie Mame was very much a star vehicle for Russell, which is not to say that the film was written expressly for Russell but that, once she had been cast, many of the scenes were scripted to feature her talents as a comedienne; her particular brand of comedy may have offered audiences another way of apprehending that gendered identities are provisional rather than fixed. Russell had had her eye on the story all along, having read it in galley proofs even before its publication by Vanguard Press (Whitcomb, 1958: 18). When plans were underway to make *Auntie Mame* into a Broadway play, Russell, acting quickly, bought a controlling interest in the production and took an active role along with director Morton DaCosta in reworking Jerome Lawrence and Robert Lee's script. Russell says she 'stole from everywhere', mostly to add visual gags: 'People thought all these bits were straight out of the novel, but they weren't. In fact, people would come backstage and say we'd got every page of the book into the play, though, in fact, we'd left out masses of it' (Russell and Chase, 1977: 192).

She and DaCosta teamed up again to write scenes and gags for the film version, and although Lawrence and Lee were again the screenwriters, Russell says she had considerable behind-the-scenes influence over the final version. Certain memorable scenes in the film suggest that Russell's gifts as a comedienne were being highlighted. By and large, she stayed with polite comedy in *Auntie Mame*, delivering her punch lines with sophisticated panache, impeccable timing, the arch of her eyebrow or the widening or closing of her eyes. But, in the next moment, her humour shifted to pure slapstick: recall the farcical hunting scene, in which Russell flops along in size-three riding boots that refused to go over her feet; her rollicking, infamous 'seat' on the killer-horse, Meditation; her hilarious, short-lived job as a switchboard operator in which she must answer several phone lines in rapid succession by repeating the tongue-twister, 'Widdecombe, Gutterman, Applewhite, Bibberman and Black'; or the frantic Vera and Mame trading high-pitched insults as Mame whirls a long twist around her head in order to make a demure coronet.

One could argue that her shifts to slapstick function as a narrative mechanism that contains Russell/Mame's counter-hegemonic appeal. By situating her in a position to be laughed at, rather than allowing the audience to laugh with her, these several scenes may operate to undermine any subversive effects of this strong figure. Clearly, there appears to be a difference in the power encoded in Russell's performance as the witty, wise, sophisticated socialite and in her image as the careening female equestrian. Yet her occasional shifts to farce can also be read not as containment, but as a sign of Russell's/Mame's multiple and fluid identities. Moreover, her style of acting stresses the performativity involved in identity formation. Alternating between the screwball aunt and the drawing-room sophisticate – one minute limbs flailing wildly, in the next, gracefully descending her grand staircase – reveals that each identity is constructed through particular mannerisms, facial expressions, bearing and clothes. Thus, rather than authorising one pattern of female identity through her comedy, Russell dominated the film with various gendered performances, oscillating between acting refined and reserved, and less graceful and less composed.

Even if there were a tendency to see Russell's slapstick as recuperatory, the film produces its own contradiction to this position by reinvesting Russell/Mame with considerable narrative power at the end of each episode. Just prior to fading to black, she delivers the final quip or knowing look, at times directed authoritatively right at the camera/audience. This is a significant departure from the novel, which privileged Patrick's voice as the narrator, whose commentary framed the beginning and ending of each chapter, often with a humorous, condescending assessment of his aunt's latest escapade. This strategy functions similarly to that which Patricia Mellencamp claims operated in the popular *George Burns and Gracie Allen Show* (1986: 80–95). Gracie's efforts to disrupt and subvert patriarchal discourses were contained through laughter, argues Mellencamp, her resistance being recuperated by a framing device similar to that used by author Dennis. At the end of each weekly episode, George recovers his 'benevolent' control over Gracie through his controlling look at the camera and his voice-over commentary. To its credit, and perhaps, again, as a means of featuring Russell, the film *Auntie Mame* dropped the framing device of Patrick's narration, allowing Mame's viewpoint to prevail.

Judging from the tremendous popularity of the film, we also may surmise that the feminine mystique, despite its persuasive cultural authority, may have been a questionable ideological investment in the late 1950s for growing numbers of women, who were no longer fully convinced that marriage and motherhood were the sole sources of personal fulfilment. Considering Mame's insistence that she is too busy being a mother to Patrick to find time to be a wife to suitor Lindsey Woolsey (Patric Knowles) or her resolve to support herself during the Depression rather than accept Lindsey's marriage proposal, we can see the striking dissimilarity between Mame and this feminine ideal. Mame is not only unconcerned about establishing a traditional nuclear family unit after Patrick comes to live with her, but she projects an image of fulfilment and accomplishment outside her relationships with men. When Lindsey Woolsey proposes, apparently for the nth time, Mame laughingly refuses him, saying, 'now let's not start that again'. True, Mame is married to southern plantation owner Beauregard Burnside (Forrest Tucker) for some eight years, but Rosalind Russell's riveting screen presence relegates both Beauregard and her persistent suitor Lindsey Woolsey to mere ancillary figures. That is, they function more or less to secure Mame's heterosexuality, thus making her – and perhaps the middle-aged, androgynous Russell – more reassuring to audiences. (Notably, Mame and Beau's eight-year marriage amounts to less than ten minutes of screen time.)

Russell was able to carry the film (and the Broadway play) to great success virtually by herself.[5] Film historian Marjorie Rosen points out that by the 1950s 'few female stars could bear a picture on their shoulders alone' and that Hollywood, in contrast to the 1930s and 1940s, was offering few productions featuring 'bright and witty women who could carry a picture because their characters astounded us with style and self-importance' (1973: 246). It would appear, then, that *Auntie Mame* was somewhat an anomaly in 1950s film production for featuring a strong, self-reliant female character, who was played by an actress whose performance alone could carry the show. Although the film did feature an ensemble cast, Russell was credited with 'swallowing the wide screen whole'; she 'continues to seize the attention and hold it', asserted one reviewer, adding, 'she is largely responsible for keeping things in shape throughout the picture' (Beckley, 1958: 13).

One could argue, though, that Mame's 'unwomanliness' as a rich, empowered, independent female may have been recuperated through her construction as an eccentric aunt. Undeniably, reviews did tend to promote her character as such, using phrases like 'unmitigated screwball', 'lovable lunatic', 'kind-hearted madwoman' and 'cukey' (sic) to describe her.[6] But her eccentricity, largely generated by her social consciousness and feminism, is precisely what makes Mame a compelling and progressive cultural figure. If eccentric means, literally, off-centre or located elsewhere than at the centre, then, in a political sense, Mame – laughable and loveable though she may have been – registered a strong critique of the mainstream values of the period. Moreover, Mame's cultural power may have derived from a more radical perspective; that is, viewers may have sensed that gender formation is not a stable entity nor a pre-determined fact; rather, what they watched on film was the fabrication of femininity and its construction through ongoing gendered acts, which necessarily take place within social interactions.

That *Auntie Mame* foregrounds such gender instability is signalled in the opening scene of the film. As the housekeeper Norah Muldoon and young Patrick first cross the threshold of Beekman Place and encounter one of Mame's spectacular parties, their attention becomes fixed on a sight directly before them. The film, through shot/reverse-shot editing, underscores the disruptive impact this scene has on the newcomers. In the first shot, as Norah raises her eyes to take in the spectacle, her face registers momentary confusion, then shocked recognition. The reverse-shot reveals what leaves her aghast: two cross-dressers (one male, one female) obviously sharing a joke. The shot then returns to Norah and a bug-eyed Patrick, showing Norah's now condemnatory expression and her protective gesture towards her charge.[7] This sequence is neither an endorsement of Norah's perspective, since, as an unworldly observer, the joke seems to be on her; nor is it merely a gratuitous spectacle. Instead, the cross-dressers present a categorical confusion of 'man' and 'woman', which disrupts, if only momentarily, the appearance of a natural continuity between sex and gender, a continuity that upholds the cultural norm of binarised sexual identities.

These images of drag in the film's opening scenes introduce *Auntie Mame*'s radical message. That is, the presence of drag reinforces Butler's notion that 'gender is drag', which is to suggest that *all* gender is 'a kind of impersonation and approximation' of an ide-alised category of identity, which becomes naturalised over time through repetition (Butler, 1981: 28). The film metonymically links the man and woman in drag, the idea of gender as drag, and Auntie Mame by juxtaposing the cross-dressing scene with Mame's initial appearance, one that is characterised by pure theatricality. She enters in costume, a black sequinned mandarin lounging outfit accented with a bright orange, jewelled coat, complete with an adjustable cig-arette holder, enormous rings, bracelets, bangles, sequins and painted nails. Russell's screen performance gives a highly stylised and staged quality to Mame's gestures as well: her body is in continuous, rapid motion; her arms reach out in wide, sweeping movements; she tilts her head back or lowers her eyelids with dramatic flair. Russell punctuates her words with her eye and hand gestures as she darts through her crowd of guests, so that the words become secondary to their delivery. Attention is displaced from what Mame says on to how she says it. This connection between Mame and performance is sustained throughout the narratives by her self-conscious use of role-playing and impersonation, which was reinforced visually with the nearly twenty costume and five wig changes required of Russell in playing the flamboyant aunt. Mame's use of spectacle and masquerade allows her to articulate a more unconventional representation of female sexual identity, one that takes as its strategic aim the disruption of stable and fixed gender binaries. Furthermore, in suggesting through masquerade that gender is performative, *Auntie Mame* perhaps gave fifties audiences another perspective about sex roles, one, according to Friedan, that many women longed to hear – that deviation from these roles was not a neurotic or dysfunctional response to one's 'natural' state.

Auntie Mame performs various gendered masquerades in different contexts and for various purposes, both to resist patriarchal power and authority and to affirm alternative patterns of female identity.[8] In one of her most potent masquerades she 'puts on' in order to undermine the authority of the conservative, class-conscious banker, Dwight Babcock (Fred Clark), who, as a trustee appointed by Patrick's late father, is charged with overseeing Patrick's schooling. Vexed that '[she] has all the responsibility, [while] Mr Babcock has all the authority [for Patrick]', and knowing that her bohemian life-style transgresses the boundaries of middle-class decorum, Mame attempts to conceal her anger and nonconformity from Babcock in order to avoid losing Patrick. Her plan is to 'pass as', thus parody, a genteel, respectable maiden aunt. Aided by the theatrical experience of best friend Vera Charles (Coral Browne), Mame transforms herself through manner, gesture and clothing, so that she exhibits 'appropriate' feminine qualities: charm, restraint and passivity. She adds a braided hairpiece – a 'halo' – in order to look 'Madonna-like', and dons a conservative camel suit with soft lines. It is perhaps no coincidence that Mame's closest friend is an actress who performs whether on or off stage. Beginning her career in a travelling burlesque show, Vera has re-invented herself as 'First Lady of the American Theatre' and member of the *haut monde*. When Patrick refers to Vera as 'the English lady', Mame corrects him: 'Oh, she's not English. She's from Pittsburgh. When you're from Pittsburgh you have to do something'.

Mame's elaborately constructed impersonation nearly fails when she and Babcock square off over Patrick's education, until Mame recognises that her challenge to Babcock's authority is counterproductive. She then reverts to a ruse of demur self-renunciation, which restores their equanimity. Babcock gives his consent to the conservative Bixby School, while Mame duplicitously agrees to abide by this decision. This act of 'putting on' empowers Mame, enabling her to reduce temporarily the threat she poses to male authority and thus to continue with her own plans to send Patrick to an experimental school where he can 'stimulate his psyche and stir up his libido'. Yet her parody of a genteel maiden aunt – one of the few culturally acceptable positions of womanhood available to older, unmarried sisters – does more than just reduce anxiety. It recontextualises this identity, exposing not only its constructedness, but also the power relations embedded within this construction. The maiden aunt(ie) Mame becomes a subversive imitation of a particular masquerade, by disclosing that such qualities as deference and fragility are part of a regulatory ideal, which women must effectively imitate in order to avoid disapproval or punishment.

Soon after, Mame masquerades again, this time as the triumph of Southern womanhood during her courtship to Beauregard. At his Georgia plantation, Mame greets Beau's family wearing a gossamer white dress of organdie and tulle and a white ornamental butterfly in her soft, newly dyed blonde hair. Clearly, this highly stylised, excessive femininity – an act of 'dressing up' – is a kind of costuming that often accompanies courtship rituals and indicates that desire is constructed partly through surface significations of the body, while giving the illusion that desire has its origins in an interior identity. There may be an anxious quality to Mame's masquerade along with the pleasure involved in this embellishment, though, since she is aware of her marginalised status as a 'Yankee'. By fictionalising her past, inventing a 'daddy' who was a Colonel and herself as an accomplished equestrian, she may hope to pass as more acceptable to Beau's family.

Interestingly, Russell does not play the Southern belle consistently, but shifts back and forth between being the belle and being the worldly New Yorker. One moment she skips across the screen, drawling about her daily romps in Central Park; in the next, she is responding to Sally Cato's 'I'll hold my breath until morning' with a gravelly voiced, sarcastic 'do that'. The emphasis here is on the stylisation and theatricality of each pattern of femininity. Furthermore, if we read Mame through Russell as having a 'masculine' edge to her femininity, her enactment of the Southern belle highlights and heightens gender as masquerade. For instance, Russell's voice was likened to 'an Ambrose Lightship calling to its mate' and 'a moose's mating call' (Hyams, 1957: 20), yet Russell managed to gush fluttery 'you-alls' and 'Beau, sugahs' for her prospective in-laws. Her flirty, delicate demeanour was further produced through various props – a parasol, frilly, white garden dress, and blonde hair. Russell's blondeness is important aspect of this parody for another reason: blondeness in the 1950s, according to Dyer, was the ultimate sign of racial 'purity' and sexual desirability; that is, it signified the 'most womanly of women' (Dyer, 1986: 43–5). An important aspect of this masquerade, then, reveals the racial component ingrained in white (heterosexual) male definitions of female desirability. Oscillating between these masquerades stresses the performative aspects of femininity, not that it springs from some natural inner consciousness of women. Rather gender identity appears to be a matter of going through the motions of social conventions or, conscientiously constructing other kinds of effects through particular mannerisms, speech, clothes, make-up and other corporeal signs.

Other instances of Mame's theatrical masquerades involve her playing the 'gracious lady' for the Upsons of snobbish Mountebank, the parents of Patrick's fiancée, Gloria. As a young adult, Patrick appreciates his aunt's multiple masquerades least of all. Fearing she will make a bad first impression on Gloria, he chides his aunt, saying, 'for five minutes try to act like a normal human being'. It would be hard for audiences to miss the point, though, that acting like a 'normal' human being is just that – acting. When Mame does act 'normal', like the maiden aunt she is purported to be, she is merely imitating or reproducing the effects of a mythical identity. Moreover, Patrick is discredited here for being a 'babbitty, bourgeois snob', since his idea of a 'normal human being' is embedded in certain ruling-class expectations of gender, class and racial identities. Normal, for Patrick, means being lady-like and reserved and certainly not letting the Upsons know about Mame's outlandish friends or flaunting of 'her new flames or old peccadilloes in front of Gloria'.

Perhaps no character in the film underscores the point about gender performativity than Mame's secretary, the hilarious and hapless Agnes Gooch. Gooch 'fails' to present herself as 'properly' feminine, meaning that she does not make herself sexually appealing and receptive to males. She appears in orthopaedic Oxfords, oversized, owlish glasses, and shapeless sweaters, effectively concealing any suggestion of sexuality or a sexed body. In short, Gooch does not 'do' her gender right. Obviously, her appearances are meant to draw laughter because they diverge so drastically from the collective ideal of female sexual identity, and if so, such humour belies an aggressive edge. Many female filmgoers would have been bombarded with advice, such as that in a 1953 *Coronet* article, advising that 'the smart woman will keep herself desirable. It is her duty to herself to be feminine and desirable at all times in the eyes of the opposite sex' (quoted in Miller and Nowak, 1977: 157). But there is other significance to Gooch's 'failure'. As Butler argues, 'the injunction *to be* a given gender produces necessary failures, a variety of incoherent configurations that in their multiplicity exceed and defy the injunction by which they are generated' (1990: 145). Therefore, what becomes reified as 'real womanhood' can be sustained neither over time nor by all women, and, if this is so, the very 'natural-ness' of femininity is suspect.

That femininity has to do with bodily signification is clearly illustrated by Gooch's imitation of Mame. When Mame is unable to accompany her ghost writer Brian O'Bannion (Robin Hughes) to a party given by her book publisher, she elects to send Agnes in her place. But in order to do so, Mame must 'create' a new Agnes, which involves giving her a complete makeover and hair style and trussing her into one of Mame's form-fitting black velvet evening gowns. By putting on Mame's clothes and make-up, Agnes is not generating a mirror image of Mame; instead she is imitating the *effects* of Mame's own gendered masquerade. For what Agnes's transformation illustrates is how Mame sustains her own performance of idealised femininity. Moreover, the stark imagistic contrast between Mame and the 'old' Agnes – acted so memorably by a slouching, gawky, squint-eyed Peggy Cass – serves to highlight Mame's theatricality and emphasis on outward appearance – her basking in jewels, flashy costumes and wigs. Gooch's hunched figure, dressed in slate blues, greys and browns, is frequently juxtaposed to Mame's, who first appears on screen with Gooch in her stylish mourning dress, which is slit down her back to the waist, then punctuated by an outrageous, oversized lavender flower.

In the following scene Mame turns up in the unforgettable shimmering, deep-burgundy floor-length dress, open in the front from waist to floor to reveal matching burgundy trousers underneath. These costumes convey a certain amount of pleasure in 'dressing up', but they also indicate Mame's willingness to play with the relationship between style and power, by wearing trousers and obviously expensive clothes. If Mame's instructions to Gooch are to 'dress up' and 'step out' in style in order to affirm the identity of a 'real woman', I contend that this is affirming a provisional identity. Within this same representation of 'womanhood' lies its contestation, for to be a 'woman' involves enacting a particular pattern of femininity.

Along with instructing Gooch 'to live, live, live', Auntie Mame attempts to convey to her a valuable lesson: if the conventional signs of gender differentiation can be masqueraded, then so too can other configurations of gender. Mame's own proliferation of gender performances affords her a certain amount of gender mobility, allowing her to claim space in a terrain that is traditionally reserved for the male subject. Although Mame is associated with spectacle and the pleasures of dressing up, which are coded as 'feminine' exhibition and to-be-looked-at-ness, she just as often reverses this process of sexual differentiation, either by turning the gaze back on handsome males or by being an active agent in 'controlling' the outcome of each episode.

While the film presents Mame's nonconformity as wholly positive, it would be misleading not to suggest that its closure retreats to safer ideological ground by introducing in the final moments a model of conventional femininity in the sympathetic, perky Pegeen Ryan, who is 'safely' middle class, college educated, and sensible. Her marriage to Patrick not only reinforces the conventions of comedy, but also reproduces the image of a white, middle-class nuclear family. The strategic placing of this image in the final scenes may have safeguarded the status quo. However, given Auntie Mame's moral force and dynamism, it is not entirely convincing that the recuperation of conventional femininity, the romantic couple, and the nuclear family unit is endorsed unproblematically. Moreover, the implication that gender is performative offers up the notion that what Pegeen's image recuperates is itself just another female masquerade.

I have been arguing here that Rosalind Russell's star image, like her character Auntie Mame, was identified with a certain amount of gender mobility and nonconformity, which gave audiences an alternative way of imagining femininity and acting 'different'.[9] In a decade in which Hollywood went about standardising the image of the desirable female, epitomised by Marilyn Monroe's vulnerability and sexual receptivity, Russell's image persisted in countering it by

offering another positive identity in her plucky attitude, her purposeful and sometimes imperious stride, and a set of facial expressions that intimated wit and wisdom. Not everyone may have found
Russell's mixture of feminine and masculine gender cues desirable,
but as evidenced by her continued popularity in post-war culture and
her record-breaking success in *Auntie Mame* we can presume that
many women and men were ready and willing to intervene, once
again, in the cultural conversation on the meaning of sexual and
gender differences. Rosalind Russell and Auntie Mame may have
been two of the power sources that fuelled this emergent discourse.

Russell's star persona and her performance in *Auntie Mame* no
doubt served to reinforce how audiences also interpreted the film as
resisting certain elements within the dominant ideology of gender
and as magnifying and extending the notion that gender is an activity or a process – *always in process* – rather than a static, fixed category. In addition to her role in *Auntie Mame*, which furthered
Russell's association with characters who acted differently, her performances in *Wonderful Town* and *Bell, Book and Candle* (1950)
show how post-war women had to masquerade an idealised femininity in order to 'pass' or find social acceptance, and in *Picnic* she calls
attention to the relentless pressure on women to marry in order to be
considered fully female. These performances, while not dismantling
gender identity, suggest that the supposedly 'natural' or 'normative'
female identity is one which all women do not easily or readily
assume. While Russell and Mame may have been read as simply
eccentric women, an exception to 'normative' femininity of the
1950s, it is important to note that they also may have been viewed as
the exception that shed light on the fact that the 'natural' is socially
constructed. As Butler points out, 'only from a self-consciously
denaturalised position can we see how the appearance of naturalness
is itself constituted' (1990: 145). This is not to suggest that 1950s
audiences had access to or articulated what they saw on stage and
screen in poststructuralist discourses of gender performativity;
rather, I wish to suggest that audiences could gain a sense of how
femininity is fabricated and performed. Filmgoers watched an
actress, whose 'self' is also a persona, play a figure who continually
manipulates gender – playing with gender, style and power – and
through the figure of Agnes Gooch, they could see how gender is
fabricated through theatrical fakery, step by step, to create an effect
of naturalness. Thus they could see that the 'natural' could be stylised

in different ways. Although Russell's image contained conflicting elements of identity that supported both hegemonic and counter hegemonic values, she did contribute in significant ways to the questioning of the dominant feminine ideal and the fifties expectations of women's roles.

Notes

1 Haskell includes Russell, along with Katharine Hepburn, Bette Davis, Joan Crawford, Barbara Stanwyck and Carole Lombard, in her list of 'superwomen', or actresses of the 1930s and 1940s who were known for their portrayals of intelligent, sophisticated, independent professional women and for their ability to 'adopt male characteristics in order to enjoy male prerogatives, or merely survive'.

2 Biskind's generalisation of the representational trends of women in post-war films is corroborated by Molly Haskell (1973: 231–76), and by Marjorie Rosen (1973: 259–318). Although recent film studies point to the contradictions within the representations of women in film, Rosen's and Haskell's reading of women in 1950s films, in contrast to those in the 1940s, is still a received perception of the 1950s.

3 For a comprehensive discussion of the relationship between Cold War ideology, gender roles and family, see May 1988. For discussions on the relationship between Cold War politics and Hollywood film representations of gender and domesticity, see Rogin 1987: 236–71.

4 Russell was forty-five years old when *Auntie Mame* was released in 1958, although accounts of her exact age vary. Producer Fred Brisson, Russell's husband, admitted after her death that she was older than the stated age in her obituaries – sixty-five and a half years old as opposed to sixty-three; Brisson said the studios were behind this change, in order to make Russell appear younger.

5 Rosalind Russell was the only member of the film cast who had leading-star status. She was joined by Forrest Tucker (Beauregard Burnside), Fred Clark (Dwight Babcock), Coral Browne (Vera Charles), Roger Smith (Patrick Dennis as an adult) and Hollywood newcomer Peggy Cass (Agnes Gooch). While Clark and Tucker were well-known character actors, neither had developed careers as leading men.

6 These descriptive phrases appeared in the *Columbus Citizen* (cited on the inside cover of the 1956 Popular Library paperback edition of *Auntie Mame*); Time, 1956: 71; and *Look*, 1957: 68, respectively.

7 For moviegoers who had read Patrick Dennis's novel (1956: 14), they would know the cross-dressers' referent: 'The man looked like a woman, and the woman, except for her tweed skirt, was almost a perfect Ramon

Navarro'. Nineties readers can not miss the implications here in recognising that sexual identities are constructed through performance: the image of a double impersonation in a woman masquerading as a (gay) man, who had masqueraded as a straight romantic male lead in silent screen performances.

8   I adopt Chris Holmlund's descriptions of masquerade (1993: 216), in order to clarify how masquerade functions according to different contexts; Holmlund's terms include 'dressing up' or embellishment; 'putting on' or parody; and 'stepping out', which refers to masquerading to contest or affirm a particular identity.

9   Michael Bronski (1984: 122) contributes another perspective on audience identification, which echoes Arthur Bell's words (at the beginning of this chapter) about Russell representing gay liberation. In discussing the importance of Russell's performance in *Auntie Mame* for gay audiences, he claims that '*Auntie Mame* may have been the last extreme in placing a hidden gay sensibility upon the Broadway stage. (It was *very* extreme . . . Rosalind Russell in her Travis Banton outfits looked more like a drag queen than an eccentric woman)'. The narrative itself further appealed to gay audiences because it emphasised 'acting different and acting out'. Bronski's insights are valuable for pointing out that audiences were diverse and brought a variety of perspectives and readings to a performance. Furthermore, since few, if any, positive images of homosexuality existed in mainstream culture in the 1950s, Bronski's calling attention to how and where gay audience members located such images adds to an understanding of how marginalised groups used popular culture in counter-hegemonic ways to meet their own needs. Rosalind Russell also may have been associated with a gay sensibility after she toured in *Bell, Book and Candle*, a play about three witches, which, Bronski claims, contained an obvious gay subtext. Of *Bell*, Bronski says: 'If it was impossible for gay people to write openly about themselves, they would find other ways to express their experiences on stage'.

References

Beckley, Paul V. (1958) 'Rosalind Russell in Movie *Mame*', *New York Herald Tribune*, 7 December.

Bell, Arthur (1976) 'A Fan's Notes', *The Village Voice*, 13 December.

Biskind, Peter (1983) *Seeing is Believing: How Hollywood Taught Us to Stop Worrying and Love the Fifties*, New York: Pantheon Books.

Bronski, Michael (1984) *Culture Clash: The Making of Gay Sensibility*, Boston: South End Press.

Butler, Judith (1981) 'Imitation and Gender Insubordination', in Diana Fuss (ed.), *Inside/Out: Lesbian Theories, Gay Theories*, New York: Routledge.

Butler, Judith (1990) *Gender Trouble: Feminism and the Subversion of Identity*, New York: Routledge.

Corber, Robert J. (1993) *In the Name of National Security: Hitchcock, Homophobia, and the Political Construction of Gender in Postwar America*, Durham, NC: Duke University Press.

Dennis, Patrick (1956) *Auntie Mame*, New York: Popular Library.

Dyer, Richard (1979) *Stars*, London: British Film Institute.

Dyer, Richard (1986) *Heavenly Bodies: Film Stars and Society*, New York: St Martin's Press.

Friedan, Betty (1963) *The Feminine Mystique*, New York: W. W. Norton.

Haskell, Molly (1973) *From Reverence to Rape: The Treatment of Women in the Movies*, New York: Holt, Rinehart and Winston.

Holmlund, Chris (1993) 'Masculinity as Multiple Masquerade', in Steven Cohan and Ina Rae Hark (eds), *Screening the Male: Exploring Masculinities in Hollywood Cinema*, London: Routledge.

Hopper, Hedda (1955) 'Ex-Career Girl Russell Starts a New Career', *Los Angeles Times*, 11 September.

Hyams, Joe (1957) 'Hollywood's Ageless Stars', *New York Herald Tribune*, 11 April.

Kerr, Walter (1956) 'Theatre Review of *Auntie Mame*', *New York Herald Tribune*, 1 November, 18.

Lane, Lydia (1958) 'Roz says: "Listen Well"', *Los Angeles Times*, 30 November.

Look (1957) 'The Wonderful Wizardry of Roz', *Look*, 28 May.

May, Elaine Tyler (1988) *Homeward Bound: American Families in the Cold War Era*, New York: Basic Books.

Mellencamp, Patricia (1986) *Studies in Entertainment: Critical Approaches to Mass Culture*, Bloomington: Indiana University Press.

Meyerowitz, Joanne (1994) *Not June Cleaver: Women and Gender in Postwar America, 1945–1960*, Philadelphia: Temple University Press.

Miller, Douglas T. and Marion Nowak (1977) *The Fifties: The Way We Really Were*, New York: Doubleday.

Pooler, James S. (1952) 'Roz's Wardrobe Tips Play Hob with Hubby', *Detroit Free Press*, 5 February.

Rogin, Michael (1987) *Ronald Reagan: The Movie and Other Episodes in Political Demonology*, Berkeley: University of California Press.

Rosen, Marjorie (1973) *Popcorn Venus: Women, Movies and the American Dream*, New York: Coward, McCann and Geoghegan.

Russell, Rosalind (1953) 'What I've Learned about Men', *Reader's Digest*, November.

Russell, Rosalind (1958) 'I'm Glad I Didn't Marry Young', *Reader's Digest*, November.

Russell, Rosalind and Chase, Chris (1977) *Life is a Banquet*, New York: Random House.

Sarris, Andrew (1976) *The Village Voice*, 20 December.

Thompson, Howard (1952) 'Rosalind Russell's Ready Repartee', *New York Times*, 30 November.

Time (1953) 'The Comic Spirit', *Time*, 30 March.

Time (1956) 'New Plays in Manhattan', *Time*, 12 November.

Wenning, T. H. (1957) 'This is the Busiest Star at Her Busiest', *Newsweek*, 13 May.

Whitcomb, Jon (1958) 'Auntie Roz', *Cosmopolitan*, 1 December.

Wilson, Earl (1956) 'It Happened Last Night', *New York Post*, 1 November.

3

'Charlton Heston is an axiom': spectacle and performance in the development of the blockbuster

Mark Jancovich

Charlton Heston is probably best known as the star of biblical or historical epics. This genre, as a number of critics have pointed out, was one of Hollywood's responses to a whole series of economic and cultural developments in the post-war period, developments which have led to the emergence of what has been referred to as 'the New Hollywood'. In short, the biblical and historical epics were one of the earliest manifestations of 'the movie blockbuster', a category of film production 'the steady rise' of which has been argued to be 'the one abiding aspect of [Hollywood's] post-war transformation' (Schatz, 1993: 8).

For Schatz, as for many others, the pivotal moment in the development of the blockbuster was the phenomenal success of *The Ten Commandments* in 1956, a film that not only starred Charlton Heston, but also firmly established the direction of his career thereafter. Indeed, while Michel Mourlet has famously referred to Heston as 'an axiom' of the cinema, whose physical presence 'provides a more accurate definition of the cinema than films like *Hiroshima Mon Amour* or *Citizen Kane*' (Mourlet, 1991: 234), the purpose of this chapter is to demonstrate that it is not just in terms of his physical presence that Heston can be seen as 'an axiom': Heston's career almost perfectly coincides with Hollywood's post-war transformation and with the development of the blockbuster.

His career therefore provides an exemplary instance through which to track the post-war American cinema, both in industrial and ideological terms. For example, Heston's association with the blockbuster is particularly interesting given that, despite the critical derision which is often directed at it by critics, Heston himself, as the Mourlet quote illustrates, has actually been able to distance himself from its more negative associations. This chapter will use Heston's career to track developments within post-war Hollywood, before moving on to examine the ways in which his star image has sought to legitimate his function as a spectacular body through a constant presentation of him as a 'legitimate' actor of the classical theatre, and through specific constructions of masculinity and heroism.

Heston and the blockbuster

In his account of the emergence of the New Hollywood, Thomas Schatz refers to three distinct periods – 1946–55, 1956–65 and 1966–75 – which he relates to various developments inside and outside the industry: 'the shift to independent motion picture production, the changing role of the studios, the emergence of commercial TV, and changes in the American lifestyle and patterns of media consumption' (Schatz, 1993: 10). The first of these periods is seen as one of transition, in which Hollywood faced a series of challenges following the five-year war-time boom during which it reaped record ticket sales and box office revenues. In fact, Heston's Hollywood career took off in the very middle of this first period and his arrival was significant in that he fought for, and was given, a non-exclusive contract. As Heston puts it, Fox 'offered me the contract. But that was the catch, you see; you had to sign an exclusive contract. Every filmmaker, actor, director or writer was the exclusive property of one studio or another. I wanted no part of that' (Heston, 1996: 91). The final contract did call for a fixed number of films, but Heston was given the freedom to accept stage and television work and to work with other movie producers. In this way, Heston's contract represented an early stage in the dismantling of the studio system, while also allowing himself and the industry to define his star image in association with the legitimate theatre. Even at this stage, he was able to present himself as more than just a Hollywood actor, and so establish claims to both 'integrity' and 'seriousness'.

Nonetheless, from very early on Heston was associated with the blockbuster. In 1952, only his second year in Hollywood, he starred in *Ruby Gentry*, a film which was clearly modelled on *Duel in the Sun* (1946), a blockbuster which, like *Ruby Gentry*, was directed by King Vidor, produced by David O. Selznick and starred the latter's wife, Jennifer Jones. *Duel in the Sun* not only took a phenomenal $11.3 million in rentals, but is used by Schatz to define the start of this transitional stage in the development of the New Hollywood because it 'signalled important changes in the industry' (Schatz, 1993: 11).

Furthermore, Heston's next film was Cecil B. DeMille's circus spectacular, *The Greatest Show on Earth* (1952). This film not only consolidated Heston's association with the blockbuster but, in so doing, put him in line for the role of Moses in DeMille's *The Ten Commandments*, a film that took an unprecedented $43 million and is used by Schatz to mark the start of the next stage of development, the stage which saw the consolidation of the blockbuster. However, during this first stage, Heston also appeared in *The Naked Jungle* (1954), an epic adventure set in the Amazon in which Heston battles against a vast army of soldier ants. It was produced by George Pal, who had made *War of the Worlds* the previous year and who would make his name as a producer of classic science fiction (SF) and fantasy films. This film is therefore significant in two ways: it was associated with an emerging taste for SF and fantasy that was largely a product of the increasingly important teenage audience and with the rise of independent production companies such as AIP (see Doherty, 1988); but perhaps more directly the film prefigured the disaster movies of the 1970s, with which Heston would also be associated.

If this first stage saw the consolidation of the blockbuster strategy within Hollywood, the second stage saw it flourish with Hollywood investing in a series of '"big" all-star projects, most of them shot on location for an international market' (Schatz, 1993: 13). Furthermore, of these films, two out of the top five grossing films starred Heston: *The Ten Commandments* and *Ben Hur*, which was described by *Variety* as 'the blockbuster to top all previous blockbusters' (Crowther, 1986: 64). However, these two films were not the only blockbusters featuring Heston. Between 1956 and 1966, Heston made an extraordinary number of big, all-star pictures: *The Buccaneer* (1958) with Yul Brynner, Claire Bloom, Charles Boyer; *The Big Country* (1958) with Gregory Peck, Burl Ives and Charles Bickford, Carroll Baker and Jean Simmons; *El Cid* (1961) with Sophia Loren, Raf Vallone, Genevieve Page, Douglas Wilmer and Herbert Lom; *Diamond Head* (1962) with Yvette Minieux, George Chakiris and James Darren; *55 Days in Peking* (1963) with Ava Gardner, David Niven, John Ireland, Robert Helpmann, and Dame Flora Robson; *The Agony and the Ecstasy* (1965) with Rex Harrison, Diane Cilento and Harry Andrews; *The Greatest Story Ever Told*

(1965) with Max von Sydow, Carroll Baker, José Ferrer, Van Heflin, Angela Lansbury, Roddy McDowall, Dorothy McGuire, Sal Mineo, Donald Pleasence, Sidney Poitier, Claude Rains, Telly Savalas, John Wayne and Shelley Winters; *The War Lord* (1965) with Richard Boone, Maurice Evans, Guy Stockwell, Niall MacGinnis and James Farentino; and *Khartoum* (1966) with Laurence Olivier, Richard Johnson, Ralph Richardson, Alexander Knox, Michael Harden, Nigel Green and Douglas Wilmer.

Significantly, however, Heston had grown tired of these projects by 1965, and began to look elsewhere for material. Such a move was opportune given that, as Schatz points out, despite the popularity of *The Sound of Music* in 1965, with its fantastic revenues of $79.9 million, 'Hollywood was on the verge of its worst economic slump since the war' (Schatz, 1993: 14). *The Sound of Music* prompted a musical binge that produced a string of flops including *Dr Dolittle* (1967) and *Hello, Dolly* (1969). However, other developments helped keep Hollywood afloat. A string of relatively inexpensive films with counter-cultural associations proved great successes, most famously *The Graduate* (1967) and *Easy Rider* (1969). They were not only made by a new generation of filmmakers that emerged from TV, theatre and film school – a generation that was greatly influenced by the European art cinema of the period – but they also spoke to, and about, an increasingly important youth audience. It is therefore interesting that in 1965 Heston had chosen to work on *Major Dundee* with Sam Peckinpah, a director who was clearly aligned with the tastes of this new generation. Heston was so committed to the project that he offered the studios his fee back if they would let Peckinpah complete the film without interference, an offer which the studios accepted, much to Heston's chagrin.

However, the importance of this generation is sometimes overemphasised, and these films did not displace the blockbuster. Indeed, Heston's career hit a new high in 1968 with a new blockbuster directed by Franklin J. Schaffner: a director who had emerged from TV, where he had directed some of Heston's early performances, and who was influenced by the European art cinema. However, Schaffner did not simply make small, low-budget productions. On the contrary, he was frequently associated with big-budget epics such as *Patton* (1970), *Nicholas and Alexandra* (1971) and *Papillon* (1973). The film they made together in 1968 was *Planet of the Apes*. *Planet of the Apes* was a SF epic that, along with *2001: A Space*

Odyssey in the same year, established the importance of the SF blockbuster of the early 1970s, a genre within which Heston would make another three films: *Beneath the Planet of the Apes* (1970), *The Omega Man* (1971) and *Soylent Green* (1973). These films are significant as they mark a point of transition between the SF film as it emerged in the 1950s, when it was largely associated with the increasingly important teenage audience and with the low-budget productions of the independents, and the post-1975 SF blockbusters that followed the success of *Star Wars* (1977). Indeed, it has been argued that many of the New Hollywood's blockbusters were simply up-scaled versions of the 1950s low-budget cinema, and these films are often awash with references to their predecessors in the 1950s. Many of the directors came of out low-budget filmmaking, or had been fans of these kinds of movies in their youth, and it has frequently been remarked that *Jaws* (1975), which Schatz uses to mark the end of the third stage of development and 'the arrival of the New Hollywood' proper, is little more than a 1950s monster movie in both structure and tone (Corman and Kerome, 1990).

The SF blockbusters with which Heston was associated, however, exist between these two moments. They are clearly indebted to the independent teenpics of the 1950s. *Planet of the Apes* was even written by Rod Serling – the figurehead of the cult TV fantasy show *The Twilight Zone* – and, in many ways, its themes and its ending were prefigured by films such as Roger Corman's *Teenage Caveman* (1958). However, it also had a substantial budget and clear intellectual pretensions. It employs a series of techniques from European art cinema, and articulates a counter-cultural politics. Heston himself plays a man who is so disgusted with human society in the twentieth century that he goes into space in the hope that 'somewhere in the universe there must be something better than man'. What he finds, however, is an allegory of political ignorance and repression, and the final proof of human folly. The planet of the apes, it turns out, is the earth of the future, a largely barren and desolate world that has been destroyed by nuclear warfare. These themes continue through *The Omega Man* and *Soylent Green*, both of which, by implication, present contemporary American society as essentially repressive and self-destructive.

Between *The Omega Man* and *Soylent Green*, however, Heston was to make another film that would again associate him with yet another blockbuster cycle, the disaster movie. This film was *Skyjacked*

(1972), a thriller about the hijacking of a plane, which Heston made in order to obtain MGM's permission for him to use battle sequences from *Ben Hur* in his film of Shakespeare's *Antony and Cleopatra* (1973). Although it is largely a thriller, the film was clearly made in response to the success of *Airport* (1970) and, as such, it marked a transition to the full-blown disaster movies of the mid-1970s. Indeed, Heston's next film in the cycle would be the sequel to *Airport* itself, *Airport 1975* (1974), and he would also go on to make *Earthquake* (1975), *Two Minute Warning* (1976) and *Gray Lady Down* (1978).

These films are significant in a number of ways. For example, they are used by a number of critics to mark a shift away from the supposedly formally and politically radical films of the late 1960s and early 1970s, and are therefore seen as films that represented a move back to formal and political conservatism within Hollywood (Britton, 1986; Wood, 1986). For these critics, these films are read as presenting traditional authority figures as the only solution to a society in a state of emergency and crisis. Hence they are seen as explicitly anti-counter-cultural. However, although some films, such as *Airport*, are clearly about the technical administration of large complex institutions by experts, this is not true of the cycle as a whole. *Earthquake*, for example, emphasises the helplessness of traditional forms of authority in the face of nature's capriciousness, and even condemns these authorities. Heston plays an architect, for example, whose father-in-law (Lorne Greene) is a contractor who, like other contractors, has been cutting corners and putting up unsafe buildings. Even the forces of law and order are presented ambiguously. While George Kennedy does play a kindly neighbour-hood cop, Marjoe Gortner plays a fascistic national guardsman who, drunk with power, attempts to rape a woman and who shoots people for fun.

Indeed, while these films do sometimes end with traditional authority figures saving the day, they finally stress the fragility of social order. They can even be seen as offering the pleasures of seeing the dull routines of modern life being swept away, and as demonstrating the need to identify 'real' and 'fundamental' priorities in a world that is presented as corrupt and compromised. In *Earthquake*, for example, not only is Los Angeles destroyed, as if by a biblical form of divine intervention, but the city is vulnerable exactly because of its corruption. This is focused in the character played by Heston, who is unhappily married to Ava Gardner despite the fact that he really loves Genevieve Bujold. However, he remains in a state of indecision about how to resolve the situation until it is too late, because his wife is the daughter of a major developer for whom he works. He is therefore seen as compromised and corrupted not only by his refusal to admit his real feelings, but also because his relationship to the developer has implicated him in the construction of unsafe buildings that the earthquake will eventually destroy.

After the mid-1970s, and the 'arrival of the New Hollywood', however, Heston's film career went into a new phase. By the release of *Jaws* (1975) he was 51 and therefore made few, if any, major motion pictures during the late 1970s and early 1980s. However, he did, as a result, become associated with other developments. In 1985, for example, he starred in *The Colbys*, a spin-off from *Dynasty*, which along with *Dallas* was almost the epitome of the big-budget primetime television drama of the 1980s. Indeed, these series were often used around the world to focus concerns about the nature of what became known as global culture. One of the complaints was that these shows were distinguished by both a melodramatic structure of feeling and a spectacle of visual opulence and excess (Ang, 1985). As a result, although *The Colbys* itself was launched as the cycle was just about to go into decline, and hence did not take off, the choice of Charlton Heston for the part of Jason Colby was telling: it suggested that he now carried an association with the glamour and spectacle of an earlier, and now nostalgically remembered, Hollywood. Indeed, in some ways it marked a return to the origins of his career in melodramas such as *Ruby Gentry*.

Rather more successful, however, was another venture by Heston 1988. In his autobiography, he writes: 'Frazer [Heston's son] pointed out that Ted Turner was about to launch a very ambitious new cable network, Turner Network Television (TNT). A new full-scale film of *A Man for All Seasons* would make a very prestigious production, for Ted and for us' (Heston, 1996: 535). The collaboration paid off and Heston went on to make two more films for TNT: *Treasure Island* (1990) and *Crucible of Blood* (1991). In this way, Turner was able to use Heston to give the network an aura of 'quality'. These films drew on Heston's associations with legitimate culture: *A Man for All Seasons* was a well-respected contemporary play that had already been successfully converted into an Oscar-nominated film (1966), and whose setting, the period of Henry VIII, carried with it classical and even vaguely Shakespearean associations; *Treasure Island* was a children's classic; and *Crucible of Blood* was based on a play about Sherlock Holmes, the British detective of Conan Doyle's popular literary classics. These films play with Heston's image as both a legitimate actor and a star of classical Hollywood. Even though, of course, he is a figure who emerges in its immediate aftermath, his presence as a star of the 'past' is of significance. In *The Colbys*, after all, Barbara Stanwyck was cast as his sister.

His status as a star of the 'past' has also enabled him to return to the Hollywood blockbuster as an almost iconic presence, and even as a kind of postmodern reference point. In *Wayne's World 2* (1993), for example, he appears as 'Good Actor'. Towards the end of the film, Wayne rushes to prevent Cassandra's wedding in a pastiche of *The Graduate,* and on the way he encounters an old man who tells him a story. Half-way through the old man's fumbling delivery, Wayne suddenly requests a better actor, and the old man is suddenly replaced by Heston, whose delivery reduces Wayne to tears.

In the James Cameron/Arnold Schwarzenegger blockbuster *True Lies* (1994), on the other hand, Heston appears as Schwarzenegger's boss. In his autobiography, Heston recalls that Cameron had claimed: 'I need you because you can plausibly intimidate Arnold' (Heston, 1996: 518). The reason why Heston could be 'plausible' as the scarred, one-eyed spymaster is, of course, because while the film clearly relies on a series of references to the past in the form of James Bond movies, Heston himself brings with him associations with earlier blockbuster spectacles. Indeed, since the 1990s, Hollywood has been awash with rumours about attempts to remake both *Planet of the Apes* and *The Omega Man*, and in both cases, Schwarzenegger has been identified as the potential star of these projects. In other words, Heston could plausibly intimidate Schwarzenegger because he signifies a kind of prototype of the spectacular action hero of which Schwarzenegger is only a newer incarnation. Like these action stars, Heston is physically 'unsuited for many, if not most, contemporary roles' (Crowther, 1986: 86), and needs the blockbuster's 'visual pyrotechnics . . . overblown budgets . . . expansive landscapes' to provide a context for his physical presence (Tasker, 1993: 76).

The blockbuster, performance and the classical actor

If, however, Heston represents an early prototype of the contemporary action star, he has always had greater critical respectability than action stars such as Stallone and Schwarzenegger. Indeed, as has been pointed out by both Cohan (1998) and Krämer (1998), similar anxieties to those that Tasker identifies in relation to the action stars of the 1980s can be identified in the 1950s. These anxieties were a response to the presence of male bodily display within Hollywood films of the 1950s, a response that saw this display as somehow unmanly; as representing 'The Crisis of Masculinity'; and as having associations with homosexuality (see, for example, Schlesinger, 1964; Cohan, 1998; Krämer, 1998). Indeed, the biblical and historical epic, the genre with which Heston was most associated during the 1950s, seems to have particularly horrified the cultural critic Dwight Macdonald. His collection of movie reviews, *On Movies*, seems almost pathologically obsessed with a hatred of the epic in general, and with the films of Steve Reeves in particular. It even dedicates a whole section to 'The Biblical Spectacular' (Macdonald, 1969).

However, it is not the absence of male bodily display that differentiates Heston from the contemporary action stars that Tasker discusses. Like them, his films frequently feature, and even revolve around, the spectacle of the body. Heston himself is clearly aware of this, and makes a joke of it in his journals when he notes during the making of *Planet of the Apes*: 'The trial scene involves, as so many of my parts seem to, another manhandling (or ape-handling, in this case). It hurts after ten takes. They're trying to think of a different way of tying me up from those used in TEN COMMANDMENTS, BEN HUR, etc., etc., etc.' (Heston, 1980: 275). However, he seems rather more defensive about the issues of nudity: 'I did an interview today on the significance of male nudity in films. I don't know why I qualify as an expert on this vital subject; I've only been nude (and that fleetingly) in four films' (Heston, 1980: 295). Actually, four nude appearances seems rather a lot by the standards of 1968, and it is perhaps not insignificant that one poster for *Planet of the Apes* advertised the film with a photo, from the trial scene mentioned above, of the virtually nude Heston.

However, while Bruce Crowther complains that Heston has 'failed to gain the level of critical approval often granted to actors of considerably less merit and distinction' (Crowther, 1986: 9), Heston has actually rarely received the kind of vilification one might expect. Indeed, despite his associations with the blockbuster and particularly the significance of bodily display to the roles that he takes, he has actually received a very positive response. The mainstream press often treats him with respect as an actor of some quality and significance, and even avant-garde critics, such as those involved with *Cahiers du Cinéma*, have taken him seriously. Indeed, as Leon Hunt has argued, Michael Mourlet's description of Heston reads like 'a virtual love poem to Heston' (Hunt, 1993: 68).

One of the main reasons for this response is that Heston has managed to legitimate his presence as a 'spectacular body' through the continual emphasis on his supposed status as a 'legitimate' theatrical actor. His journals, for example, were published under the title, *An Actor's Life* (Heston, 1980), and despite the fact that his readership was mainly interested in his film career, an interest to which the selections clearly pander, the book also makes continual references to his theatrical career to constantly reinforce the suggestion that he is, first and foremost, a professional, theatrical actor rather than a Hollywood film star. Furthermore, he is presented not simply as a theatrical actor, but as a 'classical' actor. In particular, he likes to emphasise his association with Shakespearean drama, but even when he does tackle modern plays, he avoids modern American dramatists such as Albee, Williams, Mamet or Shepherd in favour of plays and playwrights with an aura of classicism or an association with literary classics. For example, he has been in several productions of Robert Bolt's 1960 play *A Man for All Seasons*, of which he writes, 'I still don't know of any play written in that period that's as good' (Heston, 1996: 358). Another play to which he has returned a number of times is *Crucible of Blood*, a play in which he plays Sherlock Holmes.

Ironically, however, Heston's associations with legitimate drama were largely forged not through the theatre itself, but through his performances, during the late 1940s, in live television versions of classic plays and novels such as *Macbeth*, *Julius Caesar*, *The Taming of the Shrew*, *Wuthering Heights*, *Of Human Bondage*, and *Wings of A Dove*. The association with the classical has also been consolidated through his films. He has starred in numerous historical epics, in which he has played numerous 'great men' of history – Moses, John the Baptist, Mark Antony, Ben Hur, El Cid, Michaelangleo, Thomas More, Cardinal Richelieu, Andrew Jackson, General Gordon. Even the films that do not conform to this pattern often make reference to these kinds of materials. In *The Omega Man*, for example, Heston himself points to the ways in which the film emphasises his character's Christ-like qualities: he is a saviour whose blood will redeem mankind and whose death is visually presented as a kind of crucifixion.

This association is also conveyed through Heston's voice and his mode of delivery. It is therefore worth noting that references to Heston's acting frequently focus on his vocal performance. In *Wayne's World 2*, for example, he has nothing to do physically, but simply presents a speech while remaining immobile. Indeed, it is the sheer theatricality of his mode of delivery, in which every line is carefully presented as though it were a line of Shakespearean poetry or biblical scripture, which not only distinguishes him but further adds to his cultural legitimacy. Over the years, therefore, his voice has become at least as iconic as his physical image. Not only did he get to literally speak for God in *The Ten Commandments*, but recently his voice was used as the omnipotent narrator at the opening of *Armageddon* (1998) in order to lend biblical associations to the film's spectacular storyline. However, it is not just in the cinema that Heston's voice has come to signify authority and legitimacy. On Amazon's web pages, there is currently a range of audio-cassettes available that he narrated, and these further emphasise the association between his voice and issues of cultural authority. Who else would be asked to narrate: Aristotle; John Dewey; David Hume; Immanuel Kant; Soren Kierkegaard; Friedrich Nietzsche; Jean-Paul Sartre; Arthur Schopenhauer; Baruch Spinoza; Hemingway's *The Snows of Kilimanjaro*; and Herman Melville's *Moby Dick*. This is in strict contrast to body stars such as Stallone and Schwarzenegger, who are continually derided specifically through references to their supposed verbal ineptitude (Tasker, 1993).

Heston, however, not only associates himself with the classical but the British theatre in particular. Again and again, he distances himself, or is distanced by others, from American drama and American acting traditions. For example, Crowther comments:

> For a man of Heston's inclinations in the theatre, it has also proved a great handicap to have been forced to fight for the production of all but the surefire Shakespearean plays on American stages. Given his aptitude and his inclinations, to say nothing of his ambitions, it is tempting, if idle, to speculate on how his career might have gone had he been born in England. Of his ability, Olivier once told him that he was sure he could be 'a great actor . . . the only one in America in my time'. (Crowther, 1986: 67)

Here British drama is presented as both the epitome and the measure of legitimate drama, and American drama as essentially disposable, commercial and inferior.

However, it is not just Crowther who makes these associations. Heston rarely, if ever, discusses developments in the American theatre in either his journals or his autobiography, but he remains obsessed with the British theatre. He not only seems to imply that any performance that he may have given in Britain is somehow of more cultural significance than a performance given inside America, but he continually measures himself against British actors, and particularly against Olivier, who is presented almost as a father figure and certainly as a role model. Any telephone conversation with Olivier, or any chance of working with him, is used to reinforce the association: if Olivier takes him seriously, it is suggested, then so should others. As a result, his journal entry for 7 February 1960 is particularly significant. It refers to one of his rehearsals with Olivier for a theatrical production of *The Tumbler*. Heston begins by noting: 'The morning featured a long talk on acting, mainly mine, with Olivier. It's hard to pin down any truth about so intangible an art, but I remember one thing he said: "Star acting is really a question of hypnosis: of yourself and the audience."' However, Heston then moves on to observe: 'I am now the age he was when he played Oedipus. I doubt if I can quite catch up, but I'm running' (Heston, 1980: 87). The reference to Oedipus seems almost too neat, and it can hardly have escaped Heston's notice that this sentence places him in a classic oedipal relation to his mentor.

However, the association with Olivier also works in other ways – ways that further legitimate the forms of bodily display which distinguish so many of Heston's performances. For example, Heston refers to what Olivier has called 'the "Green Umbrella" method, remembering a part he was having trouble with until he saw a green umbrella in the window of a second-hand shop, and knew instantly it was the umbrella his character would own. He bought it and worked inward from there.' As a result, Heston argues, clearly distancing himself from the American method actors of his period:

> Many actors insist that they must find the *inside* of the man first, and work outwards. I'm dubious about that. I wouldn't know where to reach for the inside if I had no outside to begin with. I want to figure out what the man wears, what he uses, what he has around him. (Heston, 1996: 106)

However, this external approach to character is not limited to the props with which Heston surrounds himself, but extends also to the transformation of his body. Heston prides himself on studiously researching the look of his characters, although he has been known to get this wrong, such as when he modelled the make-up for his Andrew Jackson in *The Buccaneer* on a painting of Jackson that was painted twenty years after the period in which the film was set. Like Olivier, then, Heston uses make-up a great deal: he shapes his body in the process of shaping his characters. As he puts it: 'I realised today that I've probably worn more false noses, cheeks, wigs, beards, sideburns and moustaches than any actor since Lon Chaney' (Heston, 1980: 314). Indeed, as this passage makes clear, his journals and autobiography seem almost fetishistically obsessed with facial hair.

In this way, the presentation of Heston's body within many of these films is legitimated as part of the dramatic performance rather than as passive display. As Tasker has pointed out, one of the problems faced by action stars such as Stallone and Schwarzenegger is that the display of their built bodies has often been 'taken to signal a disturbing narcissism, a narcissism which is inappropriate to familiar definitions of manhood' (Tasker, 1993: 78). The problem is one of dealing with the male body as the focus of the gaze because, it is assumed, this converts it into an object to be looked at, a process which supposedly renders it passive and hence feminised. Such claims, however, need to be treated very carefully. These anxieties about the bodies of Stallone and Schwarzenegger, as Tasker herself notes, are largely a classed response. It is not '*familiar* definitions of manhood' to which these bodies seem 'inappropriate', but class-based definitions. These bodies may appear 'unnatural', 'excessive', or 'hysterical' to certain audiences, but they certainly do not appear so to others. Thus, the legitimation of Heston's bodily displays is specifically about his positioning within social hierarchies of taste, and the ways in which these are articulated with the conflicts between different definitions of gender.

The classical actor and the classical body

If, however, the association with classical acting provided certain solutions to the problems posed by the displaying of Heston's body, the association with the classical also produced other problems. As

Cohan has rightly pointed out, Heston 'projects a rather complicated relation to his own big body' in which it is 'celebrated for
its physicality all the while being drained of it' (Cohan, 1998: 156).
But Heston's need to transcend his own body raises as many problems as it solves. The classical body is usually seen as a disciplined
body, a body whose materiality and excesses have been contained
by form (Nead, 1992). It is a body disciplined by the head, which
dominates its lower regions; controls its bodily functions; and so
permits the construction of a clear distinction between that which is
internal to the body and that which is external. However, in post-
war America, and particularly in the post-war blockbuster, the classical body was a problem, a body that carried too many associations
with totalitarianism.[1]

The disciplined body therefore comes with its associations of
sadism and masochism. It becomes a body denied pleasure and subject to a totalitarian desire for omnipotence, or in which desire has
become so bound up with issues of repression that sexual pleasure,
in particular, can only be experienced through a desire to dominate,
degrade or destroy others. As a result, Heston's performances seem
to fall into two categories. On the one hand, he is sometimes presented as a heroic exemplar of masculinity who becomes the object
of the perverse desires of another (often the repressed homosexual
desires of another man). On the other, however, he is sometimes the
subject of these perverse desires, whose body becomes the instru-
ment of violence and cruelty. There are shades of this latter type of
performance in *Ruby Gentry* and it is definitely a feature of his circus
boss in *The Greatest Show on Earth*, but it is most pronounced in *The
Naked Jungle*. In this film, Heston's character is presented as a man
engaged in the violent repression of the natural world, a repression
that has been necessary in order to produce his empire in the
Amazon but is also needed in order to continually protect and maintain it. As this film also makes clear, this fanatical preoccupation with
dominance not only requires massive self-control, but is also linked
to misogyny. Heston's character is not only disgusted by women, but
is terrified of being humiliated by them. His massive pride is therefore only the obverse of his even more massive fear of failure. However, when failure finally comes at the end of the film, and he is
forced to destroy his empire in order to destroy the ants – he floods
the land that he has claimed from the jungle swamps and so returns
it to its original condition – the result is liberating. He finds that he

is not destroyed by the act but rather that it frees him from the fantasies of omnipotence to which he has aspired; and as a result, that he is finally able to overcome his misogynist fear of women.

A number of other films use Heston in this way, notably *The Big Country*, and it is also worth noting that he was originally offered the part of Messala in *Ben Hur* rather than Hur himself. Indeed, this film revolves around the dynamics of his sadomasochistic persona. It even revolves around a central conflict between Hur, the noble Jewish prince, and Messala, his childhood-friend-turned-nemesis. While Messala becomes the sadist who continually seeks to punish and destroy the body of the friend whom he can never have (sexually or politically), Hur becomes the object of that sadism. This is also, like other epics, given religious connotations in that suffering becomes a spiritual condition. The film is after all subtitled 'A Tale of the Christ'. Thus, when Hur is finally able to return to Israel as an avenger after years of suffering, the film repeatedly presents his desire for vengeance as a terrible mistake. In the film's terms, it makes him indistinguishable from Messala. It is only through the image of the crucifixion and the example of the Christ that Hur (who has already figured as a kind of surrogate Christ in a number of ways) finally puts aside hatred and the desire for omnipotence on which it is supposedly based, and is able to embrace the sublime transcendence which is 'love'.

Hence, the size and power of Heston's body, to say nothing of his chiselled face and jaw-line, can often be problems that threaten to signify the totalitarian forces of domination. However, they can also provide the potential solution because he is able to become the object of violence without necessarily signifying passivity. In other words, Heston's body is often signified as suffering punishment as an act of heroic self-sacrifice in which he proves his manhood through the ability to 'take the pain' and to suffer for others. (For a discussion of a similar construction of masculinity, see Walkerdine, 1984.) Nowhere is this clearer than in *El Cid*, where the major proof of the Cid's heroism is not only his abilities as a warrior on the battlefield, but also his ability to remain faithful to his king, despite repeated abuse, and most particularly, in his final decision to give up his own life and his desires for domestic happiness so that his corpse can led his men into the final battle with the enemy (Jancovich, 2000).

In this way, the film is able to convert some of Heston's most profound weaknesses as an actor into strengths. Heston's style of acting, with its focus on the externals of his characters, has meant that he has difficulty with the private and emotional lives of his characters. He therefore seems comfortable with larger-than-life public figures, but profoundly uncomfortable with scenes of intimacy, particularly love scenes which, according to Crowther, are 'not usually Heston's strongest suit owing to his natural dislike of exposing his feelings' (Crowther, 1986: 94). This is also related to a more general antipathy towards women which results, even in his heavily edited journals, in repeated attacks on the actresses with whom he has been forced to work. Indeed, Crowther quotes one particularly bitter attack that he made in the course of an interview with the *Sunday Express*:

> By and large, actresses are a different breed of cat. Most of them I wouldn't touch with a pole – or work with where I have some control of the production. It appals and disgusts me, the amateur way most of them treat film-making. The rule of thumb for most of those broads is to be 20 minutes late in the morning and ten minutes late after lunch. (Crowther, 1986: 73)

The tension between his own commitment to the public sphere and his deep discomfort and even 'disgust' of the private may also account for his fascination with Shakespeare's *Antony and Cleopatra*, which he filmed in 1973. For Heston, then, this play is crucially about the seduction and destruction of a great public figure by the exotic feminine and by his own private desires.

In *El Cid*, however, and in a number of other performances, Heston's own problems with the private are used productively. For Crowther, Heston is at his best when 'playing a man whose shell is part and parcel of his characters (Crowther, 1986: 32), but it is perhaps more accurate to say that Heston is at his best in roles where the powerful public persona of his character comes into conflict with his private desires, where his performance registers the tension of maintaining the masculine public self. This may also account for the reason he has repeatedly been drawn back to the part of Captain Queeg, in *The Caine Mutiny Court-Martial*, a man whose public persona is dismantled in the course of the play to reveal 'the quivering paranoid beneath' (Heston, 1996: 497). Heston's body is therefore a problem that can only operate as an exemplary figure of masculinity so long as it is disassociated from the dominating classical body. It may be presented as a powerful and positive image of masculinity but, in these cases, it is usually through its capacity to suffer, not to conquer, or through the sense that the masculine public persona is itself a painful and self-destructive one to maintain.

Conclusion

Nonetheless, while Heston's image may work for some audiences, it cannot work for all audiences. Indeed, the very position that it negotiates must also lead to problems. For example, Macdonald claims that he 'found *Ben Hur* bloody in every way – bloody, bloody and bloody boring' (Macdonald, 1969: 424). However, he makes this claim in opposition to the 'bellows of approval' with which the mainstream press greeted the picture. In other words, for Macdonald, this film represented the epitome of the middlebrow or 'midcult', a category which 'has the essential qualities of Masscult – the formula, the built-in reaction, the lack of any standard except popularity – but it decently covers them in a cultural figleaf . . . it pretends to respect the standards of High Culture while it in fact waters them down and vulgarizes them' (Macdonald, 1969: 37). He therefore makes special mention of Heston's performance in which, it is claimed, he 'throws all his punches in the first ten minutes (three grimaces and two intonations) so that he has nothing left four hours later when he has to react to the crucifixion. (He does make it clear, I must admit, that he disapproves)' (Macdonald, 1969: 424–5).

Heston's image as a legitimate theatrical actor can therefore become the very thing that defines him as a middlebrow star, who plays to middlebrow tastes. Indeed, as Bourdieu found in his study of French culture, the kinds of blockbusters with which Heston was associated were precisely those that appealed to middlebrow taste. Bourdieu even makes special mention of Heston's *55 Days in Peking* (Bourdieu, 1984: 271). These films, in short, appealed most to those sections of the middle class who were lowest in cultural capital and hence most culturally despised by the rest of their class. As Bourdieu argues: 'Explicit aesthetic choices are in fact often constituted in opposition to the choice of the groups closest in social space, with whom competition is most direct and immediate' (Bourdieu, 1984: 60). As a result, those sections of the bourgeoisie that are highest in cultural capital usually reserve their greatest criticism, not for low or popular taste, but rather for the middlebrow, which is attacked precisely for its aspirations or 'pretentiousness' (Bourdieu, 1984: 62).

For example, Macdonald argues that popular culture is not a problem so long as it was simply 'a parallel formation to High Culture' and the two were separated into 'fairly watertight compartments' (Macdonald, 1969: 34). The real problem, he suggests, is Midcult, because it refuses to accept its place and hence blurs the distinction between High Culture and its Other, Masscult, both of which lose their sense of integrity, outline and clear distinction from one another.

It is therefore Heston's presentation as a theatrical, classical and even Shakespearean actor, and the 'pretensions' to cultural legitimacy on which it is based, that, for some critics, marks him as a middlebrow star. However, while Heston's image becomes the target of those who wish to establish their own cultural superiority and authority over others, it should also be remembered that Heston's image is itself shaped by struggles for distinction. If some wish to assert their superiority over the tastes that he represents, his image is also based on the attempt to assert that certain tastes are superior to others. It may be true that one can never get out of this game of distinctions, but it is nonetheless important to understand how specific star images are produced in relation to, and operate within, these power relations.

Note

1 Nowhere is this clearer than in *Spartacus*, where the Roman state is clearly split into two opposing factions: the fascistic patrician class lead by Crassus (Lawrence Olivier), and the democratic mob led by Gracchus (Charles Laughton). Crassus is therefore continually associated with the classical body both through his clothing and through his frequent placing within gymnasiums and bathhouses. Gracchus, on the other hand, is distinguished by his indulgences: women and food. He is constantly positioned within the home where he is surrounded by his female slaves (whom, it is suggested, he adores rather than dominates) and there is a continual emphasis on his fleshy body. It is therefore hardly surprising that while Crassus is originally associated with the corpulent Batiatus (Peter Ustinov), and Gracchus is associated with an impressively built Julius Caesar (John Gavin), both these associates change sides by the end of the narrative. The classical body of Caesar 'naturally' gravitates towards the totalitarian Crassus, and the indulgent Batiatus gravitates towards the liberal and democratic Gracchus. In these blockbusters, the overly disciplined body becomes a sign of totalitarianism. It is for this reason that the slaves operate as the perfect resolution between the two extremes. They have none of Gracchus's

associations with corruption – he may be a democratic but he is also a politician and as such is guilty of compromise, particularly over the issue of slavery. However, to the extent that the slave's bodies have been disciplined, it is out of a position of structural inequality. The early stages of the film continually draw attention to the alienation of the slaves from their bodies as their masters train them. Indeed, Spartacus continually emphasises his desire to renounce the violent masculinity his body signifies, a desire that is repeatedly thwarted by the structures of power which require him to continually battle for his own freedom and that of others (see also Hark, 1993).

Bibliography

Ang, Ien (1985) *Watching Dallas: Soap Opera and the Melodramatic Imagination*, London: Routledge.

Bourdieu, Pierre (1984) *Distinction: A Social Critique of the Judgement of Taste*, London: Routledge.

Britton, Andrew (1986) 'Blissing Out: The Politics of Reaganite Entertainment', *Movie* 31/32, winter: 1–42.

Cohan, Steven (1998) *Masked Men: Masculinity and the Movies in the Fifties*, Bloomington: Indiana University Press.

Corman, Roger and J. Kerome (1990) *How I Made a Hundred Movies in Hollywood and Never Lost a Dime*, London: Muller.

Crowther, Bruce (1986) *Charlton Heston*, London: Columbus Books.

Doherty, Thomas (1988) *Teenagers and Teenpics: The Juvenilization of American Movies in the 1950s*, Boston: Unwin Hyman.

Hark, Ina Rae (1993) 'Animals or Romans: Looking at Masculinity in *Spartacus*', in Steven Cohan and Ina Rae Hark (eds), *Screening the Male: Exploring Masculinities in Hollywood Cinema*, London: Routledge.

Heston, Charlton (1980) *An Actor's Life*, London: Penguin.

Heston, Charlton (1996) *In the Arena: The Biography*, London: HarperCollins.

Hunt, Leon (1993) 'What are Big Boys Made Of? *Spartacus*, *El Cid* and the Male Epic', in Pat Kirkham and Janet Tumin (eds), *Me Tarzan: Men, Movies and Masculinity*, London: Lawrence and Wishart.

Jancovich, Mark (2000) '"The Purest Knight of All": Nation, History and Representation in *El Cid*', *Cinema Journal*, 40(1): 79–103.

Krämer, Peter (1998) 'The New Hollywood', in John Hill and Pamela Church Gibson (eds), *The Oxford Guide to Film Studies*, Oxford: Oxford University Press.

Macdonald, Dwight (1969) *On Movies*, Englewood Cliffs: Prentice-Hall.

Morley, David and Kevin Robins (1995) *Spaces of Identity*, London: Routledge.

Mourlet, Michel (1991) 'In Defense of Violence', in Christine Gledhill (ed.), *Stardom: Industry of Desire*, London: Routledge.

Nead, Lynda (1992) *The Female Nude: Art, Obscenity and Sexuality*, London: Routledge.

Schatz, Thomas (1993) 'The New Hollywood', in Jim Collins *et al.* (eds), *Film Theory Goes to the Movies*, New York: Routledge.

Schlesinger, Arthur M. (1964) *In The Politics of Hope*, London: Eyre and Spottiswoode.

Tasker, Yvonne (1993) *Spectacular Bodies: Gender and Genre and the Action Cinema*, London: Routledge.

Walkerdine, Valerie (1984) 'Video Replay', in James Donald (ed.), *Formations of Fantasy*, London: Routledge.

Webster, Duncan (1989) *Looka Yonder! The Imaginary America of Populist Culture*, London: Comedia.

Wood, Robin (1986) *Hollywood from Vietnam to Reagan*, New York: Columbia University Press.

4

Jim Carrey: the cultural politics of dumbing down

Philip Drake

In August 1998 *Variety* magazine awarded Jim Carrey their 'Show-man of the Year' accolade. Like a number of performers before him, Carrey moved across from ensemble television comedy (*In Living Color*, Fox 1990–94) and became a leading Hollywood film actor, achieving remarkable box-office success in a relatively short period of time.[1] His status as a major box-office draw was established in 1994 by *Ace Ventura: Pet Detective*, and followed in the same year by *The Mask* and *Dumb and Dumber*. The three films collectively earned a reported $550 million, establishing Carrey as the second-biggest-grossing box-office star of 1994 behind Tom Hanks (*Variety*, Supplement 1998: 6). In the space of just over a year Carrey there-fore managed to accumulate the economic star capital to open a pic-ture and guarantee a profitable return on a studio investment.[2] By 1996 he became one of Hollywood's star elite, able to command a $20 million fee and demand a gross percentage of film revenues.

At the same time as this meteoric rise to stardom, however, Carrey's name began to be increasingly used by cultural critics who took his success to exemplify a so-called 'dumbing down' within contemporary Hollywood cinema. In 1994 the commercial and Academy Award success of *Forrest Gump*, narrated through the char-acter of an *idiot-savant*, was attacked for its celebration of stupidity, and Carrey's film *Dumb and Dumber*, featuring two protagonists who enact childish pranks upon others, mimicking, pulling faces, sulking, belching, and engaging in gags about flatulence, urination and sexual inadequacy, became the prime target for critics accusing Hollywood cinema – and popular culture generally – of pandering to 'low' tastes.[3] Carrey's films (and those of the Farrelly brothers, and other stars of 'gross-out' comedy such as Adam Sandler and Chris

Farley) were denounced as banal, full of juvenile gags and exaggerated 'rubber-mugging' performances. An article in *Sight and Sound*,
for instance, asked rhetorically: 'isn't Carrey the epitome of dumbing
down?' (Whitehouse, 1998: 9) (their answer: 'of course he is'). A
commentator in the British newspaper *The Guardian* similarly
remarked, 'This doesn't happen often. The words "thoughtful" and
"Jim Carrey film" in the same sentence'. Richard Schickel in *Time*
even called Carrey 'both symbol and satirist of our apparently irre-
sistible dumbing down' (Schickel, 1995).

My aim in this chapter is to open up this 'dumbing down' debate
and examine how comedic performance has been understood and
judged according to the criteria set by realist modes of Hollywood
acting. Using the star career of Jim Carrey – one of the most popular Hollywood stars of the 1990s – I will suggest that these epistemological frameworks are arranged in a hierarchy in relation to
larger debates about cultural value that privilege teleological modes
of performance. Examining questions of performance more closely,
I will suggest that 'low' modes of performance (such as physical
comedy) have not acquired cultural legitimacy in popular critical
discourse, despite their recent reappraisal in academic critical writing. The popular acclaim Carrey received for his performance in *The
Truman Show*, I suggest, offers a useful example of the making of
cultural distinctions about performance, by successfully aligning discussions of 'good acting' with a teleological mode of performance.

Stardom as performance

Acting and performance have been neglected by most writing on stardom, with a particular paucity of writing on contemporary stars.[4]
Although there has been a substantial amount of work on stars and
stardom, there has been a tendency to discuss stars as personalities,
celebrities, social types, or as representations, whilst overlooking the
central place of performance in the cultural production and decoding
of the star image. To this extent, Richard Dyer's remark, originally
made in 1979, still holds true:

> While everyday critical talking about film tends to concentrate on
> performance (e.g., 'What was so-and-so like in the film you just saw?'),
> an important tradition in film theory has tended to deny that perfor-
> mance has any expressive value: what you read into the performer, you
> read in by virtue of signs other than performance signs. This makes the

lack of academic attention given to popular performance especially surprising. (Dyer, 1998: 143)

Analysis of performance is something that has presented academic film critics with considerable difficulty, and a certain amount of anxiety. It is a truth often acknowledged (if less often addressed) that film analysis lacks an adequate critical language through which to describe what it is that an actor/performer does. The precision that we are able to give to an analysis of the relation between shots, or the narrative structure of a film, contrasts with our attempt to delineate a taxonomy of performance. As Dyer remarks, this is surprising, not least because popular critical discourses are often centred on performance, debating whether a particular actor is believable in a particular role, whether they are 'over the top' and so on.

A good starting point in any discussion of screen performance is James Naremore's study of screen acting. He usefully suggests that screen performance can be considered with regard to two key sets of rhetorical conventions: 'mode of address' and 'degree of ostensiveness' (Naremore, 1988). The mode of address, he argues, can be read as operating along a scale ranging from indirect to direct address, which is loosely mapped to the continuum from representational to presentational performance. Representational performance, he suggests, tends to efface the production of the performance in order to be read as 'behaving', whereas presentational performance tends to foreground the performer *as performer*, rather than as character. Naremore uses the term 'ostensiveness' as the scale of the gestures of the performance – what we might call the 'showing' of the performance. He suggests that narrative films are usually representational (committed to realism), and achieve this in part through the use of an indirect address and a reduced degree of ostensiveness, thus giving the effect of everyday life.

Naremore's framework is a useful one, notwithstanding some difficulties in maintaining the separateness of the categories above.[5] It is helpful in establishing normative differences between different performers and helps to give some precision to performance analysis without resorting to increasingly dense levels of description. However, it is important to point out that the ostensiveness or otherwise of the performer is a recognition that is derived culturally, depending upon the cultural capital of a particular audience member. It depends on the reading of intentionality by a spectator of a particular performance, thus also on the inferential work done by that spectator. To argue that a performance was 'believable', for instance, often means to imply a particular kind of intentionality behind the performance – such as the commitment of a particular actor to conventions of naturalism. It may have very little to do with any actual 'presence' of the performer and rather more to do with the inferences made by an audience member and the interpretative 'frames' through which these are decoded.[6] Therefore, when the performer is a star, the question of inferential meaning becomes tied up in our investment in the star image of the performer. Recognition of a favourite performer clearly increases the ostensiveness of their performance signs. The *idiolect* of the star – the recurring elements of their performance that they carry from role to role – operate, for those who recognise them, as ostensive inter-textual signifiers, offering the return of familiar pleasures. Such pleasures are individualised through our memories of previous encounters, they are bound up with the social meanings of performance and the discourses of celebrity that circulate outside of the filmic text, and therefore are to a great extent resistant to formal analysis. The deliberate recurrence and specific deployment of these bodily signs gives stars a higher degree of gestural investment because their meaning is partly imported intertextually. Star performance, then, presents stars as motivated signs, and by its nature and by economic necessity, draws attention to itself as a performance even when it attempts to efface its own constructed nature.

What, then, are the motivated signs in Jim Carrey's idiolect, what we might call the 'Carrey-isms'? Most obvious perhaps is his mobility of facial expression, his kinetic bodily movement, his puppy-brown eyes, his exaggerated smile and his vocal mannerisms. Carrey's smile is particularly important to his idiolect, inducing a knowing insincerity into his performance. His physicality – using his body for comic effect – and ability to shift abruptly between different modes of performance, such as from melodramatic sentimentality to slapstick, are all major elements of his star image. His comic roles often portray a down-on-his-luck ordinary Joe type who manages to either take on supernormal powers (*The Mask, Batman Forever*) and/or pursue an impossible dream – usually a desirable female (*Ace Ventura, The Mask, Dumb and Dumber*), or else is forced to grapple with two or more different selves (*The Mask, Liar Liar, Man on the Moon, Me, Myself and Irene*, and perhaps *The Truman Show*).

Carrey's star idiolect manifests itself in such small expressive elements as the lifting of an eyebrow, or the use of a certain catchphrase (for instance 'Alrighty then!') that become invested with significance through their iteration.

Often neglected, the voice of the star is a potent sign in the idiolect in that it is often read, like the body, as the site of 'presence'. The voice is the most easily recognisable sign assignable to any star, perhaps one of the reasons why stars are frequently used to voice and thereby anthropomorphise animated characters.[7] The aura conferred through the voice-over directly draws upon an audience's investment in the star idiolect, helping to anchor the performance to a recognisable set of cultural discourses associated with the star image. Carrey's performance in *The Mask*, for instance, clearly plays with the fit between his 'elastic' facial performance and that of the Tex Avery cartoon character he represents.[8] As Dave Kehr comments, his makeup is 'a cruel parody of Carrey's features, with emphasis placed on his sunken eyes, his jutting jaw, and his big teeth' (2000: 14). These are all anchored to his body through the vocal continuity plus the apparently seamless morphing between Carrey with and without make-up, and the computer-generated effects that take aspects of his idiolect and massively ostend them for cartoon-like effect.

One of the pleasures (or irritations, depending on one's tastes) of seeing Carrey's performances is recognising signs such as those described above and recalling their contextual, memorialised meanings to us. Reading my comments above, however, what is even more apparent is just how difficult and elusive is any attempt to delineate star idiolect in a meaningful way. The investment we make in star performances is remarkably resistant to adequate textual description, and this presents a serious obstacle to our understanding of the significance of star performances. Clearly our investment in stars is individualised, yet it is also a shared discourse for aligning tastes, as is evident from the plethora of fan websites and discussion groups that populate the internet debating the merits of each performance as compared to that of previous films.[9]

Naremore's categories, though, do mark a useful attempt to move discussions of performance beyond the familiar inside–outside binaries of Stanislavsky and Brecht, both of whom focus to a greater or lesser degree on the intentionality embodied in the performer.[10] As Naremore comments, even the most naturalistic of performances, committed to a representational address, tends to involve a degree of ostensiveness that 'marks it off from quotidian behaviour' (1988: 17). The model of analysis adopted by Naremore at least recognises the problems of acting discourses that describe performance in terms of honesty or truthfulness by emphasising that a performance frame is already initiated through the placing of the actor in front of an audience. Indeed, as I shall now explore, maintaining an awareness of the star persona as autonomous from the character he or she performs is an economic imperative of star casting.

Stardom as work

Star performance clearly has an important function in the economics of post-classical Hollywood cinema. Screen performance is work, both a craft admired for its skill, and an application of labour in a larger economic process.[11] The economics of star performance are fundamental to the organisation of contemporary Hollywood cinema; stars provide a means through which films can generate immediate pre-recognition, and audiences can make judgements over whether a particular film might be worth seeing. This latter point is particularly significant, as the wide release of most major Hollywood films offers a very limited time-scale in which to make a success – hence the crucial importance of the opening weekend at the domestic box-office.[12] Stars garner recognition in international markets and are a means by which Hollywood has been able to present itself as a global rather than national film industry. Colin MacCabe, for instance, commenting on the futility of British attempts to compete with Hollywood's blockbuster strategies, comments that, 'there is a strong argument to say that the only serious assets the film industry has are stars, and at any one time there are only going to be eight to ten global stars, who will always live or be focused, as it were, through one city, Los Angeles' (Caughie and Frith, 2000: 63). In fact, the economists Arthur De Vany and W. David Walls (1999, n.p.), in a study of the effect of star power on the success of Hollywood movies, argue that at least nineteen stars consistently impact positively on a film's economic success, and Carrey ranks number four in their list of stars with the most influence. They demonstrate that stars are able to significantly extend the life of film revenue streams in other media formats as well as open up opportunities for merchandising and promotional tie-ins. So important are stars to contemporary Hollywood that the industry journal *The*

Hollywood Reporter, for instance, regularly compiles subscription-only 'Star Power' information detailing the extent of power held by Hollywood's elite, and annually publishes its rankings.[13]

Stars such as Carrey are crucial to contemporary Hollywood's post-Fordist package-unit mode of production, characterised by its flexibility of labour and mobility of capital.[14] The financing and distribution of most films directly depend on the involvement of stars and their economy of signification. The commercial strategy of Hollywood therefore requires that a star performance is recognisable to an audience. The circulation of performance signs is central to the semiotic and financial economy of narrative, establishing a set of expectations for an audience prior to the film (in the film trailer, for instance). Every performance therefore retains traces of earlier roles, histories that are re-mobilised in new textual and cultural contexts. In fact this is actually an economic condition of stardom, which relies on the continuing circulation and accretion of the star image.

Star performance, then, involves a set of processes. Firstly, it is a moment of labour production, where the performer crafts his or her performance. Secondly, it is a moment of mediation, where this performance is fragmented through the camera and reconstituted on the screen through the cinematic or televisual apparatus. Thirdly, this screen activity is decoded in the historical contexts of reception. This decoding is complicated by the signifying 'presence' of the star (a presence that is phenomenologically inferred), as the star image contains traces of other performances and a particular biography. These floating signifiers are anchored to a recognisable body, idiolect and voice, all of which act to guarantee the uniqueness and authenticity of the star and his or her performance.

The point of this is that all stars function as already-ostensive signs in the economy of contemporary Hollywood cinema, even where those signs are momentarily effaced by the demands of character. Comedic performance, particularly 'low' physical comedy, however, places the star *as a star* at the very centre of the screen, as a willed body that is to be looked at and admired for its skill or comic timing. These offer pleasures of recognition, of knowing acknowledgement, rather than of identification and effacement. The attraction of watching Carrey's films is – for those who invest in his idiolect – to a large degree centred on a fascination in watching him perform his so-called comic *schtick*. This is important because assertions about 'dumbed down' performance serve to reify discourses that assign a seemingly natural relationship between notions of authenticity, sincerity and presence to organic modes of acting. These in turn assign low cultural value to more ostensive modes of performance, such as physical comedy, stunts and action sequences.

Moments of recognition

How, then, have film theorists approached questions of performance, identification and recognition? John Ellis has argued that performance provides the 'moment of completion' for the incoherent star image, that the star promises cinema (1992: 93). He draws here upon Christian Metz's (1982) argument that cinema offers a regime of desire through which identification with the star is established. This formulation of the spectator–star relationship suggests that performance is an important place in which identification with the star is secured. The body of the star, their gestures and movement, may offer the spectator fetish points, places where we invest a particular significance in performance and through this investment are offered particular kinds of pleasure. Metz relies here on Emile Beveniste's modernist distinction between *histoire* and *discours*, arguing that classical cinema disguises its own constructed nature through its mode of address and effacement of the camera. This would suggest that we find the performance of our favourite stars pleasurable, as they are presented as idealised objects of a voyeuristic, enquiring gaze. However, star performance – especially in presentational modes of performance such as in comedy – presents itself as something to be looked at self-consciously and often, giving us pleasure in its very familiarity.

Laura Mulvey famously critiqued Metz's argument by suggesting that the directed gaze of the spectator is masculinised, and the fetish points of pleasure offered in classical cinema are points where the woman is constructed as the pleasurable object of this look (1975: 6–18). But Mulvey's article, attending to the apparatus and scopic regime of spectatorship, unfortunately avoids any specific consideration of star performance in this process. In particular it neglects to address the interesting question of how performance might function as part of this mechanism; that is, whether our pleasurable recognition of the idiolect of a favourite actor is implicated within such a process. This presents a problem as it suggests that spectators alternate between positions of identification and those of recognition.

The major problem with these influential approaches to cinema are that they offer an unsatisfactory explanation of how actual spectators with different accumulations of cultural capital and sets of expectations interact with star performance, bringing meanings from outside of the text. Neither do they help us ascertain why we remain fascinated by film stars on television or other media, which may offer different possibilities of consumption, and mechanisms of identification that are less reliant on a theorisation of the look. In addition, this emphasis on the image as the source of visual pleasure has tended to obscure the important ways in which the voice of the performer, its inflections and recognisable 'grain', underwrites the image, and often presents a point at which a dual belief can be established.[15] A star is both recognisable as a star, existing independently of the text, and as a character, existing within the diegetic world constructed by narrative. That is, the demand for visual verisimilitude in realist narrative can be offset by our recognition of the voice of the star, and the 'aura', the presence that this bestows upon the star performance, distinguishing it from that of the supporting cast.

I have elaborated these approaches as they have been central to subsequent debates on the politics of performance. Firstly they rely on a modernist concept of ideology successfully working to efface its own discourse. Secondly, and my principal point of interest here, these models assume the dominance of a mode of performance that does not acknowledge its own status as performance. In this way academic debates have themselves tended to efface questions of stardom and performance in favour of questions or representation when, as Stephen Heath acknowledges, 'all representation is performance – the time of that production and construction, of the realisation of the positions and effects' (1981: 113–30). This cues a recognition of the fictionality of the performance, questioning Metz's account of the cinema as a place of socially sanctioned voyeurism, as our place as onlooker is firmly acknowledged.

I have argued that critical discussions of performance have reproduced discourses that value teleological, effaced modes of performance. My interest, then, is in the potential challenge that comic performance might present to this model, as it ostends rather than effaces performance within the structures of narrative. To consider these questions, I now want to return to the issue of value in the performances of Jim Carrey.

Carrey's comedy value

Popular discourses of value about screen performance have been strongly influenced by the approaches laid down by Konstantin Stanislavsky and developed by Lee Strasberg and others into 'the Method'. These have largely tended to define 'good acting' in Hollywood cinema as a form of representational performance motivated by psychological realism of character. The Academy Awards, for instance, have rarely favoured comic performance. Famously, and despite both the critical approval of the critics of *Cahiers du Cinéma* and his popularity with the American public, the performances of Jerry Lewis were never rewarded with Oscar success. Even to describe a comic performance as 'acting' seems problematic; the awards for Best Actor or Best Actress seem to demand in their very nature a representational, apparently organic mode of performance. This is because, as Barry King (1987) has noted, Hollywood cinema has overwhelmingly favoured teleological modes of performance in its critical discourse.[16] It applauds, as King remarks, 'reacting rather than enacting', an economy of performance that is primarily predicated on narrative motivation and the development of character agency through notions of psychological realism.

Carrey's star career seems to support such an argument. In 1997, for instance, he won an MTV award for Best Comedic Performance, a separate category from Best Male Performance (and interestingly non-gender-segregated), which was won by Tom Cruise (for *Jerry Maguire*). We might roughly summarise the oppositions in discourses of performance set up in these debates as follows:

Realist	*Comic*
motivated by narrative	motivated by spectacle
integrated performance	autonomous performance
closed text	open text
dramatic story	elemental story
drama	comedy
serious	humorous
difficult	easy
representation	presentation
high	low
acting	performance
effaced	ostended
being	showing
identification	recognition

These oppositions are open to question, as I have already suggested. The argument that classical Hollywood realism offers a 'closed' text, for example, would be rejected by many theoretical approaches. They are, however, a useful framework of opposing *tendencies* against which we can map critical discourses of performance. As I have suggested, a performer may also be recognisable outside of a particular performance: as a star. A representational performance by a star tends at the same time to enunciate its doubleness, and hence to shift teleological acting towards the right of the grid. In this model, critical discourse of screen performance assumes a hierarchy of performance with realist modes of acting (categories on the left) privileged over comic performance (categories on the right).

Hence the oppositions outlined in my argument are also tendencies, varying from star to star and film to film. Certainly some critics have applauded Carrey's virtuoso performances, yet even they would not consider it as 'acting' in the sense favoured by the Academy. Furthermore, contemporary Hollywood cinema may have been characterised by its fragmentation and hybridisation of genre and increasingly self-conscious modes of star performance.[17] In addition, the performance is always supported by the subsidiary texts attached to the star image that circulate in the host culture. It is therefore important to retain the view, put forward by Richard Dyer, that star images are structured polysemies embodying multiple and even contradictory meanings, and able to read in different ways according to the contexts in which decoding takes place, rather than a site from which fixed or normative meanings are made.

The 'truth' of Truman

I want to return here to the comment made in the *Sight and Sound* article (Whitehouse, 1998) and its discussion of Jim Carrey and the process of cultural 'dumbing down'. The article focuses on Carrey's performance in *The Truman Show* (1998), which was reviewed as a breakthrough in his career, and raised expectations (subsequently dashed) of a possible Academy Award nomination for Best Actor, along with a move into 'serious' acting roles. Can this shift, applauded in popular critical discourse, be read as endowing Carrey with a particular cultural status, that associated with 'legitimate' acting?[18]

Certainly the press articulated it in such terms, continually affirming the higher status of teleological acting over comic performance.

Bruce Handy in *Time*, for instance, suggested that 'the film represents his first stab at Tom Hanks prestige: middlebrow respect, a possible Oscar nomination' (Handy, 1998). Similarly, *Variety* detailed how Carrey's management searched for the right 'transition' script for their star, with his agent Jimmy Miller justifying it in both commercial and artistic terms in his comment that '*The Truman Show* was a conscious attempt to broaden his audience . . . we wanted to show the world his other possibilities' (Laski, 1998: 32). David Gauntlett, looking at 236 audience reviews of the film on the Internet Movie Database (IMDB) noted the diversity of readings of the film. However, with few exceptions these engaged with the meta-narrative premise through conventions of realism, with only a few dissenting voices complaining about the lack of 'funny scenes' (Gauntlett, 1999). Richard Williams, reviewing the film in *The Guardian*, commented that 'this is a performance to impress even those whose teeth are set on edge by a glimpse of his rubber mug' (1998: 9).

The film constructs an interesting narrative premise where Truman Burbank, the central character played by Carrey, is the only authentic person in the fictional town of Seahaven. Unbeknown to him the town is actually a film set, where thousands of hidden cameras convey his life as a live 24-hour-a-day soap opera to audiences around the world. Diegetically speaking, then, all the other characters in the film are actors, performing, whilst Carrey's character, Truman, is simply 'being'. These different modes of performance are keyed in the film not just through acting but also through the use of formal devices. The artificiality of the lighting, for instance (the town appears flat and idyllically clean) and the unconventional camera angles remind us that we are watching him unaware of being watched, under surveillance. The supporting actors, then, have the interesting task of playing actors performing. This is conveyed to us by their adoption of an ostensive mode of performance keyed by a televisual melodramatic register familiar to soap opera (manic cheerfulness, for instance, and their recitation of clichéd dialogue) that seems, in its presentation to us, to emphasise their insincerity.

The narrative set up by the film, then, casts Carrey as the only person in Seahaven who is not performing, a device that clearly also functions as a comic gag, as his star image has been built around his manic presentational comic performance. This creates an awareness that we are watching Jim Carrey the star, as well as the character of

Truman. Carrey's performance mode, as some commentators have noted, seems as if he is acting for the camera. However the film leaves us unsure of which camera is being acknowledged, a device that allows Carrey to switch between direct and indirect address depending on whether the camera is supposedly concealed or not.[19] This would seem to fit with Neale and Krutnik's description of comic performance involving 'a *play* between identification and distantiation' (1990: 149). We can admire the star performance *as performance*, whilst at the same time taking up points of identification with Truman offered to us by the narrative. Here the supporting characters work to anchor the star to narrative, by insisting that the 'truth' of the film lies with Truman, even as we can enjoy watching Carrey as a star ostended within the narrative.

Despite these similarities to the processes of comic performance, Carrey's performance in *The Truman Show* is read (and has been interpreted by most readings of the film, such as those on IMDB) quite differently to his performance in *Ace Ventura: Pet Detective*. This is due to the narrative context of *The Truman Show*, which provides psychological motivation for his character's actions. A brief comparison of two scenes is instructive. Firstly, there is a scene towards the end of *Ace Ventura: Pet Detective* where Ace falls into a tank inhabited by a shark. This offers a performance enclosure where Carrey's physical and imitative skills are shown: he thrashes around in the water in an exaggerated pastiche of a shark attack scene from *Jaws*. It is worth noting about this scene that the performance has framed the action in a way so as to leave us unconcerned about narrative consequentiality; it is funny rather than threatening. In contrast, the scene where Truman almost drowns (albeit in an artificially created storm) generates anxiety through our concern to see him survive, a reading mediated through our identification with his character set up by the film.

These sequences seem to invoke different preferred epistemological frames for decoding the two performances. The first is centred around spectacle, utilising what Jerry Palmer has termed 'comic insulation'; the second retains a concern with narrative consequentiality and identification (1987: 45). In *The Truman Show* the star performance of Carrey as Truman is tied to the meta-narrative frame that works to guarantee the sincerity of Truman. It is this anchoring to narrative that makes the falling overboard feel such a tense moment. In *Ace Ventura*, by contrast, the performance is relatively autonomous; it retains a link to the narrative, but also exceeds it.

The supposed 'truth' of Truman is therefore in part keyed through Carrey's performance and the frame through which it is decoded by audiences. Interestingly this has been tied to a larger claim made by many of the reviews of the film – namely that the film presents, through the character of Truman, a stinging meta-critique of television and its effect on our perception of reality in mediatised culture. Television is portrayed in the film as an arch deceiver, concealing reality from its viewers (as evident in the sequence when the show goes off air) and from Truman. This reading of the film by many of its reviewers – perhaps even a dominant popular critical discourse – is interesting as it suggests that critical approbation for the film has been partly the result of a successful alignment with a culturally pessimistic critical position often associated with the critique of mass culture by the Frankfurt School theorists. Once again, television embodies the 'low', the 'dumbing down' of popular culture, and once again the 'high', 'authentic' and organic – as embodied by Carrey's performance – is positioned in dominance over the insincere and performed, the 'low'. Alexander Walker, for example, writing in the *London Evening Standard* comments:

> *The Truman Show* is a mental wake-up call to what the telly is doing to our perception of reality, substituting a preference for what's fictive, fabricated and antiseptic over what's truthful, plain and painful. And even a film fable that makes the medicine go down with a spoonful of its own sugar constitutes a welcome antidote to the current American cinema's almost unrelieved drip-feed of paralysing dumbness. (Walker, 1998)

This comment is typical of the critical reviews and of the kind of critical writing that has dominated the popular dumbing-down debate. What is perhaps ironic, however, is that the film in which Carrey has been praised for his authentic, narratively motivated acting has also been lauded for its criticism of the low, of the 'dumbing down' that these very same discourses considered Carrey to epitomise. The narrative framing of his performance confers upon it the legitimacy associated with 'acting', and with it the critical approbation of cultural discourses that value teleological over comedic performance.

From zero to hero? Some conclusions

People are stuck on what acting should be . . . you do need a form to work in, but you can't let that dictate or control your creativity. With *Ace Ventura*, if I had approached the role like a serious actor, it would have been ridiculous. (Jim Carrey quoted in *Variety*, Supplement 1998: 6)

I have suggested in this article that the opposition between teleological and ostensive performance can be a useful way of examining critical discourses on star performance. This focus enables us to make distinctions between performances without returning to the troublesome concepts of authenticity, presence and intention that dominate discussions of acting. Furthermore, this approach – and my case study of Jim Carrey – illustrates how such discourses privilege teleological modes of performance over comedic performance. Stars re-key performance towards an intertextual and doubled interpretative framing, maintaining a distance between star persona and character. Mobilising the idiolect of stars has always played a self-consciously important part in the narrative and fiscal economy of Hollywood cinema. In the case of Carrey, his star persona has been built on particular performances and the transference of his familiar idiolect across different films.

Stardom is a phenomenon that circulates between the industry, primary and subsidiary texts, and audiences. This suggests that there are limitations in understanding the meanings of stars through textual analysis. It cannot tell us how our investment in a particular star idiolect influences meanings, or how meanings are imported intertextually. This can be seen most overtly in fan discourse, where the affective engagement of the fan itself ostends and reframes performances signs, leading to what Barry King has termed the 'hyper-semioticisation' of the star (1985: 41).

In this chapter I have wanted to stress how performance is a cultural rather than natural experience, occurring in a particular moment, a time and space marked out as 'staged'. This may seem to be rather obvious – we all know, of course, that actors are actors, and that the characters that they perform are fictional. However, we also find that actors and critics routinely talk about performance in terms of truth to a character or role, and theorists of acting and performance have often adopted psychological, philosophical and ideological frameworks that refer to performance in terms of 'presence' and authenticity. I have suggested that critical debates have drawn upon these discourses to consider certain stars – such as Carrey – as low, dumbed-down performance. Part of the pleasure of popular performance is this kind of discriminating talk – we all enjoy discussing and judging performances using similar frameworks. Therefore questions about stardom, about whether we like or dislike a particular star, are partly about our investment in performances, in the framing that makes them so fascinating, and in the pleasures that popular culture routinely offers.

Notes

1 See, for instance, the star careers of Eddie Murphy, Robin Williams, Whoopi Goldberg, Tom Hanks, John Candy, Dan Ackroyd and Chevy Chase.

2 Indicated, after the success of *Ace Ventura, Pet Detective*, by the rise of his fee for *Dumb and Dumber* from a reported $1m to $7m. Even the much-maligned *The Cable Guy* (for which his fee was $20m), often reported as a financial flop, went on to gross over $100m internationally (*Variety*, 1998: 32). All references from *Variety* are taken from a supplement, August 24–30, 1998, unless otherwise indicated.

3 For an attack on what the authors see as this tendency see Washburn and Thornton (1998) and Moseley (2000).

4 The main exceptions to this are Naremore (1988) and Zucker (1990).

5 A high degree of ostensiveness is likely to lead at least to an indirectly presentational mode of address, leading to some interdependence between these categories. A 'histrionic' Woody Allen performance, for example, might not be formally presentational (in the sense that it uses direct address as a foregrounding device) but it may still cast some doubt about the representationalism of the performance.

6 For an exposition of 'frames' as a way of understanding how we assign intentionality to performative acts see Goffman (1974).

7 Another obvious example of this is the use of stars to provide voice-over narration to documentaries and television commercials.

8 See Klein (1998).

9 The Jim Carrey Online (JCO) website for instance (at www.jimcarreyonline.com) sends out regular email newsletters, and boasts exclusive information about Carrey's forthcoming projects.

10 See Zarilli (1995).

11 On this see King, B. (1986) and (1987) .

12 This is monitored almost obsessively by industry journals *Variety* and *The Hollywood Reporter*.

13 See www.hollywoodreporter.com/hollywoodreporter/starpower/index.jsp.

14 See Janet Staiger's analysis of this mode of production in Bordwell, Staiger *et al.* (1985: 330–7).
15 On the grain of the voice see Barthes (1990).
16 See also Blum (1984).
17 See for instance the self-consciousness of Arnold Schwarzenegger's star performance in *The Last Action Hero*.
18 A similar shift can be identified in the recent performances of Tom Hanks and Robin Williams; it would be interesting to assess the impact that this has had on their respective star images.
19 See Felperin (1998).

Bibliography

Barthes, R. (1990) 'The Grain of the Voice', in S. Frith and A. Goodwin (eds), *On Record: Rock, Pop and the Written Word*, London: Routledge, pp. 293–300.
Blum, R. A. (1984) *American Film Acting, the Stanislavski Heritage*, Michigan: UMI Research Press.
Bordwell, D., J. Staiger *et al.* (1985) *Classical Hollywood Cinema: Film Style and Mode of Production to 1960*, London: Routledge.
Caughie, J. and S. Frith (2000) 'The Film Institute and the Rising Tide: An Interview with Colin MacCabe', *Screen*, 41(1).
De Vany, A. and W. David Walls (1999) 'Uncertainty in the Movie Industry, Does Star Power Reduce the Terror of the Box-Office?', paper presented at the Annual Meeting of the American Economic Association, New York, January 1999.
Dyer, Richard (1998) *Stars* (2nd edn), London: British Film Institute.
Ellis, John (1992) *Visible Fictions: Cinema, Television, Video*, London: Routledge.
Felperin, L. (1998) 'How's it going to end?', *Sight and Sound*, 8(10): 36–7.
Gauntlett, D. (1999) 'Researching movie audiences – the armchair method', *Framework*, 41(1).
Goffman, E. (1974) *Frame Analysis*, Boston: Northeastern University Press.
Handy, B. (1998) 'Don't Laugh', *Time*, 151(21), 1 June.
Heath, S. (1981) *Questions of Cinema*, Basingstoke: Macmillan Press.
Kehr, D. (2000) 'Show Business, The Lives of Jim Carrey', *Film Comment*, 35(1), January/February.
King, B. (1985) 'Articulating Stardom', *Screen*, 26(5): 27–50.
King, B. (1986) 'Stardom as an Occupation', in P. Kerr (ed.), *The Hollywood Film Industry*, London: Routledge & Kegan Paul.
King, B. (1987) 'The Star and the Commodity, Notes towards a Performance Theory of Stardom', *Cultural Studies*, 1(2): 145–61.
Klein, N. (1998) 'Hybrid Cinema, The Mask, Masques, and Tex Avery',

in K. S. Sandler (ed.), *Reading the Rabbit, Explorations in Warner Bros. Animation*, London, Rutgers University Press, pp. 209–55.

Laski, B. (1998) 'The Three Faces of Jim, Movie Icon', *Variety*, Supplement, 24–30 August.

Metz, C. (1982) *Psychoanalysis and the Cinema: The Imaginary Signifier*, London: Macmillan.

Moseley, I. (ed.) (2000) *Dumbing Down, Culture, Politics and the Mass Media*, London, Imprint.

Mulvey, L. (1975) 'Visual Pleasure and Narrative Cinema', *Screen*, 16(3): 6–18.

Naremore, J. (1988) *Acting in the Cinema*, Berkeley and Los Angeles: University of California Press.

Neale, S. and F. Krutnik (1990) *Popular Film and Television Comedy*, New York, Routledge.

Palmer, J. (1987) *The Logic of the Absurd, on Film and Television Comedy*, London, Bristish Film Institute.

Schickel, R. (1995) 'Grossing Out', *Time*, 145(2), 9 January.

Walker, A. (1998) *'The Truman Show'*, *London Evening Standard*, 8 October.

Washburn, K. and J. F. Thornton (eds) (1998) *Dumbing Down, Essays on the Strip Mining of American Culture*, London: Norton.

Whitehouse, C. (1998) 'Bubble Boy', *Sight and Sound*, 8(8): 9.

Williams, R. (1998) 'Here's Looking at You', *The Guardian*, 9 October 1998.

Zarilli, P. B. (ed.) (1995) *Acting (Re)Considered, Theories and Practices*, London: Routledge.

Zucker, C. (ed.) (1990) *Making Visible the Invisible*, London: Scarecrow Press.

5

The rise and fall of Sandra Bullock: notes on starmaking and female stardom in contemporary Hollywood[1]

Peter Krämer

In the cover story for the December 1998 issue of *Premiere* magazine, Robert Hofler announced that in the wake of the surprise hit *There's Something About Mary* (1998), Cameron Diaz had become 'Hollywood's Next Big Thing – the first actress to be considered so in a long, long time' (1998: 98). Hofler noted that, apart from Diaz, in the previous ten years only two women had succeeded in breaking through to Hollywood superstardom – Julia Roberts with *Pretty Woman* in 1990 and Sandra Bullock with *Speed* in 1994. Hofler concluded: 'Though several male Next Big Things might be juggled at once, when it comes to young women, Hollywood tosses only one ball in the air at a time. Or none at all.'

While female stars such as Cameron Diaz may dominate magazine covers and the talk show circuit, there are numerous indicators showing that in Hollywood they usually do not amount to much. Whether it is Quigley's annual poll of exhibitors determining the top box-office attractions in the US, the Ulmer scale of international bankability for stars, or *Premiere*'s list of the 100 most powerful people in Hollywood, female stars are always few and far between, and they rarely achieve a high ranking. For example, Quigley's 1998 poll included only three women in the top ten (Meg Ryan at no. 5, Diaz at no. 9 and Roberts at no. 10) (Moser, 2000: 14). Ulmer's February 1998 list did not include a single woman in the top ten, and only two in the top twenty (Roberts at no. 15 and Jodie Foster at no. 16) (Ulmer, 1998).[2] Finally, in *Premiere*'s top 100 for 1998, there are seven actresses as compared to twenty-two actors. The highest-ranked actor (following several executives and directors) is Tom Cruise at no. 6, whereas the highest-ranked actress is Jodie Foster at no. 40 (*Premiere*, 1998: 65–81). Despite extensive publicity, then,

Hollywood's female stars do not count a lot at the box office, and, as a consequence, they have comparatively little power; at least that is what industry insiders and Hollywood's most knowledgeable observers believe.

In the light of Hollywood's extreme bias towards male stars, it is particularly important to examine those few instances where influential commentators such as Robert Hofler, who is also a senior editor for the film industry's 'bible' *Variety*, note the emergence of a major female star. It is too early to say whether Cameron Diaz's huge success in the main supporting role in the Julia Roberts vehicle *My Best Friend's Wedding* (1997) and in the lead of *There's Something About Mary* can be sustained. Early indications are that it will not, partly due to Diaz's rather uncommercial choice of often smallish parts in a series of comparatively minor, or decidedly off-beat, releases such as *Very Bad Things*, *Fear and Loathing in LA* (both 1998), *Being John Malkovich* and *Any Given Sunday* (both 1999). In fact, in early 2000 Diaz had already been replaced by Ashley Judd in the industry's talk about the Next Big Thing, on the basis of only one critically derided surprise hit (*Double Jeopardy*, 1999), which may well have no follow-up either (Schneller, 2000).[3]

However, in contrast with such temporarily hyped actresses, the careers of Julia Roberts and Sandra Bullock are well established enough to draw some preliminary conclusions about their emergence and development as major stars. Bullock has been ranked in *Premiere*'s power list from 1995 onwards (gradually sliding down from no. 56 to no. 80 in 2000), and made it into Quigley's top ten in 1995, 1996 and 1999 (at nos. 6, 5 and 10 respectively) (Moser, 2000: 14).[4] In addition to her hits, she also appeared in several box-office disappointments during this period; in 2000, for example, she had a minor role in *Gun Shy*, which grossed less than $2 million, and played the lead of *28 Days*, which grossed a moderate $37 million.[5] Similarly, despite several box-office failures (especially between 1994 and 1996),[6] Roberts has been consistently listed by *Premiere* since 1991, going as high as no. 14 in 1994 (by far the highest ranking for any female star in the 1990s, which was given to her mainly in recognition of her success with the John Grisham adaptation *The Pelican Brief* the previous year) and no. 20 in 2000.[7] Roberts also frequently made it into Quigley's top ten, achieving by far the highest ranking for any contemporary actress with her no. 2 positions in 1990 and 1997. Her ascent to the no. 1 spot in 1999, on the basis of her back-to-back summer smashes *Notting Hill* and *Runaway Bride*, is a feat that has not been achieved by a woman since 1967, when Julie Andrews was the no. 1 star in the US. While Roberts is therefore a totally exceptional female star, the ups and downs of Bullock's fortunes are more typical of the careers of actresses in contemporary Hollywood.

In this chapter, I am going to examine the general outline of Sandra Bullock's career, concentrating on the development of her star image and on her breakthrough to superstardom between 1993 and 1995 (that is between *Demolition Man* and *The Net*). It will become obvious not only that the turning point in Bullock's career, the release of *Speed* in June 1994, coincided with a decline in Roberts' box office fortunes (starting with the release of *I Love Trouble* in the same month), but also that Bullock lost her superstar status in 1997, the very year that Julia Roberts made a spectacular commercial comeback (with *My Best Friend's Wedding* and *Conspiracy Theory*). While to some extent this timing is no doubt a mere coincidence, it does suggest that in contemporary Hollywood there is indeed only ever space for one actress near the top. However, it will also become apparent that, while no longer a major box-office attraction, by 1997 Bullock had already laid the foundations for a long Hollywood career as an actress and producer.

Starmaking

Before examining this rise and fall, and consolidation, in Bullock's fortunes more closely, I want to make some general comments on starmaking in contemporary Hollywood. The dramatic, albeit mostly only temporary, transformation in the status of actresses such as Cameron Diaz and Sandra Bullock is of interest because it allows for a close examination of the complex process of starmaking, in which production decisions (casting, budget, and so on), the actress's choice of roles, her performance, film marketing (including advertising and publicity), critical responses and box-office results interact so as to select a particular performer to become the focus of intense public interest and substantial financial investments on the part of the industry. This is not a one-way process, by which Hollywood forces a performer on to the public, but rather it is a feedback mechanism, which can work positively to elevate the performer to stardom, if the various factors mentioned above reinforce her unique status, thus differentiating her from other performers. However, it can – and indeed much more frequently does – also work negatively, keeping her in the position of an undistinguished working actress, or relegating her back to that status, once she has achieved stardom.

Thus, the starmaking process is perhaps best understood in the following way. Numerous actresses offer themselves to decision-makers in the film industry (including agents, casting directors, film directors, producers and marketing executives), who in turn offer some of them as potential attractions to the press and the public. Several of these actresses are picked up by magazines as subjects for articles and even cover pictures, yet only very few also manage to attract huge audiences to their films. If box-office results do indicate that a certain actress appeals to audiences, the film industry's publicity efforts and general press and television coverage increase dramatically, thus enhancing the chances of her future films to be successful as well. Publicity and press coverage will tend to equate, or at least to draw out the parallels between, the actress's off-screen life and personality (her publicity image) and the characters she plays on screen (her screen persona), so audiences are able to imagine that by seeing the actress on the screen they get close to the 'real' person. The confluence of publicity image and screen persona constitutes the actress's star image, which is subject to change, and which also often differs quite substantially from the roles and publicity she had received before achieving stardom.[8] This is nicely illustrated by Sandra Bullock's early career.

Starlet

By the time she made *Demolition Man* in 1993, Sandra Bullock (who has been evasive about her age, but was probably born in 1964) had been a working actress for over five years. During that time, she had appeared in a sit-com (playing the Melanie Griffith role in a TV version of the 1988 romantic comedy hit *Working Girl*) and a mini-series as well as about a dozen films, including several made-for-TV movies and a straight-to-video film. Having mainly worked for television in 1989 and 1990, in the early 1990s Bullock appeared in a quick succession of theatrical features, combining lead roles in fairly low-budget productions such as the romantic comedy *Love Potion No. 9* (1992) with minor parts in bigger-budget films such as the American remake of the Dutch thriller *The Vanishing* (1993). Her roles ranged from science-nerd-transformed-into-stunning-beauty to girl-friend-in-peril, from a glamorous uptown girl (*Who Shot Patakango?*, 1990) to a waitress who is the object of affection for an old man (*Wrestling Ernest Hemingway*, 1993).

What all of Bullock's films from this period have in common is that they were disappointments at the box office, even disastrous flops.[9] Yet in an industry accustomed to far more failures than successes, the limited appeal of the films she appeared in (rarely in the lead, it has to be remembered), was not held against Bullock. Indeed, reviews of these films mention her only briefly, if at all.[10] Reviewers might note her 'genuine appeal', but in most cases acknowledged that she only has a 'brief role' (Farolino, 1992: 19; Bernard, 1993: 27). An indirect reference to her potential for stardom comes in a comment on her appearance opposite Kiefer Sutherland in *The Vanishing*. The critic introduces her as 'Sandra Bullock, an actress who bears a resemblance to Sutherland's real-life ex-girlfriend Julia Roberts – obviously a casting decision designed to provoke a weird echo' (Bernard, 1993: 27). With such indications of her potential for stardom (albeit only through her resemblance to an established star), Bullock, unlike most of her fellow actors, continued to have steady employment and regularly appeared in major releases. Her various employers thus held her in a good position for a breakaway hit that would focus media and audience attention on her and promote her to stardom.

Her status as a promising starlet was confirmed by her 1993 appearance in *Demolition Man*, a $58 million science-fiction (Sci-Fi) film that, together with the same year's *Cliffhanger*, marked Sylvester Stallone's return to the action genre after two years in which he had unsuccessfully switched from action to comedy.[11] While *Demolition Man* did less well than *Cliffhanger*, the film made it into the list of the top 20 highest-grossing films in the US in 1993, and with a $56 million gross earned about four times more than any of Bullock's previous films (and indeed much more than all of them put together).[12] While many reviews still failed to mention her, *Time* wrote that she 'has an attractive naivete' (Schickel, 1993: 98), and the *New York Post* described her as 'perky and animated. She gets some good lines and delivers them amiably' (Adams, 1993: 45).

In response to this success, a few weeks after the release of *Demolition Man* in October 1993, Bullock was selected as the focus for an article in *US Magazine* entitled 'The Making of a Starlet, 90s Style' (Kaplan, 1993). Presented as a guide for aspiring actresses, the article introduces Bullock (somewhat incorrectly) as a '26-year-old actress who seemingly came out of nowhere to nab roles in four major motion pictures this year and who has just been cast opposite Keanu Reeves in a fifth' (Kaplan, 1993: 80–1).[13] The article then proceeds to outline the secret behind her success, 'the important lessons learned on her way to the top'. Under the heading 'Get a Jump on the Competition', it is reported that Bullock already wrote and staged plays as a little girl, and in fact 'grew up on stage' while touring with her mother, a German opera singer who got her daughter small parts in her productions. After having thus had a head start, Bullock's subsequent career adhered to maxims such as 'Ignore Authority', 'Pay Your Dues', 'Get the Role – and the Guy' (by dating her *Love Potion No. 9* co-star Tate Donovan), until, finally, she made it by 'Be[ing] in the Right Place at the Right Time'. When producer Joel Silver looked for a replacement for Lori Petty in *Demolition Man*, he selected Bullock whom he had been impressed with in *The Vanishing*: 'She's sexy, she's articulate. You see the soul behind her eyes' (Kaplan, 1993: 82–4). Thus, the reasons for Bullock's rise are presented as a mixture of personal factors (talent, constant application from childhood onwards, participation in Hollywood's social networks, and so on) and pure chance. Apart from the reference to producer Joel Silver, this leaves out the crucial role of Hollywood's gatekeepers (from agents to marketing executives), yet otherwise, as my earlier comments on the starmaking process suggest, the article paints a reasonably accurate picture. In any case, the article presented Bullock as a representative Hollywood starlet.

Bullock was considered an important asset in the marketing of *Demolition Man*, with stories about her being printed in 'trend publications' and Bullock herself appearing on *The David Letterman Show* to promote the film (Kaplan, 1993: 84). In December 1993, the *LA Times* featured her in its column 'Fast Track: Up and Comers in Arts and Entertainment'. The article focuses on her sense of humour and her naturalness both on and off the screen: '[In *Demolition Man*] she manages to turn scenes of dry exposition – explaining the future to Stallone – into screwball comedy' (Newman, 1993: F1, 3). A further glimpse of Bullock's nascent star image is provided by the self-deprecating remarks she makes in an early interview; when asked about the many leading parts she has, she responds: 'I

. . . beg a lot. And I'm cheap' (Beck, 1991). It is also interesting to look at a piece on starlets in Europe's top-selling film magazine, the German *Cinema*, especially since the German market proved to be particularly important for Bullock (whose German origins – her mother is German and she spent part of her childhood in Germany – were a major selling point there). A few months after the release of *Demolition Man*, Bullock is shown here to be both sexy and quirky; the cyber-sex scene in *Demolition Man* is emphasised and her ability to do comedy is noted (*Cinema*, 1994: 50).

Thus, early publicity about Bullock portrayed her as unaffected and good humoured, as sexy but not a bimbo, as a hard-working and experienced actress with a showbiz background and a great future ahead of her; in other words: a nice young woman on the fast track to stardom. This off-screen image is mirrored in her roles as the action hero's sidekick in *Demolition Man*, where she plays a nice and humorous police officer longing for some action, and in *Speed*, where she is literally put on the fast track as a bus passenger who ends up behind the steering wheel of a speeding bus. It is important to note that in both films Bullock's character, while nominally the hero's sidekick, is in fact surprisingly close to the very centre of the narrative, which may have had a lot to do with her subsequent elevation to stardom.

Sidekick

At first sight, *Demolition Man* and *Speed* appear to be typical action films, serving as vehicles for their male stars (Stallone and Reeves) whose skilful deployment of their bodies and all manner of weapons in carefully choreographed action sequences constitutes the main attraction of the films.[14] Both films start with a violent sequence in which the protagonists confront their opponents, crazed geniuses (played by Wesley Snipes and Dennis Hopper) who don't mind blowing up buildings and killing lots of people to further their own ends. In both films, the protagonists demonstrate their determination and ability to beat their opponents in the opening sequence, yet fail to gain a decisive victory, thus setting the scene for future violent encounters. In the run-up to and during these encounters, they are helped by young women (played by Sandra Bullock, who receives third billing for both films). The protagonists have only just met these women, yet they turn out to be extremely competent and courageous helpers, while they also engage in comic banter with the protagonists as a prelude to eventually falling in love with them. Both films end with a spectacular showdown in which the protagonist kills his opponent, and a final kiss that seals the romantic union between the action hero and his female sidekick. Thus, the films would appear to be straightforward male wish-fulfilment fantasies: kill the bad guy, save the day, get the girl.

However, in each film the introduction of the young woman played by Sandra Bullock puts a very different spin on the subsequent action. After the opening action sequence set in a war-zone-like mid-1990s Los Angeles, *Demolition Man* switches to an almost totally pacified future, focusing on Bullock's bored police officer Lenina Huxley, who is nostalgic for the violent twentieth century and forcefully expresses her greatest wish in a tight close-up: 'What I wouldn't give for some action!' Immediately afterwards, violence does indeed erupt into her world in the form of Wesley Snipes's bad guy. His awakening from cryogenic sleep and all subsequent action are thus presented as the realisation of Lenina's wish. Furthermore, while she is not always allowed to fully participate in the violent action, Lenina does kick some butt, and she also has numerous lines that, wittingly or unwittingly, undercut the heroics of the action star. When Stallone's character greets an old friend with swearwords, she comments: 'This is how insecure heterosexual men used to sound'. Mangling her words, she has this to say to the hero about his confrontation with the bad guy: 'He's finally matched his meat. You licked his arse.' When they are about to pursue the bad buy, she cheerfully announces: 'Let's go blow this guy'. She also talks in filmic clichés: 'I fleshed you out as some blow-up-the-bad-guy-with-a-happy-grin-he-man-type. But now I realise that you are the moody-troubled-past-gunslinger-who-will-only-draw-when-he-must-type.' By making fun of the conventional male heroics of the action genre, and by longing for and eagerly participating in the action, then, Bullock's character allows women an entry point into this film.

Similarly, her character in *Speed*, Annie, is first shown chasing a bus, which she is only taking because she has lost her driver's licence as a result of speeding. In a conversation with a fellow passenger, she admits that she loves and misses her car, and when the bus slows down because of a traffic jam she shouts at the driver: 'Why don't you just drive all over these people, or something?' Within minutes, the narrative has moved her into the bus driver's seat, where she is forced to maintain the vehicle's high speed (so as to avoid a bomb explosion), which at times means precisely that she has to drive all over the obstacles in her way. Again, the film's narrative works to fulfil the Bullock character's wishes. Just as in *Demolition Man*, this character offers women an entry point into the action scenario of *Speed*.

In both films, the positioning of Bullock can be seen as an attempt to appeal specifically to women, who in audience surveys have consistently expressed their dislike of action-adventure and Sci-Fi, preferring romantic comedy, serious drama, musicals and melo-drama instead.[15] Since action-adventure and Sci-Fi are contemporary Hollywood's most important genres, that is the genres in which the industry invests most money, various executives, producers, writers and filmmakers, most notably James Cameron with *Aliens* (1986) and *Terminator 2* (1991), have attempted to overcome female resis-tance by moving female characters closer to the centre of action narratives.[16]

In the case of *Speed*, this strategy definitely worked. The film grossed $121 million, becoming the seventh-highest grossing film of 1994.[17] A few weeks after its release, an article in the *LA Times* reported that 'Analysts say the picture is as popular with women as with men – a departure for the male dominated slam-bang genre' (Bergman, 1994: F1, 3). According to a Fox marketing executive, the film had tested well with women, and although slightly fewer women than men eventually saw the film, their approval rating for the film was just as high (an astonishing 97 per cent) as that of male viewers (Bergman, 1994: F1).[18] To reflect this strong connection with the female audience, the advertising campaign was adjusted. While the original posters featured Keanu Reeves and an exploding bus, later on an insert showing Reeves and Bullock lying together on the ground was added (Bergman, 1994: F1). The article also quoted producer Mark Gordon: 'When we started three years ago . . . I was very interested in creating a female protagonist who was intimately and aggressively involved in the progress of the movie, rather than being saved by the man throughout the film.'[19]

The press focused a lot of their attention on Bullock, suggesting that she was more important to the film's success than Reeves. Natasha Stovall, for example, wrote in the *Village Voice* that Bullock gave a new spin to her role as 'the action flick heroine, a thankless

task usually accomplished through submissiveness and endless
screeching' (1994: 56–7). Stovall argues that, like Sarah Connor in
Terminator 2, Bullock's character in *Speed* and *Demolition Man* 'is
one of a new breed of heroines who spark action and beat bad guys
much more than they give up skin and pooch for the final lip clinch.'
Bullock is quoted as saying that she wanted to make *Speed* because
she found Annie to be a realistic, believable character. This theme is
developed in Cathy Thompson-Georges' article in *Entertainment
Today*: 'She's neither hysterical nor bitchy, and her game but scared
character is believable in a way that helps the movie tremendously:
we can easily put ourselves in her shoes, as she reacts the way we at
least hope we would under the circumstances' (Thompson-Georges,
1994). Thus, Annie is argued to be much like the female spectator,
while elsewhere she is said to be like Bullock herself. Jamie Diamond
writes in the *New York Times* that Bullock's true self always comes
through in her roles: On and off screen she's a 'klutz', 'goofball',
'kook', 'the cheerful ditz' (Diamond, 1994: H25).[20]

Following the success of *Speed*, then, Bullock's screen persona and
publicity image shifted from determined, good-natured young
working girl to a kind of idealised everywoman: highly physical and
attractive yet not reducible to her sexuality, quirky yet very familiar,
an ordinary woman coping well with extraordinary circumstances
(a speeding bus, a career that has just taken off). While the film's
makers, critics and audiences all acknowledged Bullock's importance for the success of *Speed*, the true test for her star power would
be her ability to carry a movie all on her own. As it turned out, she
passed that test in 1995 with her next two films, *While You Were
Sleeping* (released in April) and *The Net* (July), both of which
revolve almost exclusively around her character. With the success
of these films, Sandra Bullock became that extreme rarity in Hollywood – a female superstar.

Superstar

Following her success with *Demolition Man* and *Speed*, Sandra Bullock
expressed her desire to avoid being typecast as the action hero's goofy
sidekick (Stovall, 1994). So for her next two films she chose the romantic comedy *While You Were Sleeping*, which developed some of
the 'screwball' elements of her two action films, yet focused much
more exclusively on her character's fears and longings, and *The Net*, a

paranoid techno-thriller.[21] While *The Net* features plenty of technology and violent action, it is totally focused on the Bullock character's emotional experiences past and present. In fact, the generic thriller storyline about a computer conspiracy, a dissembling male killer and the electronic erasure of her identity develops the main themes of her emotional life: her abandonment by her father, the duplicity of her previous lovers, her withdrawal from most forms of direct social contact into programming work and mediated communication, the terror of not being recognised by her own mother who suffers from Alzheimer's. In this way, despite the films' huge generic differences, *The Net* is amazingly similar to *While You Were Sleeping* in which Bullock's character Lucy is an orphan, who lives with and talks to her cat, and has to do extra hours on holidays (in her job in a subway toll booth) because she is the only employee without a family.

Both films open with sequences that show their protagonists at work and outline the central importance of parents in their lives. In *The Net*, Angela is first shown working on her computer, turning down colleagues who want to meet her in person, before she then visits her mother in a nursing home, and is not recognised by her. In the first sequence of *While You Were Sleeping*, Lucy's voiceover comments on childhood memories, which are presented in a flashback: she fondly remembers her father and his deep love for her dead mother. It is this kind of love that she is looking for in her own life, and a seemingly nice, good-looking yuppie who passes her booth almost every day without ever acknowledging her is the one she chooses as her 'Prince Charming': 'I know that some day I am going to find a way to introduce myself, and that's going to be perfect – just like my prince.'

Thus, towards the beginning of *While You Were Sleeping* Bullock's character utters a wish, which the remainder of the film will work to fulfil. Soon after her prince speaks his first words to her, which surprises her so much that she can not say anything in return, he is conveniently pushed on to the subway tracks so that Lucy has to save him. In the hospital, where he lies in a coma, she is then mistaken for his fiancée, and soon afterwards she is effectively adopted by his family. When her prince finally wakes up, he is indeed willing to marry her. However, the film has a lesson to teach: Sometimes dream lovers are not the right ones. In fact, Lucy has slowly fallen in love with the yuppie's unassuming, down-to-earth brother, and it is him she marries in the end. In this way, Lucy opts for reality rather than fantasy, a choice that perhaps makes her more accessible for female identification. At the same time, male spectators are invited to place themselves in the position of the average guy who wins Lucy/ Bullock's affections, whereas the more glamorous male loses out.

The Net teaches a similar lesson about connections between people, and it also uses a dream scenario to convey it. However, in this case, the dream is a terrible nightmare, and no stable object for male identification is offered to spectators. The opening sequence portrays Angela as a woman who has withdrawn from the world – having neither friends nor lovers, keeping her distance from colleagues and neighbours, and failing to connect with her mother (due to her illness). This implicitly raises the question of whether she can maintain a sense of self without anyone knowing her well enough to confirm and appreciate who she is. The fear of losing one's identity is then played out in the remainder of the film, in which everything is taken away from Angela: her name, her biography, her house, her job, her former lover. Yet Angela manages to assert herself, regaining her public identity, and, perhaps more importantly, reconsidering her isolated private life: in a bitter-sweet ending, she is seen with her mother, who she has brought home to live with her, although the mother still does not know her. Again, this conclusion returns the Bullock character to a situation that must be all too familiar to women in the audience; at the same time, there is a marked absence of a lover in her life, a vacant spot that male fans may fantasise about.

The central themes of *While You Were Sleeping* and *The Net* (the fundamental loneliness of the central character, the joy and pain of romantic love, the centrality of family, and so on) were reflected in the vast publicity that Bullock received in 1995. The cover story of *Vanity Fair*'s September 1995 issue, for example, reports: 'A dedicated computer buff who cruises America Online, [Bullock] was determined to star in *The Net*' (Conant, 1995: 162).[22] Bullock describes herself as 'a privacy freak', and is reported to have 'no entourage, unless you count her younger sister Gesine . . . who often visits her on the set'. Her family is described as 'very close', and her 'network of friends' as an 'extended family'. About Tate Donovan, who she split up with in 1994, Bullock says: 'It's like they say, there's one person in your life, and Tate and I are closer than any two people I've ever experienced in my life. There's nobody that means more to me.' The writer comments on the split-up: 'The only thing that got her through the next year was playing lovesick Lucy in

While You Were Sleeping.' Bullock explains: 'This way I could grieve and do it in my work'. And in words that could have come from the script of *The Net*, she concludes: 'It's going to be a long time before I can trust anyone again.' Just like the two films, this construction invites identification from female fans and highlights the empty spot where, it is said, a boyfriend should be, inviting male fans to fantasise about filling that role.[23]

Thus, Bullock's rise to superstardom was achieved between 1993 and 1995 with a series of four hit movies, all of which placed her (implicitly or explicitly) at the centre of their stories, making her inner life the very source of narrative developments, while the emotional concerns addressed in the films were also at the centre of the publicity surrounding her off-screen life and personality. In this way, Bullock became one of the very few actresses able to compete with the male stars who, as we have seen, so totally dominate Hollywood. Her elevated and extraordinary position in Hollywood can be gauged by the following statistics. *While You Were Sleeping* was at no. 13 in the annual list of top-grossing films in the US for 1995, and *The Net* was at no. 29. The combined gross of over $130 million for these two films meant that the only stars whose films grossed even more money in 1995 were Tom Hanks (*Apollo 13* and *Toy Story*) and Jim Carrey (*Batman Forever* and *Ace Ventura 2*).[24]

In Quigley's poll of American film exhibitors, Bullock was listed as the sixth biggest box office attraction of 1995 (the only other woman in the top ten was Demi Moore at no. 8) (Moser, 2000: 14). In March 1996, she was also voted 'Female Star of the Year' by the National Organisation of Theater Owners (*Hollywood Reporter*, 1996: S3). Finally, in recognition of her drawing power, Bullock was ranked fifty-sixth in *Premiere* magazine's May 1996 list of the 100 most powerful people in Hollywood (*Premiere*, 1996: 77–90). Only twelve women were included in this list, and only four of those (Paramount executive Sherry Lansing at no. 15, Julia Roberts at no. 45, Demi Moore at no. 48 and Jodie Foster at no. 55) were ranked above Bullock. Furthermore, her asking price for appearing in a film had shot up from the $500,000 she had received for *Speed* to more than $10 million, which made her one the highest-paid actresses in Hollywood, although her salary was still dwarfed by the $20 million top male stars could command.

Her status as a superstar was further consolidated when she followed the commercially and critically disappointing romantic comedy *Two If By Sea* (released in January 1996, very much focused on its male protagonist and grossing only $10 million in the US) with a star turn in the big-budget John Grisham adaptation *A Time to Kill* (released in July) (*steadycam*, 1996: 12; 1997a: 19–20).[25] Bullock plays a character, Ellen Roark, who – like a star making a guest appearance – steps into an ongoing story to which she has no obvious connection and in which her role remains marginal throughout (she neither solves the case, nor does she get a man). In fact, in the novel on which the film is based (Grisham, 1989), Ellen Roark makes her first appearance after 294 pages (out of 515) and she is out of the action after page 433. Nevertheless, Bullock received top billing and was thus offered as the main attraction of the film, which became the ninth-highest-grossing movie of 1996 in the US (with revenues of $101 million) (*steadycam*, 1996: 12; 1997a: 19–20). Probably in recognition of her ability to draw people to a film in which she only does a star turn, rather than playing a key role, the Quigley poll gave Bullock her highest ranking ever (no. 5; the only other woman in the top ten was Michelle Pfeiffer at no. 10). Then, in January 1997, she won the People's Choice Award as America's favourite female movie star (Schaefer, 1997).

Falling star

At the height of her superstardom, Sandra Bullock began to prepare for the inevitable fall. In an interview in May 1996, she stated bluntly: 'My shelf life is maybe four or five years and then what do you have?' (Hensley, 1996: 54). As it turned out, her prediction was quite accurate, and instead of superstardom what she had by the late 1990s was a reduced but fairly reliable following among female cinemagoers and the ability to branch out from acting into other aspects of film production through her own company Fortis Films. Bullock set up Fortis Films in 1996, initially to write and direct the short film *Making Sandwiches*, which was premiered at the Sundance Film Festival in January 1997 (Amistead, 1996; Hensley, 1996). She also made a deal with Fox, in which she agreed to appear in the 1997 sequel to *Speed* only if, in addition to her salary (a reported $12.5 million), she received finance for Fortis Films' production of the small-scale romantic drama *Hope Floats* (released in May 1998; Bullock is credited as executive producer) (Schuers, 1997: 39). This was the beginning of what appears to be a regular production schedule for Fortis Films, combining films starring Bullock (*Practical Magic*, October 1998) with films in which she only has a minor role (*Gun Shy*, February 2000), which no doubt will be followed by films that Bullock does not appear in at all. In addition to her Fortis productions, Bullock also appeared in films produced by other companies: *In Love and War* (January 1997), *The Prince of Egypt* (December 1998; she does the voice for a supporting character), *Forces of Nature* (March 1999) and *28 Days* (April 2000).

Thus, Bullock has maintained an astonishingly high level of productivity. However, none of the above films, with the exception of *The Prince of Egypt*, in which she did not star, came anywhere near the box-office grosses of *Speed*, *While You Were Sleeping* and *A Time to Kill*. To make (financial) matters worse, the budgets of her box-office failures were particularly high. Thus, in 1997 the World War One romantic drama *In Love and War* became her most expensive film up to that point with a budget of $46 million, yet grossed only about $15 million in the US (*steadycam*, 1997a: 21; *Variety*, 1998a: 17). Her next film, *Speed 2: Cruise Control*, cost an astonishing $120 million with US grosses of about $50 million (*steadycam*, 1997b: 43). While to some extent foreign revenues made up for these shortfalls,[26] the most commercially viable of Bullock's films were the low-to-medium budget contemporary dramas which she specialised in after *Speed 2*. Her next three films, for example, while far from being blockbusters, did very respectable business: *Hope Floats* grossed $60 million in the US against a budget of $29 million, *Practical Magic* grossed $48 million against a budget of $38 million, and *Forces of Nature* grossed $53 million against a $40 million budget (*steadycam*, 1999: 33).[27]

How can the overall decline in Bullock's box-office fortunes after *A Time to Kill* be explained? It is certainly not for lack of publicity. No matter how well or badly her films perform commercially, Bullock has continued to make the talk show rounds and to command cover stories in leading magazines (for example in the April 2000 issue of *Premiere*). However, the complex, mutually reinforcing relationship between such publicity, her film characters and the stories they appear in has been difficult to maintain. First of all, as we have seen, already at the height of her star power in 1996 she began to receive top billing for films in which her character's wishes and anxieties were not central to the narrative. This continued in 1997 with *In Love and War*, in which she played the nurse that Ernest

Hemingway fell in love with during World War One, and *Speed 2*, in which she was effectively reduced to the part of the helpless female bystander or victim that her roles in *Demolition Man* and *Speed* had been so clearly departing from.[28]

Furthermore, during 1996 and 1997, the intimate link between screen persona and publicity image was being severed. While strenuous claims continued to be made in interviews and articles that her films reflected her real-life personality and experiences, her roles, especially the sexy and ambitious law student she played in *A Time to Kill* and the World War One nurse of *In Love and War*, were too far removed from the life of a Hollywood star to be credibly linked to it.[29] Furthermore, comments about her much-praised accessibility and normality – an ordinary woman in extraordinary circumstances, the superstar-next-door – rang increasingly hollow when Bullock had so clearly become just another incredibly rich member of the totally exclusive Hollywood elite. Finally, there was a backlash against the relentlessly positive reporting about her person, when starting in 1996, in the wake of her decision to replace her agent and manager, rumours began to circulate about her 'being difficult' in her business relations and on the set of her films.[30] While tales about the megalomania of stars are a standard feature of much writing about Hollywood, the backlash against female stars appears to be particularly forceful (as is evidenced, for example, by the negative publicity surrounding Julia Roberts in the mid-1990s and Demi Moore for most of her career).

As a result of these various developments in Bullock's choice of scripts and roles and in the publicity about her off-screen life and personality, she had lost much of her star appeal by the end of 1997. In line with her own prediction, her shelf-life as a major star had indeed turned out to be only a few years. It is important to note that irrespective of the particular career decisions they make, a short shelf life has been a feature of the career of most female Hollywood stars. A study of all 129 stars (81 men and 48 women) listed in the top ten of Quigley's annual polls of top box office attractions between 1932 to 1984 revealed that female stars stay at the top for much shorter periods than male stars (Levy, 1990: 255–7). The median number of appearances in the poll (not necessarily in consecutive years) is two for women and four for men. The vast majority (over 80 per cent) of female stars make fewer than five appearances on the list and none more than ten, whereas almost 40 per cent of men make five or more appearances, and almost 15 per cent ten or more, with John Wayne setting the record with an astonishing 25 listings in Quigley's top ten between 1949 and 1974. This gender imbalance has not changed in recent years; with the sole exception of Julia Roberts (six listings between 1990 and 1999) women quickly come and go, while top male stars appear year after year in the top ten (Robin Williams, for example, made it almost every year since 1988 and Tom Cruise in most years since 1983). With her two top-ten appearances in 1995 and 1996, then, Bullock fits the average career profile of female stars since the 1930s.

One of the main reasons for women's comparatively short periods as top stars might be their inability to hold on to their male following (or their unwillingness to make a special effort to service this constituency). This is certainly suggested by the ups and downs of Bullock's career. Following the *Speed 2* disaster, her films have consistently been noted for their limited, female appeal. *Variety*, for example, predicted that despite its 'dreadfully dull, completely conventional story', *Hope Floats* 'could stir up some business with a predominantly female audience since Sandra Bullock's role represents a sympathetic extension of the sort of young Everywoman part with which she's enjoyed her greatest success' (McCarthy, 1998: 57). After *Hope Floats* had indeed performed creditably at the box office, *Variety* predicted (correctly) another 'midrange success' for her next film, the 'supernatural comedy-drama' *Practical Magic*, due to Bullock's 'track record of making commercially accessible movies out of bland, schmaltzy material', primarily 'targeted at femme viewers' (Levy, 1998: 74). This track record was expected to extend to the 'neo-screwball comedy' *Forces of Nature*, which, according to the *Variety* review, was 'poised to attract enough adult ticketbuyers for a long-legged B.O. [box office] run' (Leydon, 1999: 38–9). Since the adult audience, in Hollywood's view, is led by the choices of female decisionmakers, this was another way of highlighting the particular appeal of Bullock's films to women. Finally, despite largely negative comments about the film's quality, *Variety*'s review of *28 Days*, in which Bullock plays a 'substance-abusing party girl' being transformed into a 'sober reformed citizen', again predicted (fairly correctly) a 'customarily solid midrange' box-office gross due to her 'reliable, femme-heavy fan base' (McCarthy, 2000: 43, 46).

In conclusion, then, Sandra Bullock's career exemplifies the general process of starmaking and the specific limitations of female stardom in contemporary Hollywood. After several years as an undistinguished working actress, in the wake of the success of *Speed* in 1994 she was elevated from comic action sidekick to superstar with broad appeal to diverse audience segments. During the next two years, she starred in two international superhits (*While You Were Sleeping* and *A Time to Kill*) as well as a minor hit (*The Net*) and a box-office failure (*Two If By Sea*). In 1997 she lost her superstar status and most of her male following with the two flops *In Love and War* and *Speed 2*, which were also characterised by escalating budgets. Since then she has appeared in a string of modestly budgeted female-oriented contemporary dramas (with more or less pronounced comic elements) that have been moderately successful at the box office. At the same time, in addition to her acting, Bullock has been involved in other aspects of filmmaking through her production company Fortis Films, which she formed at the height of her success in 1996 so as to gain some protection against the vagaries of female stardom in contemporary Hollywood.

Postscript

While there is a certain logic to the career trajectories of actors, there are also many surprise twists and turns. Thus, after the completion of this manuscript in the spring of 2001, both Sandra Bullock and Cameron Diaz rather unexpectedly bounced back to superstardom with genuine box-office hits (while Julia Roberts' first two releases of 2001, *The Mexican* and *America's Sweethearts*, did not perform as well as expected). Bullock was undoubtedly the main attraction of *Miss Congeniality*, which grossed $107 million in the US, while Diaz co-starred in *Charlie's Angels* ($125 million) and voiced the female protagonist of the animated blockbuster *Shrek* ($264 million).[31] Whether the two actresses can sustain their box-office appeal remains to be seen.

Notes

1 Research for this chapter was made possible by a small grant from the Arts and Humanities Research Board.
2 The list I am referring to is the one on page 71, which assesses the appeal of stars in foreign territories for films with average or above-average budgets (over $30 million). Women tend to be more bankable in lower-budget films; compare this with the list on page 72, where,

however, the columns for 'over $30m' and 'under $30m' have mistakenly been reversed. Also see discussion of worldwide bankability in Burman (1999). There are four women in the top twenty, but with the exception of Julia Roberts at no. 8, all of them are below no. 15.

3   Indeed, Judd's next films after *Double Jeopardy*, were *Eye of the Beholder*, which opened reasonably well in January 2000 but then disappeared very quickly, and *Where the Heart Is* (April 2000), in which she had only a minor part.

4   For the results of the 1999 poll, see press release by Quigley Publishing on 4 April 2000, in 'Actors & Actresses Lists' file, Academy Center for Motion Picture Study, Academy of Motion Picture Arts and Sciences, Beverly Hills. Interestingly, Ashley Judd is at no. 11 in this poll, while Cameron Diaz, the 'Next Big Thing' of 1998, does not even make it into the top 20.

5   For the most recent films, I have used financial figures from the Internet Movie Database (http://us.imdb.com). For earlier films I have used the print sources as cited.

6   US grosses for all of Roberts' films are listed in McDonald (2000: 107).

7   Thanks to Sultan Sahin Gencer for providing me with her analysis of *Premiere*'s power lists.

8   See, for example, Gamson (1994). For an overview of the extensive literature on stars and acting, on which I draw here, see Krämer (1999a).

9   For example, *Love Potion No. 9* cost $10 million and grossed only $600,000 in the US in 1992; *The Thing Called Love* cost $14 million and grossed $1 million in 1993; *The Vanishing* grossed $13 million against a budget of $17 million. See box-office figures and budgets given in the German magazine *steadycam* (which gets its data from the American trade press): *steadycam*, 1993: 12; 1994: 10. According to *Daily Variety*, grosses for some of her films were very low indeed, with the $2,000 for *Who Shot Patakango?* holding a negative record (*Daily Variety* 1995: 14).

10   Reviews from major American newspapers and magazines are conveniently collected in Ozer (1981–).

11   Having made one previous unsuccessful attempt at comedy with *Rhinestone* in 1984, Stallone released *Oscar* in 1991 (grossing $23 million and costing $22 million) and *Stop! Or My Mom Will Shoot* in 1992 (grossing $27 million and costing $21 million). See *steadycam*, 1992: 16; 1993: 12.

12   Released in May 1993, *Cliffhanger* earned $84 million against a $65 million budget, and was the ninth-highest grossing film of 1993 in the US (*steadycam*, 1994: 9–10).

13   Bullock was probably 28 at the time, and, as we have seen, had been an extremely busy working actress, rather than coming out of nowhere.

The four films of 1993 are: *Wrestling Ernest Hemingway*, *The Vanishing*, *The Thing Called Love* and *Demolition Man*. The Keanu Reeves film is, of course, *Speed*. In 1993, Bullock also appeared in the straight-to-video movie *Fire on the Amazon*.

14 For discussions of the action genre, see, for example, Tasker (1993); Jeffords (1994); and Krämer (1998a: 600–4).

15 See Krämer (1999b: 98–100).

16 Cf. Krämer (1998a). For a discussion of another strategy for broadening the appeal of action-adventure films, see Krämer (1998b).

17 Unusually for a big action film, *Speed* had only a medium-sized budget of $31 million (*steadycam*, 1995: 8–9).

18 According to the Cinemascore Movie Report 58 per cent of the opening night audience were male. Interestingly, only 33 per cent of the audience were under 25. Since action films tend to attract primarily a young male audience, *Speed*'s audience was made up of an unusually high percentage of women and older people. See *Hollywood Reporter* (1994); Grove (1994).

19 Gordon's statement was echoed by Fox executive Tom Sherak and director Jan de Bont. Sherak: 'Sandra's just like Keanu, she's also our hero. Women like to see the woman as the hero, and she's just as much a hero as he is.' De Bont: 'Sandra's playing such a different part than usual, she's not helpless . . . she's in charge of her own destiny. In fact, she's more in charge of herself than Keanu's character is' (Bergman, 1994: F1, 3).

20 Cf. the following Bullock statement: 'I'm the quirky, offbeat funny girl' (Musto, 1994: 45).

21 In some respects, Bullock thus replayed – in reverse order – the genre diversification that had worked so well for Julia Roberts in 1990 and 1991, when she followed her breakthrough hit, the romantic comedy *Pretty Woman*, with the Sci-Fi picture *Flatliners* and the psychothriller *Sleeping with the Enemy*. As we will see, Bullock later also repeated the huge success that Roberts had had with a John Grisham adaptation.

22 For similar comments see, for example, Rebello (1995).

23 Such imaginary relations with the star are actively, albeit somewhat ironically, encouraged by a lot of her coverage in the press. See, for example, the cover story of the weekend supplement of the *New York Daily News*: 'She is familiar and, to many minds, attainable. Women feel they once were, are or could be her. Men feel they could get a date with her, or at least someone kinda-sorta like her' (Nelson, 1996: 4–5).

24 Compared to the mega-budgets of $85 million and $65 million for *Batman Forever* and *Apollo 13*, Bullock's films were downright cheap, costing only $22–25 million. (*steadycam*, 1996: 11–12). In foreign markets, especially in Germany, her films did even better, earning $157

million between them. *While You Were Sleeping* was the eleventh-highest grossing film in the international market in 1995 (*Screen International*, 1996: 15); Klady (1996).

25 With a budget of $43 million, *A Time to Kill* was her most expensive film up to this point, about twice as expensive as each of her previous three films.

26 *Speed 2* grossed $105m abroad (*Variety*, 1998b: 31).

27 *Practical Magic* performed respectably in foreign markets with $8.1 million in 1998 and $34 million in 1999. *Forces of Nature* grossed $41 million abroad (*Variety*, 1999: 36; 2000: 22). The performance of *Forces of Nature* earned Bullock her third appearance in Quigley's top ten in 1999.

28 Indeed, Bullock's 'comeback' film *Hope Floats*, the first hit she had after a string of four box-office disappointments, did place her back at the centre of the story, with the action arising from, and revolving around, her decisions and her states of mind.

29 Again, it is surely no coincidence that Bullock's comeback with *Hope Floats* coincided with a (temporary) realignment of the publicity about her off-screen life and her on-screen role. She plays a woman moving back from the big city to her home town in the South to start her life all over again, not least with the help of a new lover. There were intricate connections between the film and the star's life (as reported in the press), including her move to Austin, Texas, her DIY compulsion (projected on to the male lead in the film), her alleged affair with Southern boy Matthew McConaughey, and, of course, the fact that in the wake of the *Speed 2* disaster Bullock did indeed have to re-start her (professional) life. See, for example, Leonelli (1998); MacDonald (1998); Shelley (1998).

30 See, for example, Amistead (1996).

31 Box office figures from Internet Moviedatabase, http://us.imdb.com/top_250_films, accessed 19 September 2001.

Bibliography

Adams, Thelma (1993) 'Review of *Demolition Man*', *New York Post*, 8 October, 45.

Amistead, Claire (1996) 'Sandra Bullock Shared a Bus Ride Downtown with Keanu Reeves. When She Got Off, She Was Worth a Million Dollars', *Guardian*, 6 September, Tabloid, 8–9.

Beck, Henry Cabot (1991) 'Girl Working', *Interview*, April.

Bergman, Anne (1994) 'An Equal-Rights Action Thriller Gains Speed', *LA Times*, 12 July, F1, 3.

Bernard, Jami (1993) 'Review of *The Vanishing*', *New York Post*, 5 February. 27.

Burman, John (1999) 'Star Power '99', *Hollywood Reporter*, 15 June, 23–30.
Cinema (1994) 'Die nackten Kanonen' (The Naked Guns), *Cinema*, February, 50.
Conant, Jennet (1995) 'America's Sweetheart', *Vanity Fair*, September, 156–63, 227.
Daily Variety (1995) *Daily Variety*, 18 April.
Diamond, Jamie (1994) 'On Screen She Keeps Her Head (and the Guy)', *New York Times*, 5 June, H25.
Farolino, Audrey (1992) 'Review of *Love Potion No. 9*', *New York Post*, 13 November.
Gamson, Joshua (1994) *Claims to Fame: Celebrity in Contemporary America*, Berkeley: University of California Press.
Grisham, John (1989) *A Time To Kill*, London: Arrow.
Grove, Martin A. (1994) 'Speed Accelerates Fox's Summer Hope', *Hollywood Reporter*, 20 April, 6.
Hensley, Dennis (1996) 'Making Sandwiches with Sandra Bullock', *Esquire*, May, 48–54.
Hofler, Robert (1998) 'The Year of Living Famously', *Premiere*, December, 96–104.
Hollywood Reporter (1994) *Hollywood Reporter*, 14 June.
Hollywood Reporter (1996) *Hollywood Reporter*, 6 March.
Jeffords, Susan (1994) *Hard Bodies: Hollywood Masculinity in the Regan Era*, New Brunswick: Rutgers University Press.
Kaplan, Michael (1993) 'The Making of a Starlet, 90s Style', *US Magazine*, November, 80–4.
Klady, Leonard (1996) 'B.O. with a vengeance: $9.1 billion worldwide', *Variety*, 19 February, 26.
Krämer, Peter (1998a) 'Women First: *Titanic* (1997), Action-Adventure Films and Hollywood's Female Audience', *Historical Journal of Film, Radio and Television*, 18:4 (October), 599–618.
Krämer, Peter (1998b) 'Would You Take Your Child To See This Film? The Cultural and Social Work of the Family-Adventure Movie', in Steve Neale and Murray Smith (eds), *Contemporary Hollywood Cinema*, London: Routledge, pp. 294–311.
Krämer, Peter (1999a) 'Bibliographical Notes', in Alan Lovell and Peter Krämer (eds), *Screen Acting*, London: Routledge, pp. 165–70.
Krämer, Peter (1999b), 'A Powerful Cinema-going Force? Hollywood and Female Audiences since the 1960s', in Melvyn Stokes and Richard Maltby (eds), *Identifying Hollywood's Audiences: Cultural Identity and the Movies*, London: British Film Institute, pp. 98–112.
Leonelli, Elisa (1998) 'The Childhood Scars That Made Me a Star', *Cosmopolitan*, November, 93–6.
Levy, Emanuel (1990) 'Social Attributes of American Movie Stars', *Media, Culture and Society*, 12:2 (April), 247–67.

Levy, Emanuel (1998) 'Revew of *Practical Magic*', *Variety*, 19 October, 74.
Leydon, Joe (1999) 'Review of *Forces of Nature*', *Variety*, 15 March, 38–9.
MacDonald, Marianne (1998) 'Waiting for Mr Right', *Observer Life*, 25 October, 6–10.
McCarthy, Todd (1998) 'Review of *Hope Floats*', *Variety*, 25 May, 57.
McCarthy, Todd (2000) 'Review of *28 Days*', *Variety*, 10 April, 43, 46.
McDonald, Paul (2000) *The Star System: Hollywood's Production of Popular Identities*, London: Wallflower.
Moser, James D. (ed.) (2000) *International Motion Picture Almanac*, La Jolla: Quigley.
Musto, Michael (1994) 'Sandra's Speed', *Vanity Fair*, July, 45.
Nelson, Jill (1996) 'The $11 Million Girl Next Door', *New York Daily News/USA Weekend*, 19 January, 4–5.
Newman, Bruce (1993) 'She's So Hollywood – and Proud of It', *LA Times*, 7 December, F1, 3.
Ozer, Jerome S. (ed.) (1981–) *Film Review Annual*, Englewood: Jerome S. Ozer.
Premiere (1996) 'The 1996 *Premiere* Power List: The 100 Most Powerful People in Hollywood', *Premiere*, May, 77–91.
Premiere (1998) 'The Power List', *Premiere*, May, 65–81.
Rebello, Stephen (1995) 'The Star Next Door', *Movieline*, April, 44–50, 88–9.
Schaefer, Stephen (1997) 'Sandra Gets Serious', *New York Post*, 15 January, 37.
Schickel, Richard (1993) 'Review of *Demolition Man*', *Time*, 18 October.
Schneller, Johanna (2000) 'That Touch of Minx', *Premiere*, May, 62–8, 102–3.
Schuers, Fred (1997) 'Speed Freak', *Rolling Stone*, 26 June, 38–41, 62.
Screen International (1996) 'International Star Chart', *Screen International*, 30 August, 15.
Shelley, Jim (1998) 'A Date With Sandra', *Telegraph Magazine*, 31 October, 60–4.
steadycam (1992) 'In Zahlen', *steadycam*, 21, spring.
steadycam (1993) 'In Zahlen', *steadycam*, 24, spring.
steadycam (1994), 'In Zahlen', *steadycam*, 26, spring.
steadycam (1995), 'In Zahlen', *steadycam*, 29, spring.
steadycam (1996), 'In Zahlen', *steadycam*, 31, spring.
steadycam (1997a), 'In Zahlen', *steadycam*, 33, spring.
steadycam (1997b), 'In Zahlen', *steadycam*, 34, autumn.
steadycam (1999), 'In Zahlen', *steadycam*, 37, spring.
Stovall, Natasha (1994) 'In the Driver's Seat', *Village Voice*, 21 June 1994, 56–7.
Tasker, Yvonne (1993) *Spectacular Bodies: Gender, Genre and the Action Cinema*, London: Routledge.

Thompson-Georges, Cathy (1994) 'Ticket to Ride', *Entertainment Today*,
    10 June.
Ulmer, James (1998) 'Fewer Stars Lay Claim to Fame', *Variety*, 23 February,
    1, 71–2.
Variety (1998a) 'Top 250 of 1997', *Variety*, 26 January.
Variety (1998b) 'The Top 125 Worldwide', *Variety*, 9 February.
Variety (1999) 'The Top 125 Worldwide', *Variety*, 25 January.
Variety (2000) 'The Tope 125 Worldwide', *Variety*, 24 January.

6

Rumble in the USA:
Jackie Chan in translation

Mark Gallagher

Prologue: East is met by West

The marketing in the United States of successful stars from other national cinemas has often posed problems for Hollywood studios. The marketing of Asian stars in the United States has been particularly difficult, given the limited and often derogatory and patronising connotations of Asianness in US culture. Moreover, North American cultural stereotypes about Asians typically fail to make distinctions between national or ethnic groups, corralling Japanese, Chinese, Koreans, Vietnamese and other groups into an undifferentiated, exotic mass. In Hollywood cinema since the 1930s, Asian male stars have appeared in a narrow range of roles, all circulating around a similar code of honour, tradition and family obligation: for example, Toshiro Mifune's brooding patriarchs in *Grand Prix* (1966) and *The Challenge* (1982), and Bruce Lee's scowling kung-fu master in *Enter the Dragon* (1973). Roles for Asian women, by comparison, have until recently been limited to three principal types: the diabolical 'dragon lady' (e.g., Anna May Wong in *Shanghai Express* (1932)), the happy-go-lucky prostitute (for example, Nancy Kwan in *The World of Suzie Wong* (1960)), and the sheltered 'flower of the Orient' (such as Machiko Kyo in *Teahouse of the August Moon* (1956)).[1] Because of restrictive cultural and generic conventions with regard to Asianness (and non-whiteness generally), Hollywood studios produced virtually no films with Asian leads between 1973, when *Enter the Dragon* appeared, and 1998, when Hong Kong stars Chow Yun-Fat and Jackie Chan made their respective English-language debuts in *The Replacement Killers* and *Rush Hour*.[2] Not surprisingly, all three of these films feature briskly paced action narratives geared to young and urban audiences.[3]

Given the substantial changes in the United States film industry since the early 1970s, both in terms of corporate ownership of studios and in film production, distribution and advertising, the success of Jackie Chan's films in a genre dominated by high production and special effects merits careful consideration. This chapter examines Jackie Chan's star persona as it has developed over the course of his prolific and ongoing film career in Hong Kong and Hollywood productions, particularly as US viewers interpret and respond to that persona.[4] In relation to US films' conventions for male action heroes, Chan's persona offers a progressive version of masculinity that combines skilful but playful physical dexterity with comic self-effacement. Historically, the martial-arts genre, with which Chan and other Asian stars are often associated, has been only marginally successful in the United States, and pure martial-arts narratives rarely appear in theatrical release.[5] Consequently, white martial-arts stars such as Steven Seagal and Jean-Claude van Damme have, in their more profitable films, appeared in straightforward action narratives involving gunfights, car chases, and a limited amount of acrobatics and hand-to-hand combat rather than swordplay or martial-arts kicks and punches. Moreover, in the 1990s, the appeal of professionally trained fighters such as Seagal and van Damme has been overshadowed by films that rely on expensive pyrotechnics and digital effects rather than on scenes of hand-to-hand combat.[6] The box-office success of Chan's US releases – particularly *Rumble in the Bronx* (1996), *Supercop* (1996) and *Rush Hour* – results to a great extent from the foregrounding in promotional materials of the star's acrobatic skills, which appear as an alternative to high-production Hollywood action films. Further challenging the stylised Western action-hero persona, Chan's characters function as both the source and target of physical comedy. By conveying earnestness and sincerity, his characters acquire a dimension of vulnerability rarely evident among US icons of active masculinity.[7] In contrast, Hollywood figures, from longtime stars such as Arnold Schwarzenegger and Bruce Willis to more recent action heroes played by Nicolas Cage and Will Smith, tend to perform with an air of ironic detachment, often dispensing comic asides and reassuring viewers that the screen characters are aware of their films' conventional plots and fantastic scenarios.

Genre and masculinity in the West: integrating action and comedy

Since the early 1980s, the action film has been Hollywood's principal money-making genre. Largely geared toward a young, male audience, action film places at its centre the now-conventional 'action hero'. The hero, almost always male, displays a range of character traits associated with traditional Western definitions of masculinity: physical size, strength, charisma, pronounced facial features, aggressive behaviour, and the ability to generate action. The presumed 'naturalness' of this combination of traits disguises the construction of male gender identity, an identity normalised in countless Western cultural pursuits, institutions, and media. The constructedness of the Western action hero's identity becomes apparent when one looks for evidence of the type in other genres. The male action hero does not travel well. Except in the comparable space of other 'male' genres (the war film or the western, for example), the rigid male persona swiftly assumes farcical proportions. Genre boundaries thus play a fundamental role in defining and constraining male identity. The construction of the action-hero persona depends upon complementary narrative conventions. The character type requires a formidable villain against which to test the hero's mettle; the plot must continually place the hero in danger to prove his courage and fortitude; perhaps most importantly, other characters must appear to take the hero seriously, lest the fabricated, ritualised basis of his masculinity be exposed. As Chan's films demonstrate, however, Hollywood's typology of the action hero, despite its prominence, does not reign worldwide.

The construction of masculinity in the US action genre typically involves the male protagonist's visual and narrative centrality. Laura Mulvey and others have called attention to the traditional organisation of film narrative around the male protagonist, suggesting an opposition between man as the determinant of action and woman as the facilitator or place-marker of male activity. Mulvey argues that 'the male protagonist is free to command the stage, a stage of spatial illusion in which he articulates the look and creates the action' (1990: 34).[8] The male action hero, however, demonstrates power primarily through a lack of motion. Once in motion he appears vulnerable, acted-upon rather than active. Paradoxically, male protagonists typically assert their agency and control over narrative events through physical stasis.

Film theory has not adequately addressed the paradox of male immobility. The male body on the run typically signifies escape or retreat. Films often use such behaviour to comic effect, as in *Running Scared* (1986) and *Midnight Run* (1988), and certainly in Keaton's and Chaplin's films. Virtually all of Chan's films represent flight as a survival strategy. In contrast, in Hollywood action films, only when the protagonist 'stands his ground' does he embody an uncompromised conception of male dominance.[9] The spectacle of the posturing male, fundamental to bodybuilding competitions and to other popular images such as movie posters and rock album covers, calls attention not only to the exhibition of male power, but also to the 'to-be-looked-at-ness' of the male body. In their survey of masculinity, Pat Kirkham and Janet Thumim note 'the contradiction between the vulnerable passivity arguably implicit in the state of being-looked-at, and the dominance and control which patriarchal order expects its male subjects to exhibit' (1993: 12). However, they do not address the obverse principle, the connotations of femininity that the mobile male body produces. Such connotations occur in sports as well as films: running backs in American football are usually chased, despite being positioned on 'offense', and boxers move around the ring to dodge blows. In each of these cases, another powerful male does the chasing or punching. Nevertheless, a successful escape or feint appears consistent with notions of masculine mastery over events, but only to a point. A satisfactory display of Western male power demands that the male eventually cease flight, and stand and attack.

Action films that depict male heroes in retreat usually accompany such representations with verbal comedy, legitimating the apparent violation of action-genre conventions of bravery and invulnerability. By the late 1980s, stars such as Schwarzenegger, Willis, and Eddie Murphy added comic decorations to increasingly familiar conventions of plot, character, and the representation of violence. Contemporary Hollywood action films routinely engage in parody to preserve genre conventions. Action-comedies such as *Grosse Pointe Blank* (1997) and *The Big Hit* (1998) introduce self-conscious characters and plot devices that show the problematic relations between screen conventions and the genre's absurd relation to everyday life.[10] Beginning in the 1980s, action films updated their conventions by placing well-known comic personas in the lead roles. Bruce Willis graduated from the sardonic 1980s television comedy *Moonlighting* to the *Die Hard* films (1988, 1990, 1995), and Eddie Murphy similarly made the leap from *Saturday Night Live* cast member to star of the action-comedies *48 Hours* (1982) and the *Beverly Hills Cop* series (1984, 1987, 1993). In these cases, star personas linked to a particular type, combined with the technical changes noted earlier, help shape the dynamics of genre.

Hollywood films that mix action and comedy usually subordinate conventions of one genre to the requirements of the other. As Steve Neale and Frank Krutnik observe in *Popular Film and Television Comedy*, the broad range of possible comic situations permits comedy to work well as a hybrid genre. They argue that while other genres also combine into hybrid forms, comedy 'seems especially suited for hybridisation, in large part because the local forms responsible for the deliberate generation of laughter can be inserted at some point into most other generic contexts without disturbing their conventions' (1990: 18). Though audiences accustomed to action-film conventions may find humour amid scenes of spectacular violence and destruction, comedic elements tend to be decorative rather than fundamental to narrative pacing or viewer enjoyment. Hollywood genre films usually structure the action/comedy mixture through 'fish out of water' themes, either by drawing on elements of a specific star persona or building such themes into a story. Murphy's streetwise, sarcastic persona clashes with conventional police procedures in *Beverly Hills Cop* and its sequels, and Schwarzenegger's comic vehicles – such as *Twins* (1988), *Kindergarten Cop* (1990), and *Junior* (1995) – gain their primary comedic value from placing the action star in situations that deny his trademark physique the opportunity to fend off enemy hordes. Similarly, the comic plot of *Running Scared* relies upon the appearance of the slender, wisecracking Billy Crystal and Gregory Hines as urban police officers who do not fit the mould of traditional masculinity that such roles dictate. In each of these examples, the foundations of the original genres – action or comedy – remain intact. As comedies, none of the Schwarzenegger films noted above includes scenes of torture or mass destruction, elements germane to action films.[11] Conversely, the *Die Hard* films never stray into slapstick, which might threaten the integrity and suspensefulness of the dominant action narrative.

Generic prescriptions have historically limited the interplay between action films and comedies. Comedy's inversion of social hierarchies potentially places the male hero's gender identity in distress, a transformation that poses serious structural problems for the action genre. For the action genre to retain traditional masculine

principles, comedic material must resonate outward from the protagonist; he must control the humour. If an action narrative makes
the protagonist a comedic foil, he risks becoming an inappropriate
male hero according to Western conventions, and by association the
type itself can appear unviable as a model of identity. In contrast,
when a wisecracking hero lives through beatings, gunshot wounds,
and explosions, he appears to represent a traditional male whose
fortitude and self-assurance are so absolute that he can laugh in the
face of danger. The successful action-comedy *Men in Black* (1997),
for example, puts its male protagonists in comic situations, but also
demonstrates their physical fitness, facility with weapons and bravery, conforming to action-genre conventions. Rather than critiquing
or refiguring male identity, decorative comic elements refine the
reigning model to give it the semblance of flexibility, thereby renew-
ing its appeal. In comparison, Chan's films, rather than using
comedy to reinforce conventional signifiers of self-assured male
power, mobilise comedy as an intrinsic component of the star's
masculine persona. For Chan, comedy provides male heroes with a
source of strength and autonomy and also motivates viewers to
identify with comic protagonists' vulnerability and self-effacement.

The Hong Kong film industry produces the third-largest number of
films annually of any national cinema (behind those of the US and
India) and makes genre films at a remove from the schema of classical or contemporary US cinema.[12] While genre boundaries in US films
are porous and shifting, broad parameters still appear: the settings of
westerns and science-fiction films, the underdog protagonists of
comedy, the emotional register of melodrama, the underworld milieu
of the gangster or detective film, and so forth. While Hong Kong
films tend to offer viewers either sentimental romances or crime and
action dramas, the breadth of these frameworks leaves room for a
wide range of narrative, stylistic and tonal choices.[13] Within each of
these two generic frameworks, elements from other forms such as
musicals, comedies, fantasy and historical epics often combine in a
single narrative. In the 1990s, independent American directors such
as Quentin Tarantino and Robert Rodriguez began to appropriate
elements of Hong Kong cinema in their own films. Subsequently,
with declines in Hong Kong film production and the colony's return
to Chinese rule, Hong Kong stars such as Chan, Chow Yun-Fat, and
Jet Li and directors such as John Woo, Tsui Hark, and Ringo Lam
have worked successfully in Hollywood productions.

Jackie Chan's persona, which both emphasises the performer's physical mastery and situates him as a comic underdog, challenges Western – and to some extent, global – definitions of masculinity, suggesting the tenuousness of ostensibly stable, historically rooted models of male agency and control.[14] Physically, Chan incorporates into action-oriented narratives the burlesque body fundamental to comedy. His body's continuous motion, feminised through its implied vulnerability, calls into question conceptions of the ideal male body. Chan appears simultaneously active and vulnerable, in contrast to the archetypal action hero, whose physical presence paradoxically relies upon a literal inactivity or passivity. Chan's films further avoid the erotic, and often homoerotic, treatments of the male body common in US action films. By US standards of representation, Chan's costumes and bearing do not exude sex appeal, nor does his body attain object status through displays of flexed muscles or through the slow, deliberate movements that US action films use to connote manly self-assurance and control.[15] Moreover, the comedy in Chan's films stems not merely from the actor himself, but from the actions of other characters and from the convergence of narrative circumstances upon the hero. Comedy often places Chan in submissive, masochistic positions, destabilising his characters' control over the films' humour, if not their action.

Challenging the notion that Western models of masculinity reflect a monolithic global ideal, Chan's character types and his films' narrative devices exhibit alternative modes of male heroism, modes scarcely evident in US popular culture. Since his film debut as a child performer in low-budget Hong Kong martial-arts films, Jackie Chan has appeared in more than fifty films.[16] He has been Hong Kong's, indeed all of East Asia's, largest box-office draw since the mid-1980s, serving as actor and often director, stunt choreographer, and screenwriter of films that blend furiously paced action sequences and stunts with whimsical comedy.[17] Chan's films construct a star persona at odds with the conventional male hero of the US action genre. His persona, developed over a broad range of films produced in Hong Kong and the United States, combines acrobatics, hand-to-hand combat skills, self-deprecating wit, and psychological and physical vulnerability. Prior to the successful United States releases of *Rumble in the Bronx* in 1996 (released in Hong Kong and else-where in 1995) and *Rush Hour* in 1998 (among his other US releases), Chan's films relied principally on Asian audiences for their revenues. As Chan's films enjoy greater circulation among Western audiences, his star persona operates more strikingly in contrast to US films' archetypes of heroism and masculinity.[18]

The Westernisation of Jackie Chan

Chan's films since the late 1970s set box-office records in Hong Kong and elsewhere in Asia, but until the mid-1990s he remained largely unknown to American audiences. Before New Line Cinema (controlled by Time Warner) and Dimension Films (a Miramax subsidiary) contracted for distribution rights to some of Chan's films, most of his Hong Kong productions received only limited release in the West, and his early English-language films fared poorly in the American market. He appeared as a comic supporting character in *The Cannonball Run* (1982) and its sequel and played the lead in *The Big Brawl* (1980) and *The Protector* (1985), both unremarkable B-grade action pictures noteworthy only for Chan's unusual stunt work. In *The Big Brawl*, Chan's performance includes some comedy. In one mischievous fight sequence Chan, adhering to his screen father's dictate that he refrain from fighting, adopts a passive combat style, ducking or side-stepping his opponents' blows so that they collide with each other or with brick walls. Mostly, though, he appears in the film as a sincere and serious fighter in the Bruce Lee mould. In *The Protector*, Chan plays the one-dimensional Asian Other, and his character traits include, almost exclusively, honour and solemnity.

The success of *Rumble in the Bronx* and *Rush Hour* raised Chan's profile considerably in the United States and Western Europe. *Rush Hour* was among the top ten films in US box-office receipts in 1998, a year dominated by the action blockbusters *Armageddon*, *Deep Impact*, *Godzilla*, and the late-1997 release *Titanic*.[19] Similarly, while most Hong Kong films appearing in the US play only in art houses or in Chinese-American neighbourhood theatres, Chan's first major-market US release, *Rumble in the Bronx*, received widespread American distribution, complete with a high-visibility print and television advertising campaign. The film earned $9.8 million in its opening weekend in the US and more than $30 million during its initial theatrical run, making it a great success for a modest-budget film produced outside the US.[20]

Traditionally, Hong Kong films' budgets are minuscule by Hollywood standards, so Hong Kong films can hardly compete with

Hollywood output in terms of production values or special effects. Nonetheless, unlike most Asian films exported to the West, *Rumble in the Bronx* was marketed as an action film, and its advertising, similar to that for *Supercop*'s re-release (the film originally appeared in Hong Kong in 1992 as *Police Story 3* and, re-titled *Supercop*, played briefly in the US in 1993), highlights the fact that Chan performs his own stunts. To broaden the films' appeal to American audiences, they also were dubbed into English, re-edited to emphasise action sequences and comedy over character development, and provided with new rock and rap soundtracks and, in the case of *Supercop*, a glossier set of opening credits.[21] Though *Rumble*'s success suggests that films with non-Western heroes can lure US viewers, US studios have been reluctant to finance such ventures. Chan's first five films to gain wide release in the US were produced in Hong Kong, with Hollywood-studio contributions limited to the above changes and to the films' marketing.

Chan's success in Western markets, particularly the United States, occurs not only because of the performer's comic persona but also because of his gradual redefinition as an action star rather than a martial-arts star (the latter being a restrictive category, limiting performers to low-budget productions with marginal viewerships rather than granting access to blockbuster fare with elaborate special effects and saving-the-world narratives). The progressive ironisation of the US action genre since the mid-1980s – with films such as the relatively humourless *Rambo: First Blood Part II* (1985) giving way to the more self-reflexive *Terminator 2* (1991) – produced by the mid-1990s a climate of audience awareness and expectations favourable to the broadly comic tone of Chan's films. To integrate Chan's skills into this cinematic environment, most of his 1990s films include action sequences involving chases and acrobatics – particularly jumps, flips, and falls from high places – rather than the hand-to-hand combat sequences that dominate his 1980s releases. When hand-to-hand combat does appear in films such as *Rumble in the Bronx* and *Supercop*, fight choreographers emphasise the comically dance-like rhythms of Chan's movements over the efficacy of the movements as a means to overcome opponents.

Before 1996, Chan and his films achieved only limited, primarily subcultural, recognition in the US and other Western countries. He earned recognition among martial-arts fans, who help form audiences for the films of performers such as Bruce Lee, Chuck Norris and Steven Seagal. Relatedly, Chan's Hong Kong films were released intermittently in the US throughout the 1990s for repertory theatres' 'Hong Kong festivals' in collegiate and urban locations, drawing college students, Asians and Asian-Americans, and cinephiles. Finally, Chan's films, like those of other Hong Kong stars (Chow Yun-Fat and Jet Li, for example), have appeared in Chinese-language theatres in the Chinatown neighbourhoods of Pacific-Rim cities such as Los Angeles and San Francisco. These fan groups and theatrical venues accounted for a recognisable audience base but hardly constituted mainstream recognition of Chan and his films.

To achieve recognition and financial success in the US and elsewhere in the West, Chan's films have had to overcome linguistic, cultural and generic obstacles that usually limit the appeal of non-Western films. Since major studios, particularly in the US, will not distribute subtitled foreign-language films, Chan's first four releases in the West – *Rumble in the Bronx, Supercop, Jackie Chan's First Strike* (1997) and *Operation Condor* (1997) – appeared with English dubbing.[22] *Mr Nice Guy* (1998, aka *A Nice Guy*), shot in Australia, was filmed in English, as was *Rush Hour*, his first Hollywood-studio production. Similarly, Chan's films widely distributed in Western markets have been those perceived as most accessible to non-Asian audiences, specifically those with plots or situations familiar to audiences of Hollywood thrillers and action films. *Supercop, Jackie Chan's First Strike*, and *Operation Condor* all feature Chan as a spy or adventurer, in the model of James Bond or Indiana Jones, who faces drug smugglers, global terrorists or war profiteers. These films, which include sequences in many different international locations (Australia, Thailand and North Africa, as well as Hong Kong) and rely on conventional action- or spy-film plots, mask the cultural differences apparent in many of Chan's other films. In contrast, films set in China or Hong Kong's historical past or those featuring traditional martial-arts plots, such as *Project A, Part 2* (1987) and *Drunken Master 2* (1994), while enormously popular in Asia, have not been re-released in the West because of their apparent cultural specificity. In Chan's films with plots focusing on international espionage, the prescriptions of the action genre help to create relatively homogenous narratives that downplay their cultural origins.

The dubbing and re-editing of Chan's films for English-speaking audiences also change the valences of the films' comedy, particularly their spoken dialogue, which often makes reference to Hong Kong and Chinese cultural and historical situations. *Supercop*, for example, finds humour in contrasts between urbane Hong Kong residents and traditional or rural Chinese mainlanders, contrasts that Western audiences may fail to discern. Similarly, many of Chan's films, including *Supercop*, make direct or implied references to Hong Kong's return to Chinese rule in 1997, the implications of which may be lost on Western viewers. Perhaps more significantly, *Rush Hour* introduces elements of cultural confusion into Chan's persona, casting him in the mould of a misunderstood Asian traveller – in accord with the familiar US stereotype of the quizzical Asian tourist – who must prove his mettle to his Western associates. These changes or differences notwithstanding, much of the global appeal of Chan's films lies in the actor's physical comedy, which carries a broad, comic meaning across specific cultures.

Promotional materials for Chan's US releases downplay the films' possible cultural differences or reduce those differences to high-concept images and slogans. Promotional posters and print advertisements for *Supercop*, for example, depict Chan suspended in mid-air from a rope ladder, muscles flexed and teeth clenched, surrounded by attack helicopters and the flames of an explosion. The film itself does not present a scene of such magnitude, though in a climactic stunt Chan does cling to a rope ladder attached to a helicopter. Images of explosions and advanced military hardware correspond to Hollywood action-film conventions, as does Chan's pictured attire of black T-shirt, black jeans, and black sneakers, though such a costume does not appear in the film either. Cultural difference also serves as a basis for marketing of Chan's films. For example, *Rush Hour*'s advertising slogan, 'The fastest hands in the East versus the biggest mouth in the West', reduces Chan's star persona to a single, easily apprehended idea. Similarly, the film itself relies on a monolithic conception of Asianness, introducing Chan's character and other Hong Kong or Chinese elements with stereotypical 'Oriental' music and at one point surrounding its protagonists with a busload of camera-toting Asian tourists.

Comedy in motion

US action films conventionally highlight the normative qualities of their male heroes – such as whiteness, heterosexuality and physical dominance. In addition, such films consistently avoid locating their protagonists as targets of comedy or in other feminising situations. Constrastingly, Chan's films rely on comic treatments of escape and flight that feminise his characters while reinscribing his antagonists as caricatures of 'serious' masculinity. While Chan's stunts resemble those of his predecessors Keaton, and Harold Lloyd, Chan's stunts and comedy operate in a significantly different generic context than the silent-film comedians. Keaton's small size and lean physique, for example, locate him within 1920s genre conventions for comedy rather than for action and adventure films. Chan's similar agility, grace and underdog persona translate effectively to the contemporary action genre, particularly because he combines comedy and acrobatics with displays of prowess in hand-to-hand combat. His onscreen victories ultimately 'prove' his manhood. At the same time, Chan's films import the pratfalls and feminising situations of comedy, adding a broader source of appeal to the predominantly male-centred identification that his fighting skill encourages. When Chan's films give precedence to his comic temperament, the usually serious demeanours of his opponents – criminal henchmen, gang members, bodyguards of crime lords, and other fighters who use either martial arts or cruder fisticuffs – appears as an ineffectual response to Chan's style. Resituated within conventions of comedy, Chan's adversaries play the role of straight men or comic buffoons instead of representing imposing physical threats to the protagonist. Comedy thus shifts Chan's films' emphasis away from the action film's masculine schema of mastery and control. Nevertheless, his films, like Keaton's and Lloyd's, call attention to the physical mastery required to execute dangerous stunts. (Conversely, Hollywood action films typically indicate male mastery through expensive special effects.) Notably, *Rush Hour* circumvents the representational problem of male feminisation (in other words, how to define as heroic a figure who grins youthfully and runs from his opponents) by depicting Chris Tucker's character as a fast-talking braggart who performs badly in combat or sheepishly avoids it. In comparison, Chan's character appears more conventionally heroic – and thus masculine – by default. Chan's previous films, though, foreground the star's reluctant-hero persona, making his defeats more poignant and his victories more inspiring to viewers.

Chan's persona relies heavily on uninterrupted movement as a signifier of limitless manoeuvrability. His films usually include multiple martial-arts combat sequences, applying a trademark style that fight choreographer Craig Reid identifies as the 'Perpetual Motion Technique'. Its premise, Reid observes, 'is the maintenance of continuous body motion throughout the entire fight sequence to give the impression of non-stop action' (1993/4: 34–5). In *Drunken Master 2* (1994), for example, Chan battles scores of axe-wielding assassins for nearly five minutes of screen time, remaining out of his attackers' reach by leaping, punching and kicking his way around a spacious teahouse. Fight sequences in his films typically occur amid elaborate sets, and combat covers a great deal of space, the result of Chan's traversal of horizontal and vertical distances. Chan's stunt-work directs viewers' attention to his physical interaction with surrounding architecture: his movements around indoor furniture and other obstacles, up and over walls, along the outsides of tall buildings, and clinging to moving vehicles. Such interaction makes viewers aware of the real spatial relationships and structural properties of the objects displayed. In Hollywood action films, by comparison, the protagonist dominates the spectacle no matter how disproportionately large the backdrop of action might be, and most objects function only to prove the protagonists' destructive capabilities. In a scene in *Rambo: First Blood Part II*, for instance, Sylvester Stallone's Rambo, after engaging in an explosive battle that levels a village of thatch huts, appears in medium shot while a massive fireball erupts behind him. Camera perspective allows Rambo and the fireball to appear roughly the same size, making the hero appear larger than life to the viewing eye. Rambo, bare-chested and sweating, runs toward the camera in slow motion, making his body a spectacle for erotic contemplation.

Jackie Chan's characters rarely, if ever, receive erotic or epic-hero treatment in his films. Though he engages in hand-to-hand combat throughout his films, he rarely appears shirtless or in the conventional action garb of a torn T-shirt or other revealing or form-fitting clothing.[23] Camera angles do not denote his character as an object: close-ups, conspicuously absent in his early starring roles, later highlight his comic facial expressions, eschewing 'tough-guy' reaction shots and fragmentary shots of isolated limbs or muscles. When in motion, he appears most often in medium or long shots, so his body does not dominate sceneographic space, and the camera does not devote attention to his body's proportions. The camera frames him primarily to capture him in action, to show his performance of acrobatic feats.

Chan's perpetual-motion style showcases not only the actor's combat skills but also serves as a primary component of his comic persona. His acrobatic feats parallel those of a circus performer and align him with silent-film comedians such as Keaton, Chaplin and Lloyd. As Gerald Mast observes of early screen comedies, the essential comic object was the human body, and its most interesting movements were running, jumping, riding, colliding, falling, staggering, leaping, twirling and flying (Mast, 1979: 24).[24] As Jackie Chan gained popularity and assumed directorial control of his Hong Kong productions, the films' action gradually shifted from an emphasis on kung fu to a preoccupation with stuntwork and non-violent acrobatic feats. Nearly every article about Chan written for a general-interest US publication in the mid- to late 1990s cites his interpretations of famous scenes from Keaton's and Lloyd's films, as if to remind readers that Chan was worthy of attention not merely as a foreign matinee idol but as an international performer drawing from a venerated historical tradition. In *Project A, Part 2*, Chan choreographs the spectacular fall of a huge decorative wall, updating Buster Keaton's falling-house stunt from *Steamboat Bill, Jr* (1924). In the first *Project A* (1983), Chan revisits the image from *Safety Last* (1923) of Lloyd dangling from a clock-tower arm, placing himself atop a clock-tower in a similarly perilous position. Differentiating his version from Lloyd's, and in accord with the sometimes masochistic appeal of his films, Chan, handcuffed, plummets to the ground.

Neither Lloyd's nor Chan's comic scenario fits the Hollywood paradigm of male action. Both men's stunts, like Keaton's, subordinate the heroic individual – represented visually by spectacular images such as that of Rambo noted above – to the discernible proportions of character and massive objects. Such a relationship aligns Chan again with silent-film comedians rather than with contemporary US action stars. In an essay on the history of film comedy, Tom Gunning notes Keaton's temporary helplessness amid machinery, arguing the comedian becomes 'a projectile in thrall to the laws of mechanics' (1995: 99). Devices in Keaton's films, like those in Chan's, work as comic props, affording characters the opportunity to engage in humorous struggles. With few exceptions, the Hollywood action film uses encounters with objects or machinery for dramatic spectacle, not for slapstick. Though Hollywood action films put individual characters at the centre of large-scale action, such a focus magnifies the protagonist to mythic proportions. In comparison, Chan's films, like those of the silent comedians, depict large events in relation to human dimensions. Again, the generic context provides the crucial difference: Hollywood models its action heroes after King Kong, while Chan adopts slapstick techniques and works more closely to Fay Wray's scale. Conventions of the action genre supplant viewers' everyday anxieties through fantasies of omnipotence, while comedy conventions engage directly with viewers' sense of social powerlessness. Hollywood action heroes embody fantasies of domination over natural and artificial worlds, while Chan's films establish putatively real relations with those domains. The lack of special effects in Chan's films and the regular-guy persona he typically adopts further contribute to this aura of authenticity.

Rush Hour, race and nationalism

Rush Hour, Chan's greatest success in the West to date, repeatedly enforces the notion of Chan and other Asian characters as tourists, as aliens in a Western cultural world. Unlike Chan's previous films, altered by US studios for greater appeal to Western audiences, *Rush Hour* emphasises the foreignness of its Asian star. In the film's narrative, a Los Angeles police officer (Chris Tucker) investigating the kidnapping of a Chinese diplomat's young daughter receives unwanted assistance from the diplomat's close friend, a Hong Kong policeman (Chan). As the African-American protagonist and his Hong Kong Chinese counterpart overcome their ethnic and cultural differences, they defeat the Chinese-American gang led by an evil, white Hong Kong crime lord (Tom Wilkinson). The film introduces Chan's character, known as Lee, by showing him getting off a plane, highlighting his outsider status. He appears on planes two more times in the film, re-emphasising his tourist situation. Similarly, Lee appears throughout the film in locations around Los Angeles where Asians might be expected to congregate: at Mann's Chinese Theatre, in Chinatown, at the Chinese Consulate, and at an exhibition of Chinese artefacts. Lee's integration into the American cultural world is limited and turbulent, as when he engages in a brawl in an African-American pool hall. Lee's only contact with whites is through the film's FBI agents, who are depicted as unfriendly bureaucrats. The film's displayed lack of solidarity between whites and Asians reflects the legacy of anti-Asian sentiment in the US. Significantly, it also withholds the possibility of racial reconciliation. Instead, the film

portrays blacks and Asians as victims of the white power structure's
misguided leadership, but the film's white characters appear as
conventional supporting players who do not face the consequences
of their inappropriate actions.[25] Notably, the film presents a white
Englishman as the mastermind behind its Asian criminal organisation, simultaneously applying imperialist stereotypes of Asians as
nefarious criminals and of white Europeans as habitually corrupt but
still innately qualified to lead groups of non-whites.

Outside the sphere of its white characters, *Rush Hour* establishes
connections between blacks and Asians, both at the narrative level
and through the film's marketing. Just as Bruce Lee's films performed well among black audiences in the 1970s, Chan's US releases
have attracted large non-white audiences, particularly Asians and
blacks.[26] While Asian viewers constitute a small fraction of US film
audiences, blacks represent a reliable filmgoing demographic, and
Hollywood studios in the 1990s have shrewdly cast black actors to
broaden the films' appeal.[27] *Rush Hour* characterises its stars along
racial lines: Chris Tucker's streetwise, trash-talking, sexually sugges-
tive black man (the trademark persona of this comic star) counter-
poses Chan's modest, honour- and family-oriented Asian. During
the film, racial and cultural ignorance, presented narratively through
Tucker's disdain for Chinese food and Chan's halting rendition of
Edwin Starr's soul hit 'War', give way to cultural solidarity. In a key
scene (albeit one with little narrative function), Carter (Tucker) and
Lee stake out the villains' headquarters, and Lee buys Chinese food
for the pair from a street vendor. While Carter initially complains
about the food, he soon begins eating it with relish. Carter then asks
Lee to instruct him in disarming an opponent (a skill Carter will
utilise in a later scene) and, in turn, Carter shows Lee how to perform a serpentine dance move. The scene ends with the two characters dancing in rough synchronicity on the sidewalk. The film thus
connects Tucker's physical fluidity, a principal component of his star
image, with Chan's trademark poise and agility. Because of the
scene's relative insignificance to the film's overall plot, it draws
particular attention to the characters' cultural difference.

Through its foregrounding of Chan's racial and cultural difference, *Rush Hour* reshapes the version of masculinity that Chan's
previous films develop. Chan appears less as a heroic underdog than
as an introverted, misunderstood 'child' of Asia who requires
coddling and protection from US authorities and from US cultural

rituals generally. For example, Chan's first battle in the film, a pool-room brawl, results from his own linguistic blunder (attempting to mimic the slang of another bar patron, he addresses the black bar-tender as 'my nigger', and a fight ensues). Only the tutelage of Tucker's character, the film suggests, can prevent such incidents. The comic elements of Chan's actions derive not entirely from the intrin-sic qualities of the actions themselves – for example, Chan's ability to escape from a moving bus by clinging to an overhanging street sign – but from reactions built into the narrative itself. The film repeatedly shows Carter staring at Lee in wild-eyed disbelief, adding an element of redundancy that Chan's Hong Kong films typically eschew. While such a reaction renders Tucker's character the comic straight man in a narrative sense, Tucker provides the visible source of humour, contrasting with the serious or distressed expressions that Chan's character often assumes.

Rush Hour's framing of masculine conflict and its insistence on cultural difference define the film as the product of a US rather than a Hong Kong sensibility. Unlike the majority of Chan's films, which depict his characters' simultaneous allegiance and challenges to Hong Kong Chinese values and beliefs, *Rush Hour* identifies Chan's character as a staunch defender of Chinese cultural tradition. His clashes with the film's FBI agents appear less as conflicts among men than as diplomatic struggles stemming from cultural differences, specifically from Westerners' unwillingness to permit Chan's char-acter to fulfil his duty to his countryman, Consul Han. To accom-modate Western viewers, the film also limits Chan's challenges to Western notions of masculinity. His performance – as an actor, fighter, and stuntman – is fairly restrained in comparison to his ear-lier films, with most acrobatic or fight sequences lasting no more than a few seconds. Conditions of the film's production to some extent dictate this restraint. Owing presumably to insurance require-ments, most of Chan's fights and stunts in the film are relatively unspectacular, and he wore a safety wire for the filming of a climac-tic stunt in which he falls from a great height onto a cloth tapestry. Overall, his character appears controlled and efficient, while the more flamboyant and excessive displays – including a dance after a car explodes in the film's opening scene, and much stylised mimicry of kung-fu moves – are reserved for Tucker's character.

The construction of Chan as a conventional, if highly mobile, hero and Tucker as a comic prima donna reduces the overall signification of Chan's character. Since Chan already appears culturally and racially distinct from most of the film's characters and viewers, the narrative stabilises him by downplaying his otherwise comic persona. At the same time, the film limits the visible evidence of Chan's physical strength. While both *Rumble in the Bronx* and *Supercop* intermittently picture Chan in T-shirts or muscle-Ts that display his physique, throughout *Rush Hour* he wears a loose-fitting suit in which he does not appear physically powerful. Such costuming helps define the film as comedy- rather than action-oriented. By understating the physical presence of its strongest representative of East Asia, though, the film also reassures viewers who may be wary of the economic and military power that Asian nations possess. The film similarly follows the Hollywood tradition of depicting Asian men as entirely without sexuality.[28] While Chan's Hong Kong films tend to present romance and sexuality through entirely wholesome gestures – hugs between characters, or childlike pecks on the cheek – *Rush Hour* denies Chan's character even this connection to women. (Instead, the film reinforces the convention of the hypersexual black man, making a running joke of Tucker's character's desire to have sex with a fellow police officer, played by Elizabeth Peña.) *Rush Hour* completes its neutralisation of Asian masculinity through the defeat of the Chinese gang members at the film's climax. Studios' present-day receptiveness to Chan's performances – after a series of films for the 'mini-major' New Line Cinema, he appeared next in Disney's expensive martial-arts western *Shanghai Noon* (2000) – clearly represents a step forward in terms of Hollywood's racial and cultural representation. Still, the reconstruction of Chan as naive, 'fish out of water' tourist – a character category into which Jet Li's protagonist in *Romeo Must Die* (2000) also fits – indicates the US film industry's ability to contain the culturally significant aspects of Asian male stars within particular narrative frameworks.

Male hysteria and madness

Prior to his performance in *Rush Hour*, Chan appeared in many films that use comedy to displace anxieties surrounding acceptable masculine behaviour. In many of his films, Chan temporarily plays the serious-fighter role while his opponents receive comic treatment through displays of hysterical cowardice or exaggerated masculinity. In *Twin Dragons*, for example, Chan's easy victory over a burly

biker causes his foe later to prostrate himself before Chan and proclaim him his master. Occasionally, a partner becomes the comic foil
to Chan's relative straight man. The narrative of *Twin Dragons* pairs
Chan's working-class character with a reckless, outspoken dwarf
who is repeatedly captured, threatened or otherwise victimised.[29]
The tensions surrounding Chan's character are displaced onto the
dwarf, who exhibits hysterical symptoms throughout the film: he is
boastful and abrasive, he is a failure at romance, and others scoff at
his clumsy attempts to manifest male power. As Paul Smith argues,
'the hysterical body casts a light on the powerlessness that the heroic
body lives with [and] on the powerlessness that such a body lives
within' (1993: 178). Though the dwarf displays no physical power,
his brash statements, such as the hollow threats he makes to a gang
of criminals, motivate Chan's performance of the dangerous activi-
ties he would not otherwise choose to undertake. Here, displaced
hysteria returns to its original source.

Relative to the stoic or conventionally portrayed action hero,
Chan's good-natured comedy humanises his screen characters to
promote audience identification with them and with the situations
in which they engage. US action-film conventions – which construct
heroes as products of hypermasculine fantasies – presume an emotional gap between performer and viewer. In romantic or family-
based comedies, comic elements often distance viewers from
situations that call for empathetic responses, such as scenes of
domesticity or interpersonal relations. Chan's use of comedy, however, encourages empathetic responses to action-film scenarios that
do not typically engender such reactions. Chan's version of male
agency, then, resists US action films' conservative articulation of
physical suffering. Comedy makes the pain of Chan's characters
more bearable for the viewer through emphasis on the overriding
farcical nature of action sequences or of entire narratives. Episodes
showing Chan being beaten or humiliated are always countered by
his ensuing comic triumphs. A more substantive 'don't try this at
home' disclaimer closes most of his films released since the mid-
1980s: collected out-takes show Chan and his fellow performers
filming stunts and fight sequences gone awry, giving viewers a sometimes disquieting reinterpretation of scenes that may appear car-
toonish or fantastic in the regular flow of narrative. Scenes of other
cast members grimacing in real pain or towelling off blood corrob-
orate Chan's self-mocking statement about stunt players' wariness of

his direction: 'Everybody knows Jackie Chan is crazy' (Dannen, 1995: 33–4). Chan's offhand comment hints at the larger social context in which his films appear. Though his displays of androgynous physical mastery call into question conventional formulations of masculine identity, the attribution of madness contains his subversion, situating his conduct well beyond the norms of masculine behaviour. Chan displays an excess of activity, and through his inevitable accidents during the performance of stunts, his behaviour connotes an inability to police the 'reasonable' boundaries of human aspiration. The evidence of Chan's hysteria inscribes itself across his scarred and maimed body.[30] Patriarchal order may thus reinscribe his abilities as a madman's folly. As Smith observes, one form of 'hysterical residue' apparent in some action films 'is an unresolved or uncontained representation of the body of the male as it exceeds the narrative process' (1993: 167). Chan's ability to overreach the screen, to perform beyond the requirements of a conventional narrative, has become his trademark. This activity occurs outside traditional social order, particularly the order that Hollywood action films impose. Chan's persona does not adhere to dominant cinematic models of male identity – especially the models prevalent in the action-film genre – thus marking him as an aberration. His mass appeal, however, reaffirms the resonance of his unconventional persona.

The modification of Chan's image in the West represents US studios' attempts to align Chan's persona more closely with Hollywood conventions of active masculinity. Films such as *Supercop* and *Jackie Chan's First Strike* cast him, at least superficially, in the model of the globe-trotting, James Bond-style adventurer. *Rush Hour*, by contrast, emphasises Chan's underdog status and his foreignness, which the film presents as inherently exotic. The film constructs its narrative around Chan's estrangement from the surrounding culture, a narrative strategy not utilised in his Hong Kong films. The above films alternately contain Chan's unconventional masculinity through association with a familiar model of cinematic masculinity or, in the case of *Rush Hour*, conflate Chan's masculine and racial attributes into an indistinct cluster of traits that signify his foreignness. While the visibility of Chan's films in the West does represent a progressive development in Hollywood representations of active masculinity and of Asians – albeit one motivated by profits rather than by any notion of multiculturalism or social good – the long-term consequences of this development are not yet clear. The steady flow of Hong Kong actors, directors, choreographers and cinematographers to Hollywood since 1997 suggests expanded opportunities at least at the level of film production, and further shifts in patterns of representation and narrative may slowly follow suit.

Notes

1   For more on the depictions of Asians in US film, see Marchetti (1993).
2   One conspicuous exception is *The Joy Luck Club* (1993), which, despite its box-office success, did not create substantial opportunities for Asians and Asian-Americans in Hollywood. Other Asian-American stars, such as John Lone (*M. Butterfly* (1993), *The Last Emperor* (1987)) and Joan Chen (*Heaven and Earth* (1993), *The Last Emperor*), have received occasional dramatic accolades but rarely appeared in popular, mainstream films in the 1980s and 1990s.
3   The combination in *Rush Hour* of Chan with African-American comedian Chris Tucker represents a strategy to market Chan to urban and minority audiences. Similarly, in the 1970s, Lee's films and other martial-arts narratives performed strongly in inner cities. See Kaminsky (1985) and Stromgren (1990).
4   Chan's status within Hong Kong and throughout Asia also warrants detailed study, but such analysis is outside the scope of this project. However, it should be noted that whereas Chan's films still carry signifiers of countercultural 'coolness' in the US owing to the performer's longtime cult status, his longtime popularity throughout Asia marks him as a quintessentially mainstream figure there. (For example, one undergraduate student of mine in 1998, a young South Korean man, idolised the tough-guy Hong Kong star Chow Yun-Fat but disdained Chan's films as children's fare.)
5   US-produced martial-arts films, such as those featuring American actress Cynthia Rothrock, became a staple of the straight-to-video market from the late 1980s to the late 1990s, particularly for release outside North America. In comparison, successful theatrical releases such as *Mortal Kombat* (1996) present a superficial version of martial-arts action, with their performers showing considerably more facility at posing in fanciful costumes than at hand-to-hand combat.
6   Such a trend, in turn, permits the use of bankable stars not traditionally associated with the action genre, such as Tom Cruise in *Mission Impossible* (1996), and John Travolta in *Broken Arrow* (1996) and *Face/Off* (1997).
7   For biographical information on Chan, see Chan and Yang (1998), Kehr (1988), and Dannen (1995). Many fan-based websites also

compile biographical and filmographic information on Chan and his works. Other biographical and filmographic sources appear in the references at the conclusion of this chapter.

8   In an extension of Mulvey's project, Teresa de Lauretis observes that in the male-controlled space of narrative, 'the female character may be all along, throughout the film, representing and literally marking out the place [to] which the hero will cross' (1984]: 139). In Mulvey's and de Lauretis's formulations, film narrative features active, mobile men and passive, inert women.

9   Chinese-trained film-fight choreographe Craig Reid describes a familiar situation in action films: 'Say you have a man fighting seven attackers inside a large house. An American stunt co-ordinator . . . will have the hero stand in one room and let himself get surrounded. Each opponent will attack . . . one at a time . . . Many of the attackers will let themselves get hit four or five times in a row without trying to move away, while the other attackers watch their buddy get pummelled. This is typical of Chuck Norris's films' (Reid, 1993/94: 31).

10   *Grosse Pointe Blank*, for example, features an assassin who calls his therapist while stalking his targets. In one scene in *The Big Hit*, the protagonist carries on an argument with his fiancée and her family while exchanging gunfire with a gang of killers.

11   Both *Twins* and *Kindergarten Cop*, though, allow Schwarzenegger to demonstrate his physical prowess intermittently, proving that even with a comic veneer, the actor is recognised principally as an action hero.

12   Until 1997, Hong Kong films far outgrossed their foreign competition principally from Hollywood) at the Hong Kong box office. The ready availability of new Hong Kong films on pirated video CDs, US films' increasing penetration of the Hong Kong film market, and the 1997 transition to Chinese rule have recently devastated the country's domestic film industry (Strauss, 1998).

13   Leo Ou-fan Lee categorises the principal varieties of Hong Kong film as 'the "hardcore" *gong fu*, or martial arts, movie in a pseudohistorical setting or its contemporary counterpart, the gangster film whose obvious mass appeal is violence, and the "softcore" sexual or romantic comedy featuring a beautiful actress/songstress singing the obligatory number of songs' (Lee 1994: 202). From a Western perspective, Chan's films fall most clearly into the action or kung-fu genres. For more information on Chinese and Hong Kong film history and genre, see Leyda (1972), Foronoff (1988), Berry (1991), Ehrlich and Desser (1994), Teo (1997), and Tam and Dissanayake (1998).

14   While prevailing constructions of gender identity in the US specifically and the West more broadly are by no means identical, I use 'Western' here and elsewhere to distinguish the culturally specific – in other

words Southeast Asian or, more precisely, Hong Kong Chinese – aspects of Chan's male persona from those elements that correspond to cinematic and social conventions apparent in the democratic, capitalist nations of the West, most specifically in North America, and to a lesser extent in Great Britain and elsewhere in Northern and Western Europe.

15   *Rumble in the Bronx* features a brief comic interlude of Chan flexing his muscles in front of a two-way store mirror. The scene pokes fun at the display of male vanity. Contrastingly, US action films usually present vain self-assurance as an emblem of male seriousness and fortitude.

16   Many of Chan's Hong Kong films remain unavailable to Western audiences. Nevertheless, this chapter assumes some familiarity with Chan's films. In addition to *Rush Hour* and the recent US re-releases of Chan's other films, I have chosen most textual examples from Chan's late 1980s and 1990s films, which appeared intermittently in revival theatres during the mid-1990s and now are widely available on videocassette.

17   Chan's global image as a matinee idol has been parodied in the Hong Kong film *High Risk* (1995), featuring another comic action star, Jet Li, as a stuntman for a Chan-like performer (played by Jackie Cheung) who has been made vain and cowardly by his stardom.

18   Chan's rising visibility in US media has already produced one near-duplication of his kung-fu comedian persona, in the popular ABC television series *Martial Law*, which features fellow Hong Kong actor Sammo Hung as a Chinese police officer in Los Angeles. Like Chan's character in *Rush Hour*, Hung plays a clever and physically skilled police detective whose perceived foreignness is cause for anxiety among his American colleagues. The programme's humour largely derives from the combination of Hung's rotundness with his acrobatic prowess.

19   See www.variety.com/top100.asp, accessed 22 February 1999. *Rush Hour*, with more than $136 million in US receipts in 1998, narrowly outperformed the far-costlier *Godzilla* and earned slightly more than *Lethal Weapon 4* (just over $130 million in US receipts in 1998), the latest instalment in the venerable race-pair action-comedy franchise.

20   According to box-office figures provided by the Internet Movie Database, *Rumble in the Bronx*, budgeted at US $7.5 million, earned over $33 million in the US as of August 1996 (http://us.imdb.com/Business?0113326, 21 accessed April 2000). In comparison, *Supercop*'s 1996 re-release in the US grossed just over $16 million, a profitable sum given the minimal marketing, editing, and soundtrack expenses incurred by its US distributor, Dimension Films (http://us.imdb.com/Business?0104558, accessed 21 April 2000). More impressively, *Rush Hour* earned over $33 million during its first three days of release in the US and grossed over $130

million in its initial theatrical run (according to *Variety*'s reports of domestic box-office receipts, the film had grossed $129.8 million in its first 59 days of US release (www.variety.com/dbox/index.asp, accssed 17 November 1998). Like other Chan films released in the US, *Rush Hour* opened on a weekend – in this case in mid-September, after the summer blockbuster season – when it would not face competition from a bigger-budget, higher-production Hollywood action film.

21 In terms of editing, most of Chan's US releases appear with many scenes deleted, particularly dialogue and exposition but also elements of fight sequences. The Asian version of *Rumble in the Bronx* reportedly grants a much larger role to its female lead, and the US release of *Jackie Chan's First Strike* runs approximately 25 minutes shorter than its subtitled original. For more information on the latter, see Ian D. Garlick, 'First Strike Cuts', (www.primenet.com/~tonylane/fst.htm, accessed 19 October 1998).

22 This dubbing, though relatively sophisticated compared to the inexpensive dubbing familiar to viewers of low-budget martial-arts films, produced a good deal of laughter among young audiences in the US.

23 During some sequences in *Rumble in the Bronx*, Chan appears in a black muscle-T, offering a visual referent to the ritual garb of Western action stars. More typically, displays of his body appear for comic effect. In one scene in *Jackie Chan's First Strike*, villains strip Chan's character of his clothing, and he appears naked in a long shot from behind. In another scene in the film, he appears in a pair of novelty briefs. Both scenes depict him as vulnerable and embarrassed.

24 Blends of action and comedy were commonplace in early cinema. For more information, see Crafton (1990), Gunning (1995), and Riblet (1995). The silent comedies of Keaton and Lloyd advance the action/comedy tradition and eventually expand it for feature-length narratives. In the early sound era, such performers and filmmakers as Errol Flynn and Preston Sturges also effectively balance action plots and comic flourishes. The plots of Keaton's and Sturges's films problematise the controlling male role, while Flynn's portrayals of dashing, acrobatic rogues in such films as *The Adventures of Robin Hood* (1938) and *The Sea Hawk* (1940) feminise the male hero, offering substantial material for camp interpretations of the type.

25 In one scene, the film's FBI leaders send fellow agents into a warehouse that explodes, but the aftermath of this event does not appear. Later, at the film's conclusion, the FBI men admit their mistakes to Carter (Chris Tucker), who then brusquely denies their offer of an FBI position. The agents appear in only a brief reaction shot, thus ending the dialogue.

26 As tacit evidence, studios have specifically marketed Chan's films and other martial-arts themed productions to African-American viewers.

Taking cues from the huge 1990s success of US rap stars the Wu-Tang Clan and their many spin-offs, which construct a pop mythology that combines Afrocenric ideology with kung-fu iconography, the US versions of *Rumble in the Bronx*, *Supercop* and *Rush Hour* all featured contemporary hip-hop soundtracks. Similarly, the racial combination of Chan and Tucker in *Rush Hour* recalls Lee's pairing in *Enter the Dragon* with black kung-fu star Jim Kelly (who later headlined in the kung-fu/blaxploitation films *Black Belt Jones* (1974) and *Three the Hard Way* (1974)).

27 In an *American Cinematographer* interview, black film-production manager Martin Jones offers the statistic that African-Americans account for approximately 25 per cent of all theatre tickets sold in the US, meaning that black consumers attend films nearly twice as regularly as whites (Rudolph, 2000: 122). Recognising such figures, New Line Cinema, which produced *Rush Hour*, has long geared films towards black audiences. Low- to medium-budget New Line releases such as *Friday* (1995), *Set It Off* (1996), *Money Talks* (1997) and *Blade* (1998) all feature black leads or principally black casts. Like *Rush Hour*, *Friday* and *Money Talks* both feature Chris Tucker in a jittery, hyperactive comic role.

28 Bruce Lee's US films, in which the hero devotes his physical energies solely to combat, serve as representative examples. The Bruce Lee biopic *Dragon: The Bruce Lee Story* (1993) does devote attention to Lee's real-life romance with and subsequent marriage to a white, US woman.

29 The actor in this role, Teddy Robin, is also the film's producer, a fact that largely explains his presence in the film.

30 Stories of Chan's mishaps are legion. They include a scene in *Rumble in the Bronx* in which Chan breaks his ankle while leaping from a pier onto a hovercraft, a fall during the filming of *Armor of God* that left the actor with a small hole in his skull, and an incident in which Chan, for a scene in *Police Story*, slid down a pole strung with live electrical cables, burning his hands (both are noted in Chan and Yang, 1998).

References

Berry, Chris (ed.) (1991) *Perspectives on Chinese Cinema*, London: British Film Institute.

Chan, Jackie and Jeff Yang (1998) *I Am Jackie Chan: My Life in Action*, New York: Ballantine Books.

Crafton, Donald (1990) 'Pie and Chase: Gag, Spectacle and Narrative in Slapstick Comedy', in Steve Neale and Frank Krutnik (eds), *Popular Film and Television Comedy*, London: Routledge.

Dannen, Fredric (1995) 'Hong Kong Babylon', *New Yorker*, 7 August.

Ehrlich, Linda C. and David Desser (eds) (1994) *Cinematic Landscapes: Observations on the Visual Arts and Cinema of China and Japan*, Austin: University of Texas Press.

Foronoff, Paul (1988) 'Orientation', *Film Comment*, 24(3), May–June: 52–5.

Gunning, Tom (1995) 'Crazy Machines in the Garden of Forking Paths: Mischief Gags and the Origins of American Film Comedy', in Kristine Brunovska Karnick and Henry Jenkins (eds), *Classical Hollywood Comedy*, London: Routledge.

Kaminsky, Stuart (1985) *American Film Genres*, Chicago: Nelson-Hall.

Karnick, Kristine Brunovska and Henry Jenkins (eds) (1995) *Classical Hollywood Comedy*, London: Routledge.

Kehr, Dave (1998) 'Chan Can Do', *Film Comment*, 4, May–June: 38.

Kirkham, Pat and Janet Thumim (eds) (1993) *You Tarzan: Movies, Masculinity and Men*, New York: St Martin's Press.

de Lauretis, Teresa (1984) *Alice Doesn't: Feminism, Semiotics, Cinema*, Bloomington: Indiana University Press.

Lee, Leo Ou-fan (1994) 'Two Films From Hong Kong: Parody and Allegory', in Nick Browne *et al.* (eds), *New Chinese Cinemas: Forms, Identities, Politics*, Cambridge: Cambridge University Press.

Leyda, Jay (1972) *Dianying: An Account of Films and the Film Audience in China*, Cambridge, MA: MIT Press.

Marchetti, Gina (1993) *Romance and the 'Yellow Peril': Race, Sex, and Discursive Strategies in Hollywood Fiction*, Berkeley: University of California Press.

Mast, Gerald (1979) *The Comic Mind: Comedy and the Movies*, Chicago: University o Chicago Press.

Mulvey, Laura (1990) 'Visual Pleasure and Narrative Cinema', in Patricia Erens (ed.), *Issues in Feminist Film Criticism*, Bloomington: Indiana University Press.

Neale, Steve and Frank Krutnik (1990) *Popular Film and Television Comedy*, London: Routledge.

Reid, Craig D. (1993/94) 'Fighting Without Fighting: Film Action Fight Choreography', *Film Quarterly*, 47, winter: 2.

Riblet, Doug (1995) 'The Keystone Film Company and the History of Early Slapstick', in Kristine Brunovska Karnick and Henry Jenkins (eds), *Classical Hollywood Comedy*, London: Routledge.

Rudolph, Eric (2000) 'New Millennium Studios Does It All', *American Cinematographer*, 81(3), March.

Smith, Paul (1993) *Clint Eastwood: A Cultural Production*, Minneapolis: University of Minnesota Press.

Strauss, Neil (1998) 'Hong Kong Film: Exit the Dragon?', *New York Times*, 2 August, Section 2: 1.

Stromgren, Dick (1990) 'The Chinese Syndrome: The Evolving Image of Chinese and Chinese-Americans in Hollywood Films', in Paul Loukides and Linda K. Fuller (eds), *Beyond the Stars: Stock Characters in American Popular Film*, Bowling Green, OH: BGSU Popular Press.

Tam, Kwok-kan and Wimal Dissanayake (1998) *New Chinese Cinema*, New York: Oxford University Press.

Teo, Stephen (1997) *Hong Kong Cinema: The Extra Dimensions*, London: British Film Institute.

7

Kenneth Branagh: Shakespearean film, cultural capital and star status

Nick Cox

This chapter offers an analysis of the construction of Kenneth Branagh's film persona in relation to the concept of cultural capital as it has been defined in the work of Pierre Bourdieu. Whilst there is not sufficient space, in the current discussion, for a detailed account of Bourdieu's work, it is appropriate to give some indication of those aspects of his theory of culture which have influenced the following analysis. Bourdieu's analysis can be thought of as an attempt to examine class relations from a perspective that avoids the limiting economistic determinism of some forms of Marxist analysis and the reductive tendency of Structuralism (Fowler, 1997: 2). For Bourdieu, the symbolic power exercised by classes and class fractions is at least as significant as the economic power they wield in defining their position within a social structure. Patterns of cultural consumption and appropriation function as the mechanism through which relative levels of distinction can be displayed, so that every instance of cultural practice (the food one eats, the clothes one wears, the decoration of one's home, the books one reads, even the friends one chooses) becomes a marker of an individual's position within a status hierarchy which has a complex relation to the socio-economic structure.

Cultural capital

Cultural capital is quite distinct from economic capital and most easily defined as the set of competences to make discriminating judgements about cultural products and practices. Formal education may be important in this process, but not so much for the specific qualification it affords individuals, rather because 'it really guarantees possession of a "general culture" whose breadth is proportionate to the prestige of the qualification' one acquires through it (Bourdieu, 1986: 25). Equally, if not more significant is the familiarity with a set of cultural products and practices sanctioned as 'legitimate' by the dominating classes – and the disposition one displays toward them – which is acquired through an upbringing in a household and milieu in which these cultural forms and the appropriate responses to them are sufficiently commonplace to form a seemingly 'normal' or 'natural' context for existence, what Bourdieu calls a 'doxa' (Bourdieu, 1977: 164; 1986: 471). The accumulation of cultural capital gives rise to a specific mode of subjectivity in which 'the legitimate disposition that is acquired by frequent contact with a particular class of works, namely, the literary and philosophical works recognised by the academic canon, comes to extend to other, less legitimate works . . . or to areas enjoying less academic recognition, such as cinema' (Bourdieu, 1986: 26).

Individuals who possess high levels of cultural capital are capable of making their whole lives an opportunity of displaying it by exercising powers of cultural discrimination in 'identifying what is worthy of being seen and the right way to see it', a process in which 'they are aided by their whole social group (which guides and reminds them with its "Have you seen . . . ?" and "You must see . . .") and by the whole corporation of critics mandated by the group to produce legitimate classifications and the discourse necessarily accompanying any artistic enjoyment' (Bourdieu, 1986: 26).

Bourdieu has been criticised for suggesting that the culture of the working class is relatively impoverished, defined by a 'necessity' that is 'dominated by ordinary interests and urgencies' (Bourdieu, 1986: 56; Frow, 1987: 71; Fowler, 1997: 4). However, the value of his work is that it provides a framework for the interpretation of culture which demystifies the hierarchies of taste, which work to reinforce structures of power and domination. Bourdieu's meticulous and exhaustive interpretation of cultural stratification, in a work like *Distinction*, also provides a sophisticated and subtle mechanism for the interpretation of patterns of cultural consumption which are revealed as possessing a complex relation to class and power relations.

Branagh: Shakespeare/theatre/Englishness

The concept of cultural capital is particularly useful when considering a British performer such as Kenneth Branagh since, as Sarah
Street has argued, the cinema in British culture has conventionally
been conceived by powerful cultural practitioners as a cultural mode
that is 'inferior' to the theatre, a conception reinforced by a critical
discourse that 'exuded profound reverence for theatre as a medium
capable of conferring cultural prestige on film'. One influential
definition of what constitutes a 'good British film' has been, she
claims, 'one which consciously displays its literary/theatrical origins'
(Street, 1997: 114). The theatre has been construed, in British
culture, as a relatively more significant source for the accumulation
of cultural capital than cinema, with its associations with a mass
audience and popular taste. Many British film actors, up to and to
an extent after World War Two, established a reputation as performers in the theatre before they embarked on a film career and
their status and personae were thus informed by a concept of
cultural value linked to the stage, thus reinforcing the hierarchical
relation between film and theatre (Street, 1997: 119). This has had
important implications for the way in which the very concept of the
film star has been mediated in British culture: 'there has always been
a tension', Street argues, 'between wanting British stars and resent-
ment that, as a Hollywood invention, film stardom and all its trap-
pings of gossip, fandom and scandal are somehow unseemly,
unBritish' (1997: 119).

When we examine Branagh's status as a performer this tension
needs to be kept in play. In what follows I will be seeking to address
what I see as a fundamental contradiction in the formation of his
star persona. Branagh began his career as a 'classical' actor and
his reputation as a performer was established through his success
with the Royal Shakespeare Company (RSC). He subsequently
enjoyed some success as a television actor, most significantly for
his performance in the period drama *Fortunes of War* (1987).
However, he remained closely identified with the theatre, not
least through the establishment of his own Renaissance Theatre
Company in the late 1980s.

Branagh's film roles up until 1989 were typical of the RSC-trained
actor: screen adaptations of literary texts and costume dramas. The
film role that established his reputation as a star, his adaptation of

Shakespeare's *Henry V* (1989), was entirely in keeping with this career trajectory. Moreover, the choice of this text worked to underscore the widely noted, self-conscious and almost ironic relationship between Branagh's career and that of the figure whose name continues to function as a privileged sign of 'great' Shakespearean performances on stage and screen: Laurence Olivier. Olivier's famous adaptation of the play in 1945 was not only an instance of the successful transfer of theatrical practice to the screen, it was also an example of the reinvestment of prestige acquired as a stage performer into a filmic persona. Branagh's *Henry V* performed a similar function for its actor–director, establishing him as a significant film actor who was nominated for an Oscar for best actor for his portrayal of the King, whilst simultaneously underpinning his association with a 'great tradition' of British performers whose status derived from their association with the theatre and, in particular, with Shakespeare.

Yet his 'classical' background, and most significantly his association with Shakespeare, has meant that Branagh's identity as a film actor has been caught in a contradiction in which he has sought, on the one hand, to exploit the cultural capital invested in 'Shakespeare' (not only the plays but the whole system of meanings attached to the name of the playwright in contemporary culture), whilst simultaneously seeking to generate a popular star persona.

Whilst film adaptations of Shakespeare cannot be assumed in every case to represent what, from the perspective of the dominating social faction, constitutes a cheapening or vulgar popularising of the texts which function as the most potent signifiers of cultural value in Anglo-American culture, Branagh's adaptations, I will argue, have a markedly populist or popularising tendency. This is combined, uneasily, with a concern to maintain and enhance the cultural distinction that Branagh acquires, as a performer, from his association with a 'highbrow' cultural practice such as 'legitimate' theatre and from the prestige that accrues from being recognised as an 'authentic' Shakespearean actor. This vacillation was neatly encapsulated in Branagh's own description of his objective in *Henry V* in an interview with the theatre critic Michael Billington, which was, he claimed, 'to make a popular film that will satisfy the Shakespearean scholar and the punter who likes *Crocodile Dundee*' (quoted in Bristol, 1996: 97). Branagh's shift in linguistic register from the discourse of the academy (scholar) to the deliberately demotic (punter) is indicative of the self-consciousness with which he has sought both to sustain and simultaneously broaden his impact and appeal as a performer.

In seeking to both uphold and enhance the symbolic power attached to Shakespeare by the dominant culture, whilst simultane- ously seeking to appeal to a broader audience than the habitual consumers of 'high' cultural forms, Branagh is forced to occupy a radically ambivalent cultural space. His filmic persona is imperilled, on one hand, by the potential charge of vulgarisation from those who esteem him for his theatrical background and, on the other, by the relative marginality, as far as Hollywood status is concerned, which might result from being associated with a narrowly English or culturally elitist set of concerns.

One important aspect of Branagh's film persona, at least in rela- tion to the Shakespearean adaptations which I will argue have been central in establishing his identity as a film performer, is his enact- ment of a certain Englishness. Although he was born in Ireland and has Anglo-Irish ancestry, Branagh's film roles, not least his Shake- spearean ones, have all involved the projection of an identity that is unambiguously English. Whilst, as Julian Petley has suggested, a number of British actors, including Jeremy Irons and Rupert Everett, have achieved success by rehearsing 'a familiar English stereotype: a pre-World War Two English gentleman, slightly deca- dent, preferably with an ambiguous sexual identity' (Petley, 1985: 118), Branagh's version of Englishness is not readily comprehensi- ble in these terms. Whilst there is no doubt that his performances, in these Shakespearean films at least, involve the portrayal of a cer- tain upper-class masculinity, this is less significant than Branagh's association with a particular British cultural tradition, or 'heritage', which aligns him not only with the figure widely assumed to be the greatest of English poets, but also with the tradition of British Shakespearean acting, conceptualised as the most prestigious of all 'legitimate' modes of theatrical performance. Branagh's concern with a concept of 'authenticity' in the Shakespearean theatrical pro- ductions he has been involved in is witnessed, not least, by his con- cern to present the 'full' text of *Hamlet* in his Renaissance Theatre Company's production of the play.

The cultural prestige on which Branagh draws as a film performer is thus a product of his identity as a practitioner of a prestigious and elevated cultural practice that is also closely associated with certain concepts of Englishness. This unambiguously 'highbrow' persona is exploited by Branagh in his film performances, which remain highly 'theatrical' as we shall see. This theatricality, which is reinforced by the use of highly formalised elements in the construction of the *mise-en-scène* in Branagh's films, especially in the context of those scenes where he is privileged, helps to recall Branagh's relation to a cultural mode that is granted greater legitimacy by the dominant culture than film is.

Paradoxically, then, part of Branagh's appeal, as a Shakespearean film performer, is that his performances are designedly other than those of established (Hollywood) film actors who play alongside him. The Shakespearean films are thus a mechanism through which the cultural primacy of theatre and the hegemonic position of Shakespeare within Anglo-American culture are reinforced. This is, I suggest, important in understanding the appeal of these films to a certain kind of audience.

Cultural capital and star status

To claim, however, that Branagh's appeal and his persona as performer are simply and unambiguously 'highbrow' would be a misreading of what is in fact a more complex relation to his audience. Whilst Branagh's status is, I suggest, heavily dependent on his theatrical background, his association with Shakespeare and his Englishness, all of these elements are rendered meaningful in the films only through a process in which Branagh is both aligned with, and yet also importantly differentiated from, co-stars whose appeal is importantly different from his own. Certainly Branagh has been supported, in his most recent Shakespeare films (*Much Ado About Nothing* (1993) and *Hamlet* (1993)), by English actors who have equal (if not greater) prestige as Shakespearean stage performers (Richard Briers, Emma Thompson and Brian Blessed in *Much Ado About Nothing*, Briers and Derek Jacobi in *Hamlet*). Given the account of Branagh's exploitation of the conceptual matrix of Shakespeare/theatre/Englishness outlined above, it could be argued that such performers provide further signifiers of the highbrow character of the films and confer further legitimacy on both Branagh and the whole enterprise. Yet these performers have been supplemented in both films by actors whose nationality (and ethnicity), relation to Shakespeare and to high culture are very different from Branagh's;

performers whose star personae are the product of the Hollywood system. The cast of *Much Ado About Nothing* contained American performers such as Denzil Washington, Keanu Reeves, Michael Keaton and Robert Sean Leonard, that of *Hamlet* Hollywood 'greats' such as Charlton Heston and Jack Lemmon.

The casting of figures such as these can be understood as part of a strategy of popularisation in which the pleasures associated with mainstream films are promised by a text whose meanings are conventionally understood to be far less accessible. Yet the effect of the conjunction of Branagh with these American popular performers is, simultaneously, to emphasise his difference from them. Paradoxically then, the inclusion of figures whose status is an effect of their popular success works to reinforce the 'highbrow' character of Branagh's persona. It is possible to suggest that the involvement of performers with considerable symbolic power within the Hollywood system in Branagh's films can be explained as an effort to derive a certain 'legitimacy' by drawing on the cultural capital invested in his persona. In a sense, however, that persona is itself an effect of their involvement, since it manifests itself through the difference the films establish and reinforce between Branagh and these others. Branagh's status is thus characterised by a certain vacillation between the apparent claim to popular stardom suggested by his association with successful mainstream performers and the simultaneous need to maintain a conception of his own performance as an effect of quite different domains of cultural production.

This has important implications for an understanding of the kind of audience these films seem to address. Whilst the films transfer canonical literary texts to a middle- or low-brow medium there is an important sense in which they seek to reinforce, rather than dilute, the cultural superiority of both the literary 'classic' and of the theatre over and against the 'easy' pleasures of the cinema. More fundamentally they seek to enhance the feeling of cultural distinction of which the bourgeois sector of their audience are possessed. Again Branagh's persona can be understood as both an appeal to and a construct of this audience. His function in the films is to reassure the bourgeois audience that vulgarisation and contamination of high art by popular taste has not been permitted. Branagh's identification with the concept Shakespeare/theatre/Englishness means that he is able to operate as a kind of guarantor of legitimacy even whilst the text admits the presence of TV comedians, Americans and actors from the popular cinema. This explains the likely appeal of these films to an audience whose members would not regard mainstream cinema as part of their cultural domain. A (British) bourgeois audience which frequents the theatre and would be willing to watch certain art-house or heritage films finds, in the Shakespeare/Branagh couple, the imprimatur of legitimacy that marks these films out as distinct from the cinematic mainstream and thus enables them to function as markers of cultural distinction for their consumers. Branagh's function (along with Thompson, Jacobi and Briers) is to prevent the translation of Shakespeare from stage to screen and the inclusion of performers whose very names carry connotations of popular pleasure and sensation from radically disturbing the cultural hierarchies that are intrinsic to the habitus of the middle class. For this group the privileging of Branagh, in a fashion that alludes to a certain concept of theatricality and simultaneously reinforces his Englishness, guarantees the authentically Shakespearean character of the object they are invited to consume. Branagh's function is to proclaim to an audience who are suspicious of mere entertainment that these films offer something more than the quotidian delights of popular cinema.

Nonetheless, Branagh's Shakespeare films were promoted as mainstream and were financed by major Hollywood production companies (Samuel Goldwyn in the case of *Much Ado About Nothing*, Columbia Tristar on *Hamlet*). Clearly, part of the project of both films was to have box-office success and appeal to major distributors and the mass audiences they target. The inclusion of established Hollywood stars, in this context, was a vital element in the success of the films. Branagh's cultural capital was relatively less significant than the popular appeal of performers such as Reeves, Washington, Billy Crystal and Robin Williams or the status as film performers of figures like Charlton Heston and Jack Lemmon. Commercial success and popular appeal might have the effect of enabling Branagh to be recognised as a performer who can be seen as attractive by the very Hollywood system certain aspects of his persona are designed to hold at bay. Here the ambivalence of the Shakespearean adaptations can serve a different function to that described above. It could be argued Branagh occupies the hybrid space of these films, which merge 'high-' and 'low-brow' elements, in order to negotiate a transition from the culturally powerful but relatively narrow appeal of the Shakespeare/theatre/Englishness persona to a more popular, film-star identity. In this context the association with American film actors, which functions as a mark of Branagh's distinction for bourgeois spectators, can also operate as the mechanism through which he becomes aligned with these popular stars and so acquires appeal for a wider audience. Cultural capital thus becomes the mechanism through which Branagh gains entry into the Hollywood star system. This account of the ambivalence of Branagh's persona can now be illustrated, through a more detailed analysis of its construction in the film which is taken as a case study for this chapter.

Much Ado About Nothing

Theatre

The association between the film and theatre, which I have suggested is so fundamental to Branagh's persona in the Shakespearean adaptations he has made, was reinforced in the case of this text by a number of elements. Firstly, the film transferred a successful stage production of the play, by Branagh's Renaissance Theatre Company, to the screen and a number of the cast were members of the ensemble of performers who were identified with the company. One very important trace of this theatre production can be discerned in the film, with important implications for the way in which Branagh is projected within it. The choice of setting for the film, a Tuscan villa, had a significant influence on the meanings generated by the film, one of which was the sense of artifice and of theatricality it repeatedly exploits. The spatial dynamics of the villa – formal gardens, courtyards, arches, cellars, balconies, avenues, statuary, fountains – and the spectacular opportunities it affords for painterly tableaux and vistas over the surrounding countryside, help to enhance the sense of the film's action taking place in a self-consciously artificial *mise-en-scène*. These spatial elements are combined with other elements such as masquerade, song and dance to generate an implicit, but nonetheless insistent, sense of the theatrical that reminds the audience – particularly those members who frequent the theatre – that they are watching a Shakespeare play.

We can consider in a little more detail how this aspect of the film contributes to the production of a particular kind of persona for Branagh. A crucial moment in Branagh's interpretation of the role of Benedick in the film takes place in the gardens of the villa in an enclosed, rectangular garden with a fountain at its centre. The garden is bordered at the sides by cypress trees and at the back by clipped yew hedges, which, at one point, form an avenue opening onto the garden and fountain. The space operates very explicitly as a stage-set with a view down the formal yew avenues forming the opening to a sequence in which Branagh is central. Branagh as Benedick enters the formal garden and speaks directly to the camera, delivering the longest soliloquy in the film. This is broken by the entry of Don Pedro (Washington), Claudio (Leonard) and Leonato (Briers). Branagh retreats behind the yew hedge and then reoccupies the garden with the fountain to deliver a second long speech to the camera.

In this sequence Branagh commands the most overtly theatricalised space in a self-consciously theatrical film. Other characters enter the stage-like garden but once they have done so they are limited by it. Washington, Briers and Leonard sit on the side of the stone fountain, whilst Branagh moves into, out of and around the fountain and the garden, dominating the frame. When Emma Thompson as Beatrice enters the space Branagh remains centrally positioned beside the fountain and later he wades jubilantly in it. If this formal garden is deployed in the film as a kind of stage then it is clear that Branagh is represented in the text as the performer most clearly and closely associated with it, reinforcing the link between him and the theatre. Other figures in the film are associated with particular locales: Keanu Reeves, for instance, is repeatedly portrayed in the villa's cellars. This helps to reinforce the marginality and malevolence of the character he plays, Don John, but also provides a suitably sultry, candlelit space within which his oiled torso can be displayed to mutedly eroticised effect. Branagh's occupation of the most explicitly theatrical locus in the film, meanwhile, works to underscore visually the notional association between him, the theatre and Shakespeare that the audience always already assumes; an impression reinforced by his deployment of the discursive mode that is least congruent with cinematic realism and most readily identified with the 'legitimate' and especially Shakespearean theatre, the soliloquy, when he occupies this space in the text.

Englishness
If Branagh's association with the theatre is reinforced in the text, so is his enactment of and association with Englishness. As I have already suggested, the casting of American performers alongside Branagh works to establish his difference from them. This difference

is, paradoxically, reinforced by the use of identical costume (vaguely nineteenth-century cavalry uniforms) for the four young male characters in the film, the roles played by Branagh, Washington, Leonard and Reeves. Branagh's Englishness is reinforced when he appears in this cohort of identically dressed American actors. Early in the film, for example, Branagh is seen walking towards the camera slightly behind and flanked by Washington and Leonard. Washington's ethnicity might be thought to function as the most significant marker of difference in this shot, but the alignment of him and Leonard in the foreground stresses their alliance with one another. It is Branagh – who stands in the centre of, but some way back from, the other two – who is differentiated by the disposition of bodies in this instance. Branagh's difference from his American co-stars is marked here and elsewhere in the film sartorially as he introduces a note of informality into his dress which is never matched by Washington and Leonard, who remain symmetrically dressed in almost every scene. In the first scenes Branagh's waistcoat is unbuttoned whilst the other actors remain buttoned up; later, in the scene in the stage-like garden, Washington and Leonard are identically dressed whilst Branagh, wearing the same costume elements, has his shirt sleeves rolled up in another mark of relative casualness.

Whilst helping to mark Branagh's difference from his American co-stars and thus to underline his Englishness, these visual signifiers perhaps also have the effect of suggesting to the audience that Branagh is relatively at ease in the Shakespearean role while Washington and Leonard are united in their conformist submission to the costume designer's concept, demoting them to elements of the background against which Branagh is defined.

Another important element in the projection of Branagh's Englishness in the film is provided by his pairing in the film's love-plot with Emma Thompson. Thompson and Branagh, as Beatrice and Benedick, have some of the most intricate, verbally playful and amusing speeches in the play. This means that their performances are readily associated with verbal dexterity, wit and sophistication. Thompson and Branagh's identities as English performers are therefore linked in the text to this discursive register, with its connotations of linguistic mastery and rhetorical fluency. In contrast Washington is cast as the likeable but stolid Don Pedro, Claudio (Leonard) is alternately insipid and histrionic, Reeves as Don John is, necessarily, marginal and Michael Keaton's idiosyncratic performance as

Dogberry is confined to the subplot, which is typified in the film by 'low' comic strategies such as visual humour and absurd accents. Consequently Branagh and Thompson are marked out in the text as performers who operate successfully in a distinct linguistic field that is marked as the verbal terrain in which English actors speak. There is also the potential, for members of the audience who are equipped with the cultural capital to make such comparisons, to align Branagh and Thompson's performances with those of other established (British) actors who have played these parts successfully, Derek Jacobi and Judi Dench's for the RSC in the early 1980s may have been significant for Branagh.

Tuscany and cultural capital

I want now to return to consider the setting of film and its capacity both to denote cultural distinction and also to invite a section of the audience to identify Branagh with a certain form of cultural capital which they either possess or aspire to possess. The Tuscan countryside plays a significant role in the cultural imaginary of the British middle class. As the location for holidays it functions as a site of leisure, the other to the realm of work and often highly competitive struggle that structures their everyday experience. Tuscany's significance as the most important centre in the production of the high culture of the Renaissance and as the site in which that culture is mediated and displayed today makes it a privileged location for displaying cultural competence and for the accumulation of cultural capital by the bourgeois subject. The Tuscan landscape is endlessly represented in British broadsheet newspapers, novels, magazines, advertising and the kind of television programmes designed to appeal to the middle-class preoccupation with taste (cooking, wine, interior and garden design, travel). It has been constructed through this system of representations as a locale invested with peculiar significance: as a site for the cultivation of complex and elevated pleasures and the opportunity to display one's distinction through the consumption of food and wine, visits to architecturally or aesthetically significant centres and (more or less) fluent use of a foreign language.

Vital to this habitus is the villa, a term now used indiscriminately to describe almost any form of property given over to use by tourists. Property functions as a medium through which financial capital can be translated into cultural capital with the villa (owned or rented, large or small, nobleman's dwelling or converted cowshed) operating as perhaps the most significant element in a system of meanings whose function is to designate gradations not just of income but of taste (whilst all bourgeois stay in villas, not all villas are alike: position, decor, history are all important markers of difference).

This is why the villa in Branagh's film (Villa Vignamaggio, Greve in Chianti) is one of its most important signifying elements. Whether as the object of recognition and identification or of aspirant fantasy, the villa and its painterly representation in the film operate to generate pleasures that are linked to concepts of leisure, taste and prestige which reinforce distinction and which are richly appealing to a middle-class audience. Branagh's identification with the villa in and through the film is therefore another way in which he is himself invested with cultural value as another purveyor of the fantasy of Tuscany, which is a central element of the consumption practices of the British middle class. Since the action of Shakespeare's play is set in an urban context, the city of Messina in Sicily (something the film is happy to recognise at the level of discourse, whilst utterly ignoring its implications for the production) the use of the Villa Vignamaggio in the film can best be explained as part of its attempt to appeal precisely to this audience through the projection of a visually enticing version of its ideologically constituted notion of Italy as a rural setting for its leisure time. Branagh successfully penetrates this fantasy and collaborates in its promulgation.

Cultural capital and popular taste
Reading the text as productive of these interrelated concepts of theatricality, Englishness and cultural capital, Branagh's persona could be thought of as functioning to offer a form of stardom that is meaningful as a signifier of distinction for an audience with the cultural competences to situate it in relation to these fields. In this account the American co-stars are really foils, whose function is to constitute Branagh's status, which is defined in its difference from them. Yet, as I have already suggested, Branagh gains little, in the domain of cinema, by simply underscoring his association with cultural fields that are extrinsic to it. In order to be acknowledged as a *film*-star he must acquire prestige within cinematic cultural practice. Branagh cannot simply 'cash in' the cultural capital accumulated through an association with theatre or with bourgeois taste, for these aspects of his appeal are (by definition) confined to a powerful but limited audience, whose broad cultural disposition is to disparage film.

Branagh's identity as a film-star must involve a delicate manoeuvre in which he is rendered attractive to a 'popular' audience whilst simultaneously avoiding too radical a dilution of the cultural capital that provided him with his initial entry into film. The function of the Hollywood stars in *Much Ado About Nothing* can be understood as crucial to this project.

Whilst I have stressed the manner in which the spatial disposition of Branagh and his American co-stars differentiates him, it could also be argued that the film also works to align them in ways that reinforce their alliance. Branagh's first appearance in the film, for instance, is in a sequence of shots in which he, Leonard, Reeves and Washington are seen riding side by side towards the camera, unified by a gesture of victorious fist-raising. Moreover, the sartorial signifiers I have mentioned as a mechanism for differentiating Branagh are easily overlooked and the dominant signification of the uniforms worn by both him and his co-stars is sameness. Whilst the markers of difference are there, they are encoded in a manner that simultaneously signals similarity: buttons undone on identical waistcoats; the sleeves rolled on a shirt that is otherwise indistinguishable from those of Washington and Leonard. Even the linguistic difference I have suggested is crucial in defining Branagh's Englishness might be said to be subsumed within the more fundamental speech genre that we could call 'Shakespearean English', within which all the performers operate. The peculiarities of the Branagh–Thompson exchanges are, again, not insignificant but these differences are never so radical as to make it impossible for them to be interlocutors in exchanges with American performers.

The point is not that Branagh is *or* is not differentiated from his American co-stars, rather that he is *and* is not differentiated from them. The text's modulation between highbrow and lowbrow is, moreover, not only an effect of its incorporation of Hollywood actors. Importantly, those British actors who played alongside Branagh in the film, such as Richard Briers, Brian Blessed and Emma Thompson, were already familiar to sections of the British audience for television performances as much as for their theatrical success. Briers, in particular, had a well-established TV persona as a highly successful sit-com and television drama actor during the 1970s and 1980s. Whilst a certain section of the audience might possess the cultural competence to associate him with his successful portrayal of the Shakespearean comic part of Malvolio in one of the

Renaissance Theatre Company's earlier productions, others recalled his performance as Tom in *The Good Life*. Briers could therefore have a double signification in the text and Branagh's deployment of him in the role of the genial Leonato may have been informed by an awareness of his popular comic associations. The casting of the 'alternative' comedian Ben Elton as Verges is certainly explicable in these terms. As Verges, Elton retains the round-rimmed glasses and estuarine verbal register that are integral elements of his television comedic identity, which is simply grafted onto the film text. Branagh's alignment with performers who were so familiar to the British TV audience may be thought of as possessing as ambivalent a meaning as that with his American co-stars. At one level Branagh's persona can again be seen as defined in its difference from such vulgar entertainment as an 'authentically' canonical interpretation of the role. Yet the presence of Briers and Elton (Blessed had also appeared in one of the *Blackadder* series that Elton co-scripted) situates the film within an intertext that incorporates television culture. Branagh's performance can then never be wholly dissociated from this level of meaning in the film and, it might be argued, is informed by it.

Indeed, Branagh himself had established his reputation co-starring with Thompson in a television drama series, *Fortunes of War*, in the late 1980s. Subsequently, Branagh and Thompson's familiarity to a television audience but their identification, nonetheless, with 'legitimate' theatre made it possible for the makers of the satirical puppet-show *Spitting Image* to routinely parody them (along with Blessed) as stock 'luvvies' in the late 1980s and 1990s. This ambiguous presence of Branagh in the popular doxa is perhaps telling since it suggests a degree of popular recognition precisely for being a practitioner of 'highbrow' culture. This conception could only be reinforced by a film like *Much Ado About Nothing* in which Branagh operates in a popular medium and is surrounded by a variety of popular performers, but nonetheless retains his association with 'high' culture since the film is an adaptation of a canonical text and the skills he is asked to display in his role within it are unambiguously those of the 'Shakespearean' actor.

Even if we can argue, then, that his role in *Much Ado About Nothing* works to extend Branagh's appeal to a broader audience it remains the case that the very basis for his success in this film remains his association with cultural practices which are not readily absorbed within popular cinema: the literary text, theatre and the British bourgeois habitus that is evoked by representations of the Tuscan landscape. Branagh, to say clearly what has been implicit throughout this chapter, is popular, insofar as he is popular, for not being (too) popular. For a bourgeois audience Branagh's whole appeal as a film actor lies, paradoxically, in his putative distinction from the medium in which he operates. For this group too much success – too much exposure, box office impact, Hollywood status – would be interpreted as a capitulation to commercialism, a prostitution of 'talents' initially associated with high art, a pandering to 'low' taste and the indulgence of the unsophisticated appetites of the masses, a degradation, in short, of the cultural values they hold dear. The audience that is condemned by this conception of cultural distinction would also, for different reasons, read Branagh's transformation into a more popular performer as problematic, I suggest. Branagh's association with 'high' culture and thus with an aesthetic that presents itself as demanding a range of cultural competences which are intrinsic to the dominating class, with a life-style that is antagonistic to and oppressive of the subordinate classes and their habitus, would render him anomalous, absurd, alien in the context of an unambiguously popular genre such as action films, for instance.

Therefore, Branagh, in his Shakespearean film roles, occupies a fairly specific cultural space, which is neither sufficiently popular to warrant dismissal as 'bad taste' by the middle-class consumer, nor so uncompromisingly elitist to be considered simply inaccessible, or pretentious. A film such as Peter Greenaway's *Prospero's Books* (1991) provides a useful contrast to Branagh's adaptations here since its overtly innovative and experimental relations both to the Shakespearean text and to mainstream cinema are likely to appeal to a smaller, self-consciously 'artistic' or 'intellectual' audience than that for Branagh's *Much Ado About Nothing*. The cultural domain within which these films seem to operate is quite different from this one. On the one hand they are dominated by what Bourdieu calls 'bourgeois taste', defined in opposition to the more 'scholastic' and 'daring' culture of the intellectual fraction but also distinguishing itself from aspects of 'middle-brow and popular taste' (Bourdieu, 1986: 267). Simultaneously, however, the appeal of these films to such 'bourgeois taste' seems to be compromised or modified by the absorption of more popular elements and figures into them. These gestures in the direction of 'popular taste' are crucial in constituting a version of Branagh which is not bounded by the Shakespeare/theatre/ Englishness structure I have outlined. At the same time, however, these elements cannot be permitted to subvert the hegemonic status of the Shakespearean text and the culture that appropriates it as its privileged signifier of distinction. This is not surprising, since his currency as a performer, at this point in his career, was always already premised on that relation between Shakespeare and the dominant culture and the cultural capital, as a performer, this yielded to him.

Subsequently, Branagh has sought to modify the association between his own persona and the Shakespearean/theatre/Englishness triad. An early indication of this shift was *Dead Again* (1991), in which Branagh plays a character (or characters) whose identity is split between a German past self and an American current one. The text clearly operates as a vehicle for Branagh to display his 'versatility' and to sever the association with theatre and Shakespeare, since the film's intertexts are Hitchcockean suspense films and *film noir*. *Dead Again* is nevertheless self-conscious in its pastiche and is intended to appeal to an audience with the cultural competence to recognise its generic allusions to film texts, which are ascribed an unusual degree of significance by more or less 'intellectual' elements of the bourgeoisie. Moreover, it deploys a moderately 'experimental' technique to suggest temporal differences through the use of black and white and colour. This, combined with the presence in the cast of Emma Thompson and Derek Jacobi, suggests that Branagh, in this text, is still to be read as a performer who is to be associated with films that can be ascribed legitimacy within the sphere of bourgeois taste.

More recently Branagh has been cast in far more mainstream films such as *Wild, Wild West* (1999), which stars Will Smith, a performer associated with big-budget action films such as *Men in Black* (1998) and *Enemy of the State* (1999). *Wild, Wild West* is a text that is intended to appeal to a popular audience in both Britain and America, and Branagh's role in the film marks his most radical break with the Shakespeare/theatre/Englishness matrix on which his career was founded: he plays a white racist megalomaniac from the American south intent on overthrowing the US government. This role might establish Branagh as a performer with mainstream Hollywood appeal. Yet, as I have already indicated, this is a potentially hazardous move for him, since popular success would certainly imperil the persona he has established as a figure who can transfer some, at least, of the cultural capital identified with 'legitimate' cultural modes like theatre to film. It is worth noting that whilst he tests the Hollywood system in a bid to establish a filmic identity amongst a popular audience, Branagh has also worked on another Shakespearean adaptation, of *Love's Labours Lost* (2000). It seems, then, that the vacillation between popular status and cultural capital remains the defining element of Branagh's persona.

Bibliography

Bourdieu, Pierre (1977) *Outline of a Theory of Practice*, Cambridge: Cambridge University Press.

Bourdieu, Pierre (1986) *Distinction: A Social Critique of the Judgement of Taste*, London and New York: Routledge.

Bristol, Michael (1996) *Big-time Shakespeare*, London: Routledge.

Fowler, Bridget (1997) *Pierre Bourdieu and Cultural Theory*, London: Sage.

Frow, John (1987) 'Accounting for Tastes: Some Problems in Pierre Bourdieu's Sociology of Culture', *Cultural Studies* 1(1): 59–77.

Jenkins, Raymond (1992) *Pierre Bourdieu*, London and New York: Routledge.

Petley, Julian (1985) 'Reaching for the Stars', in Martin Auty and Nick Roddick (eds), *British Cinema Now*, London: British Film Institute.

Street, Sarah (1997) *British National Cinema*, London and New York: Routledge.

8

'Baby I'm a star': towards a political economy of the actor formerly known as Prince

Lisa Taylor

Prince[1] reaped tremendous success in his debut feature film *Purple Rain* (1984). But the feature that followed, which he both directed and in which he starred, *Under the Cherry Moon* (1986), was, in terms of audience popularity, a flop. This chapter sets out to ask why Prince decided to return more firmly to his musical career after *Under the Cherry Moon* and seeks to explore why Prince's musical star persona was not able to cross over into Hollywood with the same kind of ease that stars such as Frank Sinatra, Harry Connick Junior, Elvis Presley and Madonna have enjoyed.

Media critics have taken various approaches to star images. Using the critical work on Madonna, I argue that political economy approaches, which find it unfeasible to isolate the film 'text' from the rest of its multi-media production-line, offer the most useful perspectives. For these critiques, a film text's narrative form or its aesthetic features are shaped by economic imperatives. However, interpretative readings offer a valuable insight into why certain cultural commodities fail to enlist audience agency. Prince's star text presented a radical challenge to mainstream ideas about gender, sexuality and race in ways that proved unpopular with compartments of the audience. Yet such readings must be couched in the context of the contemporary media marketplace: the corporate imperatives that construct, repackage and distribute star texts across multi-media sites are a key dimension for analysis. As Meehan argues: 'No business means no show and doing business means constructing shows according to business' (Meehan, 1991: 62). Nonetheless, business is not always successful and commercial strategies can sometimes fail to finance the right show for the right corporate plan, as exploration of Warner Communications Inc.'s handling of the Prince star persona reveals.

Cultural analysis and star studies: the case of Madonna

Music stars make the most effective transference to mainstream cinema when the character played draws upon the star persona already established by the music and culture industries. Madonna's music and film career is a case in point. In 1983, Madonna released her eponymous debut album. Subsequently, the videos of the major hits culled from this album – 'Holiday' and 'Lucky Star' – were featured on MTV. These products established Madonna as an outrageous female icon known for her individuality, sexual rebellion, impudence, non-conformity and willingness to experiment with fashion and alternative lifestyles. Her continual change of image across these early music and video outputs promoted the idea that female identity was a construct that could be orchestrated and manipulated at will. Indeed, it is precisely these traits that the character of Susan (Madonna) embodies in *Desperately Seeking Susan* (1985). The narrative drive of the film hinges on the desire of the central character Roberta (Rosanna Arquette), to emulate Susan by changing her identity in terms of her image and behaviour, in order to live life on her own terms.

With Madonna, transference relies on the credibility of her chimera-like persona. In contrast, the meaning of Prince's star vehicle is only effective when his musical persona is used virtually wholesale, as in the case of *Purple Rain*, *Sign o' the Times* (1987) and *Graffiti Bridge* (1990). In *Under the Cherry Moon*, his attempt at a character role was unsuccessful because the stylistic features of his musical persona – the camp element of his performance repertoire for instance, so well-wrought in more abbreviated forms such as the short music video – simply could not be effectively developed in a traditional feature-length production, which required causality and coherence.

These elements have been partially examined in recent cultural analyses. Star studies that utilise cultural studies approaches have tended to blend textual readings of star personae with attention to an understanding of stars via their consumption (Fiske, 1989; Stacey, 1994). Fiske's interpretation of Madonna in 'Reading the Popular' (1989) has been attacked for surrendering a truly critical standpoint in favour of a depoliticised, crass celebration of popular media culture (Kellner, 1995; McGuigan, 1997). The methodological approach to the cultural consumption of Madonna, with its blend of ethnographic audience research and semiotic textual analysis, has been dismissed as ultimately simplistic. 'How much more difficult', McGuigan tartly remarks, ' it would be to combine the analysis of consumption with other dimensions and levels of analysis' (McGuigan, 1997: 149). Kellner also criticises Fiske's reading as far 'too one-sided' and argues, trenchantly, that the analysis, such as it is, is impaired by 'focusing too intently on cultural texts and audience reception' (1995: 36).

Perhaps even more problematically, Fiske tends to find a neat congruence between his own semiotic textual readings of Madonna (Madonna = bad girl who subverts patriarchal meanings) and the positive comments he unearths from ethnographic work among young consumers (therefore Madonna empowers girls through her bad-girl image). The problem with this kind of simplistic over-emphasis on textualism and consumption is that the dominant ideas which clearly exist alongside whatever radical meanings reside in the commodities produced by Madonna are ignored and rendered harmless. As Kellner argues: 'Such studies might also lose sight of the manipulative and conservative effects of certain types of media culture, and thus serve the interests of the culture industries as they are presently constituted and those groups who use the culture industries to promote their own interests and agendas' (Kellner, 1995: 38–9). Fiske had earlier argued that a political economy approach was obsolete for his analysis of Madonna, since, as a critical method, it tends to dismiss young consumers as dupes, manipulated by the culture industries (Fiske, 1989: 96). Yet the danger with this kind of argument is that the reader or audience becomes the only source to unlock the meaning of the text, and, as a result, factors such as the institutional production of commodities are marginalised. Kellner and McGuigan argue that political economy is precisely the approach that needs to be imported back into cultural studies generally and star studies in particular. If more complex readings of commodities are to be conducted, cultural goods require an analysis of production in the context both of economics and the system of production.

Kellner's review of Madonna's career offers a complex, multi-layered analysis of a pop icon, focusing on the uneven struggle the industry has undergone to continually re-invent strategies in the relentless pursuit of profits. The strength of his account is to merge the political economy of her stardom with interpretative analysis to assess the success of her career both culturally and economically. The changing semiotic meaning of Madonna's image is therefore set into the context of marketing strategies, public relations exercises and the pursuit of audiences. Her change of image – which has appealed to a range of audiences in terms of race, age, gender and sexuality – is read as a planned set of astute marketing moves to generate difference and maintain the turnover of capital. Indeed, it can be seen that Madonna achieved mega-stardom during a historic moment when music videos and MTV played a key role in conferring fame within the music and culture industries. Her success can thus be attributed to the successful marketing of image and the manipulation of the grand spectacle of her live concerts and music videos as opposed to any extraordinary talent as either a vocalist or dancer. Ultimately, if we are to understand why certain cultural goods are produced by the media and culture industries, we must foreground the system of production and the political economy of culture, since it is that very system which determines the boundaries, constraints and possibilities for production. As Meehan argues: 'Profit, not culture, drives show business: no business means no show' (Meehan, 1991: 48).

Prince as star vehicle

Prince has enjoyed an extremely prolific and, at certain moments, very popular musical career. A glance at his discography serves to underline his extraordinary output, both in terms of his collaboration with such groups as Grand Central Station, The Time and New Power Generation, as well as his solo career as both 'Prince' and 'The Artist'. Prince has struck an interesting figure: he is admired as a musical virtuoso and a skilled composer and producer. He is also known for his clean anti-drugs and -alcohol image and for his incredible capacity for hard work. More recently, he has gained a certain notoriety for the stance he took against Warner for the restrictions placed upon his artistic career.

Prince has responded to the idea of 'media synergy'. As Meehan argues, contemporary conglomerates 'view every project as a multimedia production line' (1991: 52). Like many other stars who work within the music industry, his image has been used to produce a large variety of by-products, which capitalise on his star persona. These range from the mundane and instantly obsolescent – calendars, T-shirts, biographies – to the New Power Generation (NPG) shop opened in Camden in 1994 selling Prince and NPG merchandise, and the major film productions *Purple Rain*, *Under the Cherry Moon*, *Sign o' the Times* and *Graffiti Bridge*.

Some commentators have argued that Prince's star persona rests on a fundamental set of oppositions. Pauline Kael, for example, pointed out in *New Yorker* in 1984, that Prince represents, 'godliness and promiscuity, machismo and effeminacy, spirituality and material ostentation, futurism and nostalgia, black rhythm and white rock' (quoted in Hill, 1989: 158). Yet Prince's ability to contain contradictory elements simultaneously amounts to perhaps the most important feature of his persona: his ambivalence. Prince doesn't so much swing from one opposition to the other, rather his persona tends to nestle somewhere in between, balancing, sometimes effectively, sometimes dangerously, mid-way between the two poles of the opposition. In this way, elements of his persona refuse to completely cohere: they represent clues and enigmas as opposed to complete meanings. Prince's version of heterosexual masculinity is never played 'straight'. The lyrics of 'If I Was Your Girlfriend' (1987), for example, articulate an ambisexuality which challenges traditional ideas about masculinity: 'Can't you trust me? If I was your girlfriend you could oh yeah I think so/ Listen for you naked I would dance a ballet would that get you off? Tell me what will?/ If I was your girlfriend would you tell me? Would you let me see you naked then?/ Would you let me give you a bath? Would you let me tickle you so hard you'd laugh and laugh?' Heterosexual masculinity is presented – as it is so often traditionally constructed – as essentially voyeuristic, but here it recognises the unique pleasures and erotic intimacy to be gained if only it could locate its viewing position from the one occupied by a female friend. Yet more radically these lyrics are about developing the type of relationship with a woman that might well be scorned by a fiercely conventional type of masculinity, for these words yearn for the kind of emotional bond with a lover that is usually only the preserve of close female friends: 'If I was your best friend would you let me take care of U and do all the things that only a best friend can/ . . . If I was your one and only friend would U run to me if somebody hurt you even if that somebody was me?'

Ambivalence has been an important, much exploited trading-tool for the careers of a range of music stars in an age where the maximisation of profit through the endless pursuit for new audiences is paramount. As Ellis argues, stars must refuse the presentation of themselves as fully formed or resolved if they are to successfully generate the necessary enigmas required for audiences to resolve them by purchasing star merchandise: 'The star image is . . . an *incomplete* image. It offers only the face, only the voice, only the still photo, where cinema offers the synthesis of voice, body and motion. The star image is paradoxical and incomplete so it functions as an invitation to cinema' (Ellis, 1982: 2–3). The members of British boy-band 'Take That', for example, were contractually bound never to admit to their sexual orientation. In this way their producers ensured that their star images refused fixity. As a result, they were able to generate a dominant public relations image based on good, clean, boyish heterosexuality, whilst ensuring that other possible meanings of their personae were not precluded. Clearly aware of their gay following, their producers ensured in their music video 'Pray', for example, that pleasures of the male gaze were not excluded. This strategy enabled them to garner 'pink pound' revenues with great commercial success.

In like manner, Prince's tendency to evade fixed sexual and racial identities has provided him with a wide set of marketing options and a means of appealing to a wide set of audiences. Prince, in the context of the music, television and film industries, is certainly 'different'; nowhere is this more apparent than when his persona is placed alongside the other black music and film stars in circulation since the late 1980s. Black militant rap artists such as Public Enemy based their identity on an overtly political African-American cultural identity. The science-fiction utopianism of funk artists Parliament and Funkadelic covertly articulated black consciousness and political action. A glance at some of Funkadelic's song titles and at the images of women that decorate their album sleeves confirms their brand of machismo. Pedro Bell's cartoon of a black woman with gigantic breasts and buttocks, featured on Funkadelic's 1978 album sleeve for 'Hardcore Jollies', testifies to a taken-for-granted, sexualised objectification of women. Prince breaks away from these notions of black masculinity. He offers a less bellicose instance of maleness. His eschewal of traditional masculinity appeals to audiences who seek something other than staunchly aggressive male personae. For example, college-educated women, who have encountered feminism, might find Prince's persona in 'If I Was Your Girlfriend' powerfully attractive: where else could one find notions of a non-threatening male confidante who might well become a lover?

However, while ambivalence can crack open commercial possibilities, it can also prove to be an extremely high-risk strategy. Few can
deny the sheer wit of Prince's ability to probe the marginal, slightly
more taboo aspects of sexuality – witness for example the Edwar-
dian coat, the sexy pout and the mock-innocent upward look Prince
wears on the album cover of *Controversy* (1981). Here, as elsewhere, Prince plays with the potential eroticism of perversion by
fashioning the coat into the 'flasher' pose. Yet he is too small and
lithe to ever qualify as a dominant, conventional macho male;
indeed, his physicality places him on rather more equal terms with
women. More at home as the 'switch', he occupies a number of
sexual subjectivities, often moving between dominant and submissive roles at will, demonstrating the non-fixity of heterosexuality.
Clearly, these more radical elements of Prince's persona have held
tremendous appeal for mainstream audiences. However, I would
argue that the more radical strands of Prince's persona have more
efficacy within the formal boundaries set by song lyrics, music videos
and album concepts. Mainstream audiences have been receptive to
these strands in the context of generic forms which deliberately foreground the artificiality of performance. Viewed in this context radical elements can be made 'safe' by coating them with fantasy. The
camp body-language that characterises Prince's performance techniques in the 1980s – his tight-buttocked swagger, his mock histrionic strut with head thrown back, his splits in high heels – can be
appreciated by audiences viewing his short music videos on MTV,
but, perhaps in some cases, only just. As RZA of the Wu-Tang Clan
commented in *The Face*, 'I might be flamboyant and shit, but Prince
is walking about with his arse hanging out of his pants. I'm not
saying he's gay, but how do you interpret that stuff?' (quoted in
Jones, 1998: 12). Comments such as these provide hints as to why
Under the Cherry Moon, a film which serves to stretch the boundaries of possibility for heterosexual masculinity still further, might
have proved disappointing at the box office.

Purple Rain

While the story of *Purple Rain* draws a loose mythical parallel with
Prince's early musical career, its narrative is fashioned rather awk-
wardly so as to platform concert footage from The Revolution. In
this sense, *Purple Rain* is a generic hybrid that draws as much from
the dream-like elements of 'rock'n'roll' movies as it does from other

mainstream narrative feature films in its cycle. For example, the antecedents of *Purple Rain* are apparent in a film such as *The Song Remains The Same* (1976), which intersperses images of Led Zeppelin's rock stars acting out their fantasy ambitions with clips from their 1973 Madison stage performances. *Purple Rain* is also part-fantasy tale in as much as its narrative hinges on the anticipation of Prince's imminent stardom, indeed on his birth as a 'rock messiah'. Thus, *Purple Rain* offers a safe yet inventive showcase at a vulnerable point in Prince's career: it provides a means of documenting Prince's rise to stardom while at the same time enabling him to perform becoming a star. Yet, in the final analysis, Purple Films Company and Warner Communications Inc. (WCI) minimised the financial risks of *Purple Rain* by virtually lifting Prince's already established musical persona. The film is a loose docu-biography. While Prince is given a pseudonym – 'The Kid' – Morris Day, Jerome Benton, Wendy, Lisa, indeed, the rest of the musical cast, play themselves. In this way, *Purple Rain* can hardly be credited with being the film that allowed Prince to cross over into mainstream Hollywood cinema as a character actor. Rather, WCI tested out the possibilities of Prince's mainstream cross-over possibilities using a number of fail-safe strategies that tended to empty Prince's persona of its radical potential, particularly in relation to race and gender. The real cross-over challenge still awaited Prince in *Under the Cherry Moon*.

For WCI, Prince's package of musical abilities as multi-instrumental composer, singer and producer was reminiscent of Stevie Wonder, another black artist, who had broken out of the black music charts in the mid-1970s into the far more profitable musical compartments that American leisure capitalism had developed. *Purple Rain* illustrates a similar attempt to lift Prince out of the black music 'ghetto' across to a white leisure audience. Prince had already chosen to construct a racially ambivalent identity in ways that have ultimately allowed him to service as many markets as possible: in terms of race he looked to where maximum profits lie. His musical lineage comprised black artists such as Sly Stone and Jimi Hendrix who were out to prove that they too could 'do' rock. They were exceptional black musicians who were able, arguably, to outplay their lumbering white rock counterparts. From Minneapolis, Minnesota, Prince already came from a part of the United States where black people were in a minority. Hill claims in his biography, *Prince: A Pop Life*, that it was commonly known as a 'vanilla market' (1989: 6). Prince started out playing in two kinds of arenas: small funk venues, and larger clubs with pre-dominantly white audiences. His strategy of holding black audiences, while always aspiring to cross over to the far more profitable white leisure audience, has informed the construction of his image through-out his career. Unlike 1970s funk artists such as George Clinton – the driving force behind Parliament and Funkadelic, whose identity was black without apology – Prince has never been overtly political about being black. While it would be wrong to rule out the possibility of 'rad-ical' moments in his career, which might render central ideological positions unstable, several of Prince's early interviews testify to a will to consciously opt out of a black identity: 'My mum is a mixture of a bunch of things. I don't consider myself part of any race. I'm just a human being, I suppose' (Hill, 1989: 72). Indeed, Hill argues that the industry strategy in the early 1980s was about laundering Prince to predominantly white audiences as 'un-black' (1989: 83). It was cer-tainly a strategy that was to enable Prince to open markets that an artist like Clinton could never access. In *Purple Rain*, the actors who play his parents were selected precisely so that the Kid (Prince) would look as though he was the offspring of a multiracial marriage. While Prince's parents both define themselves as black, a black actor played the Kid's father (Clarence Williams III) and a Greek actress his mother (Olga Karlatos). Clearly this decision was made so as to appeal to a main-stream audience whose preference was for a whiter skin. It is more likely, however, that Prince's producers were more concerned with holding on to the opportunities racial ambivalence might spawn: *Purple Rain* illustrates a will to allow audiences the prerogative to interpret Prince's racial identity in multiple ways. And, in the same way that the film anticipates Prince's stardom, it also projects the birth of that stardom taking place in front of a predominantly white American audience with only a smattering of young African-Americans. Closer inspection of that audience reveals a desire to include rock, new wave and indeed new romantic trends: men and women sport lace, make-up and white frills – Steve Strange would not be out of place in these audience panoramas.

Purple Rain measures up to the more rigidly conventional aspects of heterosexuality. Just as The Time are pitched against The Revo-lution in a contest of musical talent, Morris and the Kid are roman-tic rivals for the affection of Apollonia (Apollonia Kotero), but she resists Morris's cloying attempts at seduction. Portrayed as a fawn-ing admirer, Apollonia is shown gullibly succumbing to every courtship trap that The Kid lays for her, which includes stripping naked by a lake at The Kid's command. In her desire to seek fame she accepts The Kid's violent treatment and she is shown, albeit clothed in a basque, in full frontal position during the sex scene in the Kid's bedroom. *Purple Rain*, as Hill remarks, 'is not a feminist film' (1989: 149). In dialectical opposition to the way in which the film represents women, the film's men play out their roles in typically macho fashion. Prince's body in concert footage, though frequently undercut by purposeful high-heeled walking backstage to his dressing room, is often shot in ways which highlight the muscularity of his well-oiled (albeit miniature) chest. We also see him mock grinding in missionary position during his performance of 'Darling Nikki'. As is so frequently the case in mainstream popular cinema, there were no radical risks here in terms of the way in which *Purple Rain* represents gender.

However, although it is important to consider the kind of text that the industry was prepared to back, it is relevant to bear in mind Meehan's maxim that, 'For much of American culture, corporate imperatives operate as the primary constraints shaping the narratives and iconography of the text as well as the manufacture and licensing of the intertextual materials' (1991: 48). Meehan documents that between 1982 and 1989 WCI developed from being a diversified conglomerate, which included media interests, to becoming a highly concentrated and integrated media conglomerate. In 1989, WCI merged with Time Inc. to produce Time Warner, the largest media conglomerate in the world. In the years prior to 1989, to guarantee its expansion into a big media conglomerate WCI had to increase profits. In real terms this meant maximising revenues from each project, whether from box office sales or from 'recycling through WCI's non-film outlets' (Meehan, 1991: 51). Thus, film soundtracks offered recycling possibilities as repackaged CDs and music videos, which in turn could be distributed as recorded music or given airplay via MTV networks. Indeed, it is precisely this backdrop of corporate action that forms the conditions surrounding the production and distribution of Prince's star persona in *Purple Rain*. WCI distributed not only *Purple Rain* but also its attendant, recyclable, star-based products including several music videos, an album and multiple publishing projects. In fact, WCI declined the offer to finance the film; instead it was independently made by Purple Films Company. WCI's decision to distribute *Purple Rain* was made purely because of its potential to offer revenue from a vast array of related products. Therefore, as far as WCI was concerned, *Purple Rain* did not warrant ownership or a significant budget since the film itself was only one component in a production line that extended way beyond the boundaries of the cinema. Indeed, one could argue that the film merely acted as an advertisement for related Prince and *Purple Rain* multi-media products, from music videos to ephemera such as key-rings and calendars. Certainly, the viability of *Purple Rain*'s distribution was assessed according to the potential the project offered for leverage in other markets. Arguably, these criteria demonstrate that industrial interests actually became etched into the very fabric of the film; economics dictated the aesthetic choices that contributed to the overall 'look' of *Purple Rain*. As Meehan suggests, 'WCI's reluctance to finance the film project may explain why *Purple Rain* looks like half a dozen videos stitched together by a loose narrative' (1991: 52). Ultimately, Prince's star vehicle was only of interest to the industry insofar as it presented opportunities for what Schatz calls 'multimedia reincarnation' (1993: 31). Whether or not *Purple Rain* held any narrative integrity bore little consequence for the film's producers. Indeed, the meanings of Prince's persona were of scant interest, as long as they held sufficient cultural cachet to ensure that they were open to multimedia exploitation. In the end, *Purple Rain* was a commercial success in its own right (it made $65 million in its first year alone) and the host of revenue-earning reiterated products it spawned persuaded WCI to finance *Under the Cherry Moon*, with twice the budget of its precursor.

Under the Cherry Moon

As William Goldman famously remarked in 1983, 'nobody knows anything' when it comes to forecasting the market value of cultural commodities (Goldman, 1983: 39). As Schatz suggests, 'despite all the market studies and promotional strategies, the kind of public response that generates a bona fide hit simply cannot be manufactured, calculated or predicted' (1993: 28). The industry, therefore, acts paradoxically by taking risks and working to minimise them. In order to do so, it works by a basic set of rules which are designed to both supplement and counter Goldman's maxim. *Under the Cherry Moon* already met the terms of these rules at the time of its release: it had a star vehicle; risks were minimised by previous hits – a film, a number of pop songs and complementary music videos, published materials and a host of related ephemera; and like *Purple Rain* it had the same potential for multi-media reiteration. In order to assess why the film flopped, taking with it WCI's $12 million investment, we need to examine both the textual organisation of Prince's star persona as well as the efficacy of the co-ordination of the diversified products that *Under the Cherry Moon* generated.

Under the Cherry Moon is an interesting example of a film that attempts to break with conventional portrayals of black men in mainstream cinema. Set on the French Riviera, the film is loosely modelled on romantic comedies of the 1930s and 1940s, yet there are also sufficient contemporary references to make one think that the film might be set in the present day. Prince plays Christopher Tracy, a playboy-cum-gigolo who works as a bar pianist. He and his partner Tricky (Jerome Benton) have travelled from Miami in the hope of marrying money.

In this context, Prince's role is problematic. Traditionally, the playboy is a predominantly white construction. Barbara Ehrenreich argues that during the 1950s white men grew tired of the patriarchal ideal of masculinity, based on caring for wife and children, and instead sought an escape in the idealised role of the playboy:

> They had stealthy affairs with secretaries, and tried to feel up their neighbors' wives at parties. They escaped into Mickey Spillane mysteries, where naked blondes were routinely perforated in a hail of bullets, or into Westerns, where there were no women at all and no visible sources of white-collar employment. And some of them began to discover an alternative, or at least an entirely new style of male rebel who hinted, seductively, that there was an alternative. The new rebel was the playboy. (Ehrenreich, quoted in hooks, 1992: 95)

Ehrenreich's envisaged playboy, here undoubtedly a white figure, might well explain why musical stars such as Sinatra and, to some extent, Elvis were able to take on playboy film roles with relative ease. Both Sinatra and Elvis were solid, straightforwardly hetero-sexual, white men whose popularity was virtually guaranteed in the films in which they starred. Prince's part as a black playboy is more difficult when one considers that he had no tradition of black play-boy roles within which to set himself. While Prince could quite safely play with images of active sexuality in terms of his musical career, following in the footsteps of a tradition of overtly sexual black 1970s funk artists such as the Ohio Players and Rick James, to take on a character role of this kind was far more risky. Yet his attempt to set a black lounge lizard in the context of the South of France as opposed to an urban setting, such as New York, works as an alternative image of black masculinity. More pertinently though, Prince's version of the black gigolo-cum-playboy stretches the boundaries of heterosexual masculine identity. Christopher's clothes in the film deserve mention here: in the first scene he sits behind his piano, in a head-dress reminiscent of 1920s women's flapperwear, and later, after a pre-coital drive around a race track with Mary (Kristin Scott Thomas), he runs in pursuit of her in a white lace outfit and high heels. Indeed most of the outfits he wears are flouncy and sensuous, fashioned from 'feminine' fabrics in pastel shades, and decorated with pearls, diamante or lace. Buttons are big, collars are high and bell bottoms are wide; these are not the clothes one usually associates with masculine forms of dress.

However, there is yet more subversion. Christopher's version of a playboy is not the sexual predator in this narrative; rather it is the women he encounters who prey sexually on him. The opening shows Christopher rapturously playing his piano for the delight and patronage of Mary's rich and beautiful mother (Francesca Annis): he must dance to the tune of the women who pay for his favours. Towards the end of the film, Mary's father Issac (Steven Berkoff), shouts his disapproval of her relationship with Christopher after her, 'that man's a gigolo, do you know what that means? It means he's a whore.' Christopher's behaviour prompts those around him to curse him with swear words usually used pejoratively against women. Moreover, Christopher comes to Nice in the hope of finding a woman whose fortune he can mine – whereas it is traditionally women who are portrayed in cinema as amoral, heartless gold-diggers.

Prince further subverts our expectations of the genre by injecting black-American cultural mores into the language of the lounge lizard. The script is replete with jokes, mostly played out between Christopher and Tricky, that snipe at the disdain whites associate with black culture. Using Southern accents and a set of culturally different idioms previously unknown to the genre, Christopher and Tricky play two quick-witted black pranksters who manage to undermine the priggish white world in which they find themselves. The pair knowingly parody the stereotypes of black people that abound in white culture, particularly in relation to language, music and sexuality. For instance, between courses at an expensive restaurant, Christopher insists that Mary read his phonetic spelling of the place where, as he phrases it 'you would buy a Sam Cooke album'. Christopher and Tricky fall into paroxysms of mirth as Mary, in an eloquent English accent is forced to repeat, in a way that reveals her complete lack of cultural competence, the words 'Wrecka Stow'. Prince's direction of these scenes testifies to an impudent will to flout the conventions of a genre where black people had previously been marginalised or stereotyped.

Unfortunately, while these strands of potential radicalism show an attempt to represent black heterosexuality differently, Prince's use of a particular kind of camp in his performance tends to overlay his role with the kind of mannered, narcissistic overstatement that corrodes the audience's sympathy for his character. Camp could have supported the subversiveness of the role, but it needed to be sharper and more conscious of its own sense of exaggeration. As a result, critics at the time were vitriolic in their attack – one called Christopher 'a self-caressing twerp' (quoted in Jones, 1998: illustration 11) – and it is likely that large sections of the audience found the pouting vanity of Prince's performance alienating. In the final analysis, however, it was the culturally progressive aspects of Christopher's representation of black masculinity within a genre so traditionally preserved for white actors that mainstream audiences found hard to swallow.

However, it was also the co-ordination strategy of Prince's related products that played a major role in the film's poor box-office returns. Probably as a result of the success of *Purple Rain*, WCI agreed to finance the film's production in the knowledge that the film had potential commercial spin-offs. However, the decision was made to shoot some of the music videos independently as opposed to recycling aspects of the film; the music video for 'Kiss', for example, features only Prince and Wendy Melvoin in a pared-down musical stage performance. It might well have been the case that WCI decided that videos carved out of *Under the Cherry Moon* featured Prince's persona in a way that was too bound into the character and narrative development of the film to successfully market his musical off-shoots. In his discussion of New Hollywood, Schatz argues that 'Competing successfully in today's high-stakes entertainment marketplace requires an operation that is not only well financed and productive, but also diversified and well coordinated.' There has been a trend, therefore, towards what he calls 'tight diversification' so that commercial success in the cinema can be positioned closely alongside related products showcased by record companies, network television and magazine publishing (Schatz, 1993: 29). This kind of co-ordination ensures that hits can market the other reiterated products in the synergy chain to their maximum potential. Considered under these terms, the commercial intertextual management of Prince's persona in the *Under the Cherry Moon* project is found wanting. Audiences at that time were used to seeing Prince's rock persona performing hits such 'Kiss' on MTV, only to be faced with the culture-shock of black and white images of a 1930s-style camp lounge-lizard performing the same track in the cinema. That, coupled with the very different representational messages about gender, race and sexuality that *Under the Cherry Moon* carried, proved too much for audiences to handle. Yet, as far as WCI were concerned, the failure of the film component of the project was probably no great loss in commercial terms. Off-shoot merchandise – for example, the album *Parade*, with its attendant singles and videos – would form the commercially successful aspects of the commodity repertoire. In true conglomerate fashion, WCI merely used *Under the Cherry Moon* as a product line to satisfy its hunger for profits among its internal markets in television, print, music and video.

Under the Cherry Moon was the last feature where Prince would take on a true character role. Subsequently, Prince turned back to being a music star whose concerts were recorded. The films that followed, *Sign o' the Times* and *Graffiti Bridge*, are even less ambitious in narrative terms than *Purple Rain*. The former is an unapologetic recording of the album tour; the latter a sequel to *Purple Rain* which contains little more than concert footage scenes of 'The Symbol' aka Prince and The Time engaged in the same kind of musical jousting that had characterised the earlier film.

These later productions merely continued the industry strategy that WCI had exercised with *Purple Rain* and *Under the Cherry Moon*. Yet again, WCI's key aim was to intensively mine their stock of materials for further off-shoots. These later films gave visual backing to the aural experience of Prince's music products in yet another commodity package to an MTV-loyal, 15–35–year-old, chiefly white, middle-class audience. The crucial difference was that WCI had decided to ensure that Prince could still be a star, but this time in strictly musical terms. If any one of the executives at Warner had ever re-considered the idea of backing Prince in a character role that stepped outside the terms of his musical persona, they need only think back to the reviews of *Under the Cherry Moon*. 'For all those who can't get enough of Prince, *Under the Cherry Moon* may just be the antidote', the *New York Times* had remarked. 'Don't even turn up in the same continent where this is playing', said *USA Today* (quoted in Jones, 1998: 105–6). For WCI, Prince's star vehicle was too commercially valuable to ever suffer that kind of damage again.

Note

1   Prince has used a number of names throughout his career, I use this name throughout for simplicity.

Bibliography

Ehrenreich, B. (1984) *The Hearts of Men: American Dreams and the Flight from Commitment*, New York: Doubleday.

Ellis, J. (1982) *Visible Fictions*, London: Routledge.

Fiske, J. (1989) *Reading the Popular*, London: Routledge.

Goldman, W. (1983) *Adventures in the Screen Trade*, New York: Warner Books.

Hill, D. (1989) *Prince: A Pop Life*, London: Faber and Faber.

hooks, b. (1992) *Black Looks: Race and Representation*, London: Turnaround.

Jones, L. (1998) *Slave to the Rhythm*, London: Warner Books.

Kellner, D. (1995) *Media Culture: Cultural Studies, Identity and Politics Between the Modern and the Postmodern*, London: Routledge.

Kellner, D. (1997) 'Critical Theory and Cultural Studies: The Missed Articulation', in J. McGuigan (ed.), *Cultural Methodologies*, London: Sage.

McGuigan, J. (1997) 'Cultural Populism Revisited', in M. Ferguson and P. Golding (eds), *Cultural Studies in Question*, London: Sage.

Meehan, E. (1991) '"Holy Commodity Fetish, Batman!": The Political Economy of a Commercial Intertext', in R. E. Pearson and W. Uricchio (eds), *The Many Lives of The Batman: Critical Approaches to a Superhero and his Media*, London: Routledge/British Film Institute.

Schatz, T. (1993) 'The New Hollywood', in J. Collins *et al.* (eds), *Film Theory Goes to the Movies*, New York: Routledge.

Stacey, J. (1994) *Star Gazing: Hollywood Cinema and Female Spectatorship*, London: Routledge.

9

Cynthia Rothrock:
from the ghetto of exploitation

Andy Willis

Yvonne Tasker observes that 'Cynthia Rothrock has repeatedly been described as an unlikely action heroine' (1993: 24). This may be because she is blond and petite; however, due to her impressive credentials within the related worlds of martial arts competition and the Hong Kong film industry she has forged something of a unique career. There have been other female martial artists who have attempted to establish themselves in films, such as kick-boxing champion Kathy Long, but none has managed to equal the standing of Cynthia Rothrock, who has appeared in over thirty films and television programmes. For this alone she is a rare performer. However, her achievements have been largely ignored by critics who have chosen instead to concentrate their thinking on the muscle-bound male heroes of the 1980s and 1990s. This might be explained by the fact that since her return to the USA from working in Hong Kong, Rothrock has worked almost exclusively in what might be described as exploitation cinema. In this chapter I want to explore the idea of exploitation cinema and consider the forces that come to bear on, and help mould, a 'star' who has chosen to work in the field of martial arts cinema in the USA.

Cynthia Rothrock made the move into action cinema following a successful career within competitive martial arts. This is an important aspect of her career, as it laid the foundation for her acceptance by the fans of martial arts movies who place a great deal of store in the idea of 'authenticity'. Her website (www.cynthiarothrock.org) proudly proclaims that 'From 1981–1985 she was the undefeated World Karate Champion in both forms and weapon competition', going on to state, impressively, that 'She is a consummate performer with such Chinese weapons as the Chinese Double Broad Swords,

Staff, Chinese Nine-section Steel Whip, Chinese Iron Fan, and an assortment of Okinawan Kobudo and Japanese Bugei Weapons'. It followed that producers began to think that if she can become a world champion she should be able to translate those moves onto the screen. In 1985, after making her acting debut in an advertisement for Kentucky Fried Chicken, Rothrock, the holder of five black belts in Eastern martial arts, began her career within the Hong Kong film industry. This is significant due to the fact that in Hong Kong it was possible for female performers to be widely accepted in the lead and supporting roles in action movies, in a way they were not in the USA. Yvonne Tasker acknowledges this when she says that 'The different conventions and traditions of the Hong Kong cinema allow all sorts of characters . . . to be fighters' (1993: 25). Rothrock's first appearance was as co-lead in a production entitled *Yes, Madam* (1985). Here she appeared alongside Michelle Khan, who would later find international stardom as Michelle Yeoh. Directed by Corey Yuen (Yuen Kwai), the film was a big hit at the Hong Kong box office and was followed by a series of other films directed by Yuen, including *Blonde Fury* (1988) and *No Retreat, No Surrender II* (1989). She was firmly established on the Hong Kong action scene, and other successful projects saw Rothrock appear alongside high-profile Hong Kong performers such as Sammo Hung in *Shanghai Express* (1986) and Yuen Biao in *Righting Wrongs* (also directed by Corey Yuen; 1987). In this period, Cynthia Rothrock had quickly become one of the few western performers to successfully take lead roles in Hong Kong martial arts film productions.

This success in Hong Kong led producers at Golden Harvest, a major player in the Hong Kong film industry, to consider Rothrock as having the potential to 'cross over' into the lucrative US market place. They had previously attempted this by offering Jackie Chan to US audiences as the new Bruce Lee in *The Big Brawl* (directed by Robert Clouse; 1980). However, they thought the fact that Rothrock was actually American might give her an advantage over failures such as Chan. Once again Golden Harvest employed Robert Clouse, who had made the enormously successful *Enter the Dragon* (1973), to direct the film, hoping that he would be able to work some of the fading magic from his collaboration with Bruce Lee. They chose to make two films back to back, which became *China O'Brien* (1988) and *China O'Brien 2* (1988). The approach, as with *The Big Brawl*, involved creating a more 'American' format for the performer. Here, Rothrock plays Lori 'China' O'Brien, a cop who leaves the force after an accident and ends up 'cleaning up' the corruption in her father's town. As Yvonne Tasker points out, the film is put together in such a way as to offer narrative moments that showcase Rothrock's martial arts talents, such as a fight in a bar (1993: 25). These sequences reveal the tension between the creation of action and the importance of femininity to Rothrock's image, as she performs her fights wearing high heels. However, once again Golden Harvest's attempt to break into the US market failed as both films under-performed at the North American box office. Significantly, the films were able to take advantage of the growing video rental market as they both became huge successes in this format. This new development marked the future direction for Rothrock's career in the US, establishing her as a bankable action performer in this form of distribution, and leading to her being dubbed 'the video queen of martial arts' by her own website.

As Brian A. Austin has argued, videocassettes provided another important mode of distribution for feature films. Introduced to the North American consumer market in 1975, the major boom in VCR ownership took place in the 1980s. According to Austin, 56 per cent of North American homes owned VCRs by 1988, which coincided with Cynthia Rothrock's move into the US action movie market. Because of this new technology, fresh patterns of consumption emerged in this period. Low-budget, exploitation filmmakers who had previously placed their products in drive-in theatres and inner-city cinemas now saw a new distribution network emerging. Video, initially seen as a minor threat by the Hollywood studios, was embraced by exploitation movie moguls. Again as Austin notes, 'the impact of home video . . . may have important consequences for independent [those not tied to the studios] filmmakers. In particular, new markets for the products of the Hollywood outsiders could result. Already we have seen independent production of horror/ slasher films targeted to the teenage audience in the home' (1990: 340). The impact of video consumption on the audiences for type of martial arts films that Rothrock was making was equally great. They were primarily consumed by under-23s, and in particular teenage males. According to Austin, research showed that this group quickly took to video consumption: 'teenagers spend more than twice the number of hours watching films on videocassette than in movie theatres' (1990: 342). This change in audience consumption patterns paved the way for video stars, whose films, whilst either poorly received at cinemas or even unreleased theatrically, were now bankable in the home viewing market. As Yvonne Tasker notes, 'Rothrock was important on the video martial-arts scene' (1993: 24): a performer whose films may fail in the theatrical market place but whose work found a dedicated and enthusiastic audience in the realm of video releases.

It is therefore possible to argue that the poor response by audiences to the theatrical release of the China O'Brien films, along with their popularity on video, pushed Rothrock firmly into the confines of North American exploitation cinema. Here producers were able to exploit her talents by delivering a very particular martial-arts-based product to a niche market of fans. However, this has created a situation where Rothrock has been forced to accept that success in this market has meant her opportunities to cross over into mainstream, Hollywood, productions have become limited. The demands of a martial arts performer, as I discuss later, are very particular and, it might be argued, have forced Rothrock into what might be termed a 'ghetto of exploitation' – one from which, whilst she has made over thirty features, she has found it difficult to escape.

Exploitation cinema, some definitions

The term 'exploitation cinema' is certainly not easy to define. Whilst there may be some clear elements that make a film 'exploitation', the limits of the term and the political potential of exploitation films have made any clear assertion of meaning difficult. Amongst this, the relationship of exploitation films to the so-called mainstream is probably the most difficult element of this struggle for definition. Thomas Doherty argues that the term 'exploitation' operates in three distinct and sometimes overlapping ways within the American film industry. Firstly, it refers to 'the advertising and promotion that entices an audience into a theatre (1988: 3). However, he argues that the film industry generally operates in this exploitative way. Its advertising and promotion is clearly aimed to entice an audience to its product. This point is reflected in Justin Wyatt's (1994) work on 'high concept', in which he argues that contemporary Hollywood is marked by this type of exploitation:

> The high concept films therefore depend upon the visual representation of their marketable concepts in advertising. Advertising is the key

to the commercial success of these films through representing the mar-
ketable concepts of the films, but, more basically, advertising as a
medium of expression is fundamental to the very construction of the
high concept films. (Wyatt, 1994: 23)

As has traditionally been argued with regard to exploitation films,
Wyatt argues that the importance of marketing, advertising and promotion has gone so far as to impact upon the actual construction of
the films themselves. This definition of 'exploitation' therefore
becomes limited, as it does not distinguish exploitation films from
those produced within the so-called mainstream. Other uses of the
term exploitation are more focused on creating a distinction between
legitimate mainstream products and those that are produced within
the less central parts of the industry. Jim Hillier argues that

> The term 'exploitation' differentiates a certain kind of overly exploita-
> tive product from the supposedly non-exploitative product of the
> majors, and implies that movies thus labelled take advantage of their
> audiences, for example by promising more than they deliver – in effect
> by cheating. (Hillier, 1992: 40)

This links with Doherty's second way in which the term exploitation
operates within the American film industry, 'the way the movie
endears itself to that audience' (1988: 3). Whilst again he argues that
this type of exploitation was present in the Hollywood film industry
generally, in so much as 'the wise moviemaker "exploited" what he
knew about an audience by catering to its desires and meeting its
expectations' (Doherty, 1988: 6), it is this manipulation that Doherty
sees as particularly exploitative. The marketing of exploitation
movies therefore demands a certain level of mutual knowledge on
behalf of the filmmakers and their audience. The promotional materials produced for exploitation films had to create a sense of dialogue
between filmmaker, film and potential audience. This dialogue was
dependent upon the marketing departments knowing who their
potential audience was in some detail. Hillier picks up on this point
when he explains that exploitation movies could be targeted 'not at
a general audience but rather at the youth market that the majors,
particularly in the 1960s and 1970s, were failing to cater for'. He
also discusses the ways in which new outlets for exploitation pictures
impacted upon their reaching particular audiences in this period. For
instance, downtown movie houses now became an important outlet
for the exploitation product because they 'attracted a predominantly

male, working-class audience' (Hillier, 1992: 40). Many of these theatres would have a reputation for showing martial-arts-based films, anything from 'blaxpolitation' movies that included martial arts, such as *Cleopatra Jones* (1973), to dubbed Hong Kong imports, such as *Five Fingers of Death* (1973). Martial arts had therefore been a mainstay of exploitation cinema since the 1970s.

Whilst these points lead to an understanding of why certain films exploit both the audience and production staff, it is Doherty's third use of the term exploitation within the Hollywood film industry that is most relevant in relation to martial-arts films. He argues that it is used to define 'a particular kind of movie' (Doherty, 1988: 3) and that by the 1950s this kind of movie was commonly seen in a negative light. According to Doherty this related closely to subject matter that was 'timely and sensational'. This linked to a growing appetite amongst certain elements of the audience for 'the bizarre, the licentious, and the sensational' and led to the growing division between exploitation films and the more 'serious' products of the Hollywood majors, which in turn fostered the idea that exploitation fare was certainly a less serious product. Doherty argues that in the 1950s the exploitation formula had three strong elements that often contributed to its being seen as a lesser form of filmmaking,

> (1) Controversial, bizarre, or timely subject matter amenable to wild promotion (exploitation potential in its original sense); (2) a substandard budget; and (3) a teenage audience. Movies of this ilk are triply exploitative, simultaneously exploiting sensational happenings (for story value), their notoriety (for publicity value), and their teenage participants (for box-office value). Around 1955–56, 'exploitation film' in this sense had become fairly common usage within the industry. (Doherty, 1988: 8)

Martial-arts films, produced in America, seem to fit these definitions well. They appeal to young audiences and often offer the promise of violence. Bearing in mind this tradition of low-budget filmmaking it is not surprising that when performers have become very closely associated with such filmmaking styles they are unable to reinvent themselves in the mainstream. A good example is the actor David Carradine, who, even though he has worked with the likes of Ingmar Bergman, is widely seen as an exploitation actor. Cynthia Rothrock is in a similar position. However, in her case this is due to the very particular demands on martial-arts films and performers made by their target audience, as I discuss below.

Exploitation films and martial arts

Roger Corman is often seen as the king of the exploitation movie. Indeed, he himself has promoted himself in such a way, calling his biography, *How I Made a Hundred Movies in Hollywood and Never Lost a Dime* (1990). In 1970, after a career in the exploitation field, Corman formed a production company, New World Pictures, with his brother Gene and with Larry Woolner. Since then, Corman and New World have become the focus of some of the most important academic work on the exploitation field (Hillier and Lipstadt, 1981, 1986; Hillier, 1992), which provides some useful insights into the links between traditional genres and the exploitation 'cycles' favoured by production companies such as New World. One of the most significant aspects of the company was that from the outset it was concerned with distribution as well as production. The control of both areas was of particular concern to Corman, who had been pushed towards the formation of the company in an attempt to prevent what he perceived as the mishandling of his pictures by others. This position had certainly been arrived at following the fact that his film *Gas-s-s* (1970) had been re-edited against his wishes by its distributor American International Pictures.

The early development of New World between 1970 and 1973 set certain important trends for the company that, it may be argued, are still typical of the practices of exploitation production companies more generally. New World's first film *Student Nurses* (1970) proved to be an enormous success and, according to Hillier and Lipstadt, encouraged the company to initiate a series of films that dealt with 'groups of professional (and of course reputedly titillating sexually) women. All featured three or four heroines and dealt with their professional / romantic problems; all ran between 81 and 87 minutes; all were set in the present, usually in California; all were rated R' (1981: 3). During this period New World also initiated a series of women in prison films following the success of *The Big Doll House* (1971). The importance of prison films to the exploitation tradition generally and Corman's companies in particular is something that would later link with an interest in martial-arts-based films.

The importance of cycles within exploitation cinema is noted by Aaron Lipstadt, who argues that a cycle

> has a life of its own; it appears, as indicated by the definition of exploitation films, on the heels of an event or successful movie. Several

independent companies, and maybe even some of the majors, will quickly commission a script and shoot a film which apes the prototype, particularly in the details that are thought to contribute to its success. Speed of production and widespread bookings are typical, especially in the summer months when school is out, the drive-ins are open, and the kids are looking for excitement. (Lipstadt, 1981: 10–11)

The exploitation of mainstream success, however, is no longer simply the realm of the so-called exploitation companies. The major studios now also attempt to create financial success out of models that have in the past proved successful for others. This partly explains the continual promotion of sequels to even moderately successful major productions. Often these sequels are put into production before the financial success of the original has been fully calculated.

The quick follow-up of success is also evident within martial-arts film production, and this aspect places it firmly within the exploitation tradition of filmmaking. This is particularly evident in relation to martial-arts film production in the late 1980s. For example, the success of *Blood Sport* (1987), Cannon films' vehicle for Jean-Claude van Damme, led to the production of a large number of films that used the martial-arts competition to structure their narratives. This then subsequently forms a 'cycle' in the manner outlined by Lipstadt. Certainly this is supported by the fact that Pyramid Entertainment exploited the success of the earlier film by quickly producing another van Damme film that focused on a martial arts competition, 1989's *Kickboxer*. Other films that 'exploited' the success of *Blood Sport* in particular and van Damme's image more generally include *Death Match* (1993); *King of the Kickboxers* (1993); *Rage: Ring of Fire II* (1994); and *Savate* (1994). Indeed, the competition narrative played an important, but not singular, role in the narrative of van Damme's next film *AWOL* (1990) (also known as *Lionheart* and *Wrong Bet*). Again, this shows how once initiated a cycle can have a longevity well beyond the period of the initial film's, or films', success. In the case of martial-arts films, competition narratives were still being produced well into the late 1990s. It is this emphasis on cycles, and the fact that production companies demanded the inclusion of certain 'vital' ingredients and little else, that potentially allowed space for those involved in exploitation film-making to, should they wish, explore a number of what might be broadly labelled 'political' issues within their productions.

Rothrock's the 'real deal': authenticity and the martial-arts performer

One of the main criteria used by martial arts fans to select those performers they champion is 'authenticity'. The fact that much of the fan material about Cynthia Rothrock highlights her real-life martial-arts achievements, and that many publicity pictures have her posed with weapons from her championship disciplines, indicate that this is an important aspect of her as a performer. In his article, '*A Star is Born* and the Construction of Authenticity', Richard Dyer argues that the idea of authenticity in relation to film stars leads to their being associated with words such as 'sincere, immediate, spontaneous, real, direct, genuine and so on'. He goes on to say that 'it is these qualities that we demand of a star if we accept her or him in the spirit in which she or he is offered' (Dyer, 1991: 133). This may be related to martial-arts film performers in a number of production contexts. The idea that martial-arts performers can actually perform the actions we see them do on screen is their mark of authenticity. Jackie Chan, for example, always includes a series of out-takes at the end of each of his feature films. These out-takes often show Chan performing dangerous stunts that have gone wrong, and amazing feats of athleticism. For example, the ending of *Supercop* (also known as *Police Story 3*) (1992) shows Chan being accidentally hit by a passing helicopter as he attempts to perform a stunt whilst on the top of a moving train. We then witness him being eased down from the train to the medical support team who have been standing by. These out-take endings clearly work to reinforce the idea that Jackie Chan performs all his own stunts on his productions, even those which are highly dangerous and would have other actors calling for a stand-in. Through these important moments *he* becomes the authentic action performer, offering us confirmation of this through our witnessing his 'accidents'. These sequences, and Chan's commitment to stunt work, are used by fans as a way of demarcating between the 'real' and the 'play' action men. Jackie Chan's star persona relies very heavily on this creation of an almost mythic authenticity, continually the subject of talk-show appearances and magazine articles. Indeed, his break-out US box-office hit *Rumble in the Bronx* (1994) was marketed in some places with the line 'No doubles, no stuntmen, just Jackie Chan' emblazoned across posters.

If martial-arts movie fans therefore seek out this confirmation of a performer's authenticity, it helps explain why Jackie Chan is held in such high regard. As Dyer argues, 'we no longer ask if someone performs well . . . but whether what they perform is truthful, with the referent of truthfulness not being falsiable statements but the person's "person"' (1991: 133). For many martial-arts movie fans then, the actuality of experience and 'real' martial-arts skills are at the heart of their admiration for an actor, the rather problematic assumption at work here being that the 'real' skills of the performer are simply transposed onto the screen. Of course they cannot be, so a great deal of effort is spent in the creation of an authentic persona through other related media texts. For example, at the height of his popularity in the 1990s, Jean-Claude van Damme often appeared on chat shows promoting his latest releases. When he did it was likely that he would be asked to perform a trademark high kick. He almost always obliged, usually missing the presenter's head by inches, and achieving some level of authenticity by doing so. It would be fair to assume that van Damme realised that the appearance of such actions in these related media texts acted as a guarantor of his authentic martial-arts skills, proof that he could actually 'do it'. In a similar vein, a variety of unconfirmed stories circulated concerning the involvement of another action star, Steven Seagal, with the CIA in Asia. Whenever this topic is raised in interviews he carefully neither confirmed nor denied these stories, rather he refused to talk about them. The 'refusal' here worked to create a myth suggesting that the stories may well be true. In a similar fashion to van Damme, he thereby reinforced his authentic action persona.

As many martial-arts fans prefer Hong Kong films, seeing them as in themselves 'more authentic' because of their origin, those working in the US film industry have similarly sought to create auras of authenticity for their performers. Cynthia Rothrock has two things that her persona has sought to exploit: her real-life martial-arts skills and her cinematic origins in the 'real' Hong Kong film industry, where as noted earlier she had worked with 'real' performers such as Sammo Hung and Yuen Biao. Rothrock, as a female performer appearing in martial-arts-based action films, has had to employ similar strategies in an attempt to create a genuine, 'real' and authentic persona. In her case these strategies have manifest themselves in two distinct ways.

The first strategy can be seen through interviews in specialist magazines such as the British based *Impact*, which is devoted to action cinema, and the North American *Black Belt* and *Inside Kung Fu*, which are primarily for martial artists. Such magazines in their interviews and features regularly focus on the fact that Rothrock was a star performer in the Hong Kong action movie industry, carrying films herself and holding her own with the stars of that industry. As I have noted earlier, many martial-arts movie fans prefer a more authentic action cinema, often based on their assumptions about performers skills discussed above in relation to Jackie Chan. Indeed, in a small research project I undertook through the letters pages of *Impact*, all respondents claimed to prefer Hong Kong martial-arts films to those produced in the USA. I believe this preference has hardened through the increase in availability of Hong Kong films on DVD and video in the UK. This has been facilitated over recent years by DVD and video distribution companies such as Made in Hong Kong, Eastern Heroes and Hong Kong Legends, and the fact that stores such as HMV and Virgin now carry specialist sections devoted to such titles. This is a reflection of the consumer power of such supposedly small fan groups. Rothrock's position as a performer with a Hong Kong track record therefore assists the acceptability of her US films with fans in the UK and elsewhere.

The second key strategy in creating an authentic performer of Rothrock has been the highlighting of the fact that she has been a weapons and forms champion. Whilst this too is brought up in interviews, this authentic skill also has to be integrated into the films themselves. Often this takes the form of training sequences. This narrative device was particularly favoured by Hong Kong filmmakers in the 1970s and 1980s as a way of displaying performers' talents, and can be seen in such landmark titles as *Invincible Shaolin* (1978) and *36th Chamber of Shaolin* (1978). However, as North American martial-arts movies are more driven by action than the historical epics of the Hong Kong industry, which conventionally include the more static training sequences, these moments of display can be seen to interrupt the narrative flow. This is certainly the case in relation to Cynthia Rothrock. Arguably, the need to authenticate her martial-arts skills is heightened because she is a woman operating in a very male-centred genre. The fact that her 'real' martial-arts skills are in the area of forms and weapons, a particularly static practice, demands this sort of narrative disruption and almost invites the audience to step outside the narrative progression whilst the display takes place. For example, her 1992 film *Undefeatable* contains sequences that work in this manner. A member of a street gang involved in inter-gang rivalry, Rothrock's character is seen practising with martial-arts weapons outside her mobile home. She stands facing, and looking at, the camera in a full-length shot as she goes through her display. The camera is static and the sequence contains little editing. The purpose is simply to show the audience what Rothrock can do. The lack of editing and the static camera show that no special effects or doubles have been used, that what we are seeing is the 'real' thing.

The desire to create a truly authentic martial-arts persona leads me to another area of interest in relation to Cynthia Rothrock: the inability to transfer her success and persona in a popular exploitation genre to mainstream roles. The desire to prove the authenticity of female action performers is less prevalent within mainstream Hollywood films. Here, audiences are willing to accept performers such as Sigourney Weaver, Geena Davis and Linda Hamilton in action roles, if they look right. There are few sequences in their films that authenticate their skills in the manner used within Rothrock's. Interestingly, Michelle Yeoh, Rothrock's co-star from *Yes, Madam*, was cast in the James Bond film *Tomorrow Never Dies* (1997) based upon her reputation within the Hong Kong film industry. However, she was cast alongside Terri Hatcher, who was clearly identified in the marketing of the film as the sex interest. Yeoh, alongside Hatcher, was marketed as being there simply for action. Perhaps the idea of an Asian actress holding her own in fight sequences and being feminine enough to catch James Bond was too much for the producers.

One of the most negative effects of popularity in the exploitation field is that audiences for this type of cinema have, like all audiences to some extent, certain, very fixed expectations of performers. For performers with a very high profile within exploitation films, such as Rothrock, this impacts upon the projects that are seen as suitable for them. The performers themselves are very conscious of these expectations, and how this translates into expectations regarding content and authenticity. Rothrock herself has shown an awareness of the demands made of her and her films by her primary audience. Indeed, this is reflected in an interview with *Impact* magazine where, when discussing the opportunity to play a 'straight', non-martial-arts role, Rothrock commented that 'The company sent me a script for that movie [*Deep Red*, 1992], in which I'd have played a co-lead part. It wasn't an action piece. I said "I'll do it if you don't bill me. Don't put me in the credits." I don't want people saying "This is a

Cynthia Rothrock movie" and people seeing it and going "oh she just acts."' (Logan, 1995: 25). It seems therefore that Rothrock herself is very aware of the fact that as an exploitation action performer she brings a lot of baggage to the screen. This means that any new film that may be outside her normal product range, such as an erotic thriller for example, needs to be marketed in a way that does not put off audiences for either the erotic thriller or a Cynthia Rothrock movie. This seems to suggest that within the field of exploitation films there is an increasing awareness of the fragmentation of markets, whereas in the 1970s there was much less differentiation between elements of the audience in the marketing of exploitation films. The Rothrock persona, established through the authentication of her martial-arts skills, satisfied her primary target audience of martial-arts movie fans. However, in satisfying that primary market Rothrock moved herself into a ghetto of exploitation cinema. The few roles that Rothrock has been given within mainstream productions have been very predictable. For example, she appeared in the thriller *Eye for an Eye* (1994) as a karate instructor. There has been a resistance to cast Rothrock in roles in medium- or big-budget films, as her image is seen to be 'cheap' due to her work in the US exploitation field. However, in Hong Kong the appearance in lower-budget films did not automatically mean marginalisation, as generally budgets are lower in that industry. Sadly, the time when Cynthia Rothrock could have arguably transferred into the mainstream given the right vehicle may have passed. This is because the action movie in Hollywood has changed. One of the main reasons for this change has been the long-awaited breakthrough of Hong Kong superstar Jackie Chan into the US market.

Conclusion: Jackie Chan and Hollywood[1]

Whilst Jackie Chan had failed in his first two attempts to break into the US market (the already mentioned *The Big Brawl* was followed by another failure, *The Protector* (1985)), his third effort was to prove a success. Ironically, after studio heads felt the need to attach an American director to his earlier efforts, Chan's breakthrough came in the form of a Hong Kong film, directed by longtime associate Stanley Tong and shot on location in Vancouver, Canada: *Rumble in the Bronx* (1994). When the film was released in North America, in a re-scored and re-dubbed version, it shot to number one at the box-office. This led to the same process being applied to another Tong film, *First Strike* (1996). However, this time the film was heavily re-edited, which led to complaints from Tong, who was told by New Line, the US distributors, that 'we know the American market better than you' (Odham Stokes and Hoover, 1999: 130). The extent to which Chan had become a box-office success is reflected by the fact that New Line Cinema re-titled the film, *Jackie Chan's First Strike*, leaving the audience in no doubt about who the star of the show was. Chan, with his comic action persona, contributed to a significant change in the tone of action movies in the late 1990s. This change is reflected in the casting of comedian Chris Rock and Hong Kong martial arts star Jet Li in the action film *Lethal Weapon 4* (1998) alongside established stars Mel Gibson and Danny Glover. Indeed, Chan's first post- breakthrough Hollywood-produced film, *Rush Hour* (1998), cast him alongside US comedian Chris Tucker. The knock-on effect of this success has been an increased interest in Hong Kong cinema within Hollywood. Directors such as Ronny Yu and Kirk Wong have been invited to work in the US, but perhaps the most high-profile transfer outside of Jet Li and Jackie Chan has been another Chinese-opera-trained star, Sammo Hung. Hung and director Stanley Tong found unexpected success with the television series *Martial Law* in 1998. Reflecting the new trends in action production, *Martial Law* teams Hung with comedian and talkshow host Arsenio Hall. The po-faced action heroes of the 1980s and early 1990s now seem to be well and truly out of fashion.

This change in fashion within the martial-arts cinema is of course no surprise. If the fans want authenticity then Hong Kong performers provide it. These shifts, however, have left Rothrock in a marginalised position. Now she is removed by a number of years from her period in the Hong Kong industry, many within her potential audience will only be familiar with her from low-budget US productions. Ironically, as she is a real martial artist, the success of Hong Kong performers in the US has meant her opportunities have been severely limited. This in turn has led her to drastically reduce the number of projects that she is involved in, struggling to find suitable vehicles for her talents. 2001 saw her involvement in a project for TV, for which she also acted as an executive producer, *Outside the Law*. This film cast her as an ex-CIA operative on the run. However, the confines of television severely limited the opportunities for the bone-crunching martial-arts action of her earlier work, and so the satisfaction on offer for her fans. In another interesting development, the Internet Movie Database lists her as being involved in a video game *The Untouchable 2* (2002); perhaps this medium will offer her a new place to display her many martial-arts talents. One thing is for sure: if Hollywood makes a film of the game it is unlikely that Cynthia Rothrock will be required to return from the ghetto of exploitation where her career has so often existed.

Note

1   For more on Chan see chapter 6 of this collection.

Bibliography

Austin, B. A. (1990) 'Home Video: The Second-run "Theater" of the 1990s', in Tino Balio (ed.), *Hollywood in the Age of Television*, London: Unwin Hayman, pp. 319–49.

Corman, Roger and J. Jerome (1990) *How I Made a Hundred Movies in Hollywood and Never Lost a Dime*, London: Muller.

Doherty, Thomas (1988) *Teenagers and Teenpics: The Juvenilization of American Movies in the 1950s*, London: Unwin Hayman.

Dyer, R. (1991) '*A Star is Born* and the Construction of Authenticity', in Christine Gledhill (ed.), *Stardom: Industry of Desire*, London: Routledge, pp. 132–40.

Hillier, Jim and Aaron Lipstadt (eds) (1981) *Roger Corman's New World*, London: British Film Institute.

Hillier, Jim and Aaron Lipstadt (1986) 'The Economics of Independence: Roger Corman and New World Pictures 1970–1980', *Movie*, 31/32, winter: 43–53.

Hillier, Jim (1992) *The New Hollywood*, London: Studio Vista.

Lipstadt, Aaron (1981) 'Politics and Exploitation: New World Pictures', in Jim Hillier and Aaron Lipstadt (eds) *Roger Corman's New World*, London: British Film Institute, pp. 9–21.

Logan, B. (1994) 'Lethal White Female: Inside Cynthia Rothrock', *Impact*, January: 24–6.

Logan, B. (1995) *Hong Kong Action Cinema*, London: Titan.

Odham Stokes, L. and M. Hoover (1999) *City on Fire: Hong Kong Cinema*, London: Verso.

Tasker, Yvonne (1993) *Spectacular Bodies: Gender, Genre and Action Cinema*, London: Routledge.

Teo, S. (1997) *Hong Kong Cinema: The Extra Dimensions*, London: British Film Institute.

Wyatt, Justin (1994) *High Concept: Movies and Marketing in Hollywood*, Austin: University of Texas Press.

Index

Note: 'n' after a page reference indicatess a note number on that page.